The Persuasive Negotiato

Negotiation permeates every aspect of our lives, from our home to our work. Whether you consider yourself a novice or expert, there is always room to improve your negotiation performance. With easily replicable tools throughout, this book offers everything you need to know for an MBA in negotiation, but without the expense and time-consuming study. It will help you improve both your confidence and ability, and equip you with all the skills and tools needed for successful negotiation.

Negotiation is more than buying and selling, more than winning and more than streetwise manipulation; it's creating a successful deal that will lead to a fruitful relationship with the other party. In this book, the author demonstrates how we can all become more effective negotiators in business, and our everyday lives, by combining theory with real-life examples and offering practical tips. At the end of each chapter, your knowledge will be tested and the learning reaffirmed to enable you to walk into any negotiation confidently.

This book is essential reading to all students taking part in an MBA programme, as well as anyone with an interest in negotiation. Whether you need help negotiating a new kitchen installation, a better salary or a multi-million-pound business deal, this book will give you the competitive edge to get there.

Florence Kennedy Rolland is an international negotiation consultant and Managing Director of Negotiate Ltd, offering specialised bespoke training in Negotiation Skills from the shop floor to board level for over 20 years. She has taught the Negotiation MBA module at The Edinburgh Business School since 2005, and the Strategic Negotiation module since 2014. She has a wide range of experience in every industry, from small family companies to large multi-nationals, and in both the public and private sectors in the UK and across the world. Some recent clients include large oil and gas organisations, financial institutions, digital tech firms, public services organisations, university development departments and IT companies.

The Persuasive Negotiator
Tools and Techniques for Effective Negotiating

Florence Kennedy Rolland

First published 2021
by Routledge
2 Park Square, Milton Park, Abingdon, Oxon OX14 4RN

and by Routledge
52 Vanderbilt Avenue, New York, NY 10017

Routledge is an imprint of the Taylor & Francis Group, an informa business

© 2021 Florence Kennedy Rolland

The right of Florence Kennedy Rolland to be identified as author of this work has been asserted by her in accordance with sections 77 and 78 of the Copyright, Designs and Patents Act 1988.

All rights reserved. No part of this book may be reprinted or reproduced or utilised in any form or by any electronic, mechanical, or other means, now known or hereafter invented, including photocopying and recording, or in any information storage or retrieval system, without permission in writing from the publishers.

Trademark notice: Product or corporate names may be trademarks or registered trademarks, and are used only for identification and explanation without intent to infringe.

British Library Cataloguing-in-Publication Data
A catalogue record for this book is available from the British Library

Library of Congress Cataloging-in-Publication Data
A catalog record has been requested for this book

ISBN: 978-0-367-45987-1 (hbk)
ISBN: 978-0-367-56592-3 (pbk)
ISBN: 978-1-003-02688-4 (ebk)

Typeset in Baskerville
by Newgen Publishing UK

For my father, Gavin, who taught me how to negotiate,
And for my son, Alexander, who teaches me everyday.

Contents

List of figures   x
List of tables   xi
Foreword   xii

1   What is negotiation?   1
Introduction 1
Alternative methods of making decisions 3
What is negotiation? 8
Conclusion 11
Checkpoint 1 13

2   Distributive bargaining   14
Introduction 14
Distributive bargaining 16
Entry and exit prices 17
Settlement range 18
Negotiators with overlapping entry prices 20
The negotiators' surplus 22
Conclusion 26
Checkpoint 2 30

3   Integrative bargaining, part 1: Preparation   31
Introduction 31
What do we need to do first? 36
What are we negotiating about? 38
What are Interests? 39
What are the negotiable Issues? 40
What are the priorities for each Issue? 42
What are the negotiable ranges for each Issue? 51
Positions – setting entry and exit points 51
Tradables 53

viii *Contents*

    Conclusion 55
    Checkpoint 3 56

4   Integrative bargaining, part 2: Debate   57
    Introduction 57
    What is debate? 60
    Types of destructive debate 62
    Constructive debate behaviours 68
    How not to disagree 75
    Conclusion 87
    Checkpoint 4 89

5   Integrative bargaining, part 3: How to propose   91
    Introduction 91
    What is a proposal? 94
    How to make proposals 98
    How to receive a proposal 103
    Summarising issues 108
    Conclusion 110
    Checkpoint 5 111

6   Integrative bargaining, part 4: How to bargain   113
    Introduction 113
    From proposals to bargains 114
    Linked trading 119
    Bargaining to close the deal 125
    The agreement 128
    Conclusion 129
    Checkpoint 6 130

7   The styles of negotiation   132
    Introduction 132
    Trust in time 135
    Negotiator's dilemma 138
    Red, Blue and Purple styles of negotiation 141
    The difficult negotiator 146
    Making progress with a Purple style in a Red negotiation 151
    Conclusion 157
    Checkpoint 7 158

8   Rational bargaining   159
    Introduction 159
    John Nash and Utility Theory 160
    The benefits of bargaining 166

The real bargaining problem 167
Fisher and Ury on principled negotiation 169
BATNA 178
The negotiator as mediator 179
Conclusion 180
Checkpoint 8 181

9   Ploys and tactics   182
Introduction 182
Learning about ploys 182
Three types of ploys 186
Dominance ploys 187
Shaping ploys 190
Closing ploys 195
Conclusion 197
Checkpoint 9 199

10 Culture and negotiation   201
A negotiating tale of two cities 201
Cultural relativism 202
Do people negotiate using different processes? 203
What is culture? 204
The cultural relativist's challenge 206
Conclusion 214

Appendix 1: Glossary of terms   217
Appendix 2: Checkpoint answers   221
Index   228

Figures

1.1	Negotiation	11
2.1	Entry points	17
2.2	The gap between the negotiators' exit points	18
2.3	The negotiators' exit points meet	18
2.4	The negotiators' exit points overlap	19
2.5	Negotiators with overlapping entry prices	19
2.6	The negotiators' surplus when exit points overlap	22
3.1	The Negotek® Preparation Phase Planner	35
3.2	Comparative priorities – differing	50
3.3	Comparative priorities – similar	50
3.4	Comparative priorities – mixed	50
6.1	Distinction between a proposal and a bargain	115
7.1	The Red–Blue continuum	144
9.1	Relationship between your perceptions of power and your expectations of the outcome	185
10.1	A simple model of the relationship between behaviours, attitudes, beliefs and values	210

Tables

1.1	Ten alternative decision-making methods	7
1.2	Three types of bargaining	10
3.1	Data on invoice accuracy and time spent correcting those errors	38
3.2	Forth's list of negotiable Issues	42
3.3	Forth's list of negotiable Issues and their priorities	45
3.4	Forth's Issues prioritised	46
3.5	PDQ's Issues prioritised	48
3.6	Forth's and PDQ's Issues prioritised	49
3.7	Farmer Jones's and Farmer Morgan's Issues prioritised	49
3.8	Forth's and PDQ's Issues with entry and exit points	52
3.9	List of potential Tradables for Forth	54
4.1	Time sheet: argument behaviour	62
4.2	Time sheet: constructive debate behaviour	69
5.1	Components of a proposal	97
7.1	Payoff diagram for Susie and Bob	134
7.2	Payoff diagram for Rodney and Bob	136
7.3	Sequence of choices for four rounds of the pottery game	136
7.4	Red or Blue?	139
7.5	Red and Blue conditionality	146
7.6	Choice of styles	146
7.7	How Thompson is currently handled and how he should be handled in the future	147
8.1	Louise's flip chart	161
8.2	Utilities before trading	163
8.3	The Nash solution in a Negotek® PREP format	164
8.4	Net utility positions for Bill and Jack after trading across their varying priorities	165
8.5	The four prescriptions of principled negotiation	170
8.6	Airport runway	176
10.1	Hofstede's cultural differences using four indices	207

Foreword

Sometimes you are blessed to meet someone who has a profound effect on your life, someone who teaches you and mentors you and inspires you to learn and grow as a person. Someone who shapes the focus of your career and willingly gives you opportunities to develop your own career path with that knowledge. I have been extremely fortunate to have that person with me my entire life, until recently, my father.

Professor Gavin Kennedy, as he is known the world over, has been a leading figure in the world of negotiation since he first started researching for his PhD in 1972, the year I was born. He'd created his four-phase model by the time I was a toddler. I suppose you could say that I was always fascinated, even as a young child, in what he was doing. It seemed incredibly cool that he would travel the world to teach people about negotiation. He would come home with foreign trinkets and endless stories. I'm sure I didn't listen to them all, but the extraordinary enthusiasm he always had somehow contaminated me.

I'd always worked for him (cleaning, filing, printing course materials, packaging courses, mailing, database entry, etc.) as I was always keen to make money – but it wasn't until I was 16 or 17 that I actually realized that the subject was so interesting and that Dad was really an expert. It was during the summer holiday from school and, as usual, I was working in his office. He wanted an old book of his, *Superdeal: How to Negotiate Anything!*, to be typed into the new computer. He didn't have it on file, as when he had written it originally he had done so on a typewriter. Initially I was annoyed at the task as it seemed incredibly dull to a teenager to retype an entire book, but as soon as I started I was gripped. It was a brilliant book about dealmaking around the globe, and I wanted to learn more.

I then read one of his other best-selling books, *Everything is Negotiable*, and thought I knew everything there was to know about negotiation. I was still at school, though, so all thoughts of becoming the next international globetrotting negotiator had to be put on hold. After completing a degree in Business Studies at university, I opened my own small business using all the negotiation skills I had learnt. Dealing with landlords, suppliers and customers wasn't quite so easy as it appeared in the books, but I enjoyed every interaction, celebrating the victories and learning from the failures. Dad was working on another project with a few of his colleagues at Heriot Watt University – they started the Edinburgh Business School with the aim of teaching an MBA by distance learning. It became one of the most successful MBA programmes in the UK.

It was then my father had his first stroke. Everything changed. He didn't want to travel so much, and teaching tired him. I had sold my business, and he asked me to help him at work 'for a few months', until he was back on his feet. That was 21 years ago. I have never looked back or regretted the decision, though sometimes it is hard. My first time teaching was terrifying, but his advice got me through. I asked him how long it would take to get over the nerves before the day's teaching started, and he said, 'If you ever stop being nervous, you should stop teaching'. I understand now what he meant, though at the time I was really frustrated that his advice seemed so useless!

Through his guidance and help I have taught over 20,000 students, from all kinds of businesses, from all corners of the world. Through it all the lessons of negotiation have helped me not only in my teaching, but in running my business. I'm not going to say it helps negotiate with my son because, as with all children, his natural ability to get his own way in any situation is utterly remarkable.

When Dad died last year he left me with this legacy. It is a huge responsibility to make sure that I do it justice, and I hope that this book goes some way in starting that. I wish he were here to read it, and no doubt 'improve' it, but most of all I wish he could see that I have taken his work a little further with this publication.

The book itself is based on his 1991 MBA Negotiation text, which we have both taught over the years to many students across the globe. I have made a lot of changes, and – dare I say it – improvements, but it is still very much a text worthy of post-graduate study. Having said that, the book is also a valuable tool for any budding negotiator, with practical tips and tools to help you in any negotiation situation, from multi-million pound deals to deciding who is this weekend's designated driver, and everything in between. Check your learning with questions at the end of every chapter, and if you want details on taking your learning further with a training course, contact me on florence@negotiate.co.uk.

Florence
Ex bona fide negotari
20 February 2020

1 What is negotiation?

Introduction

When it comes to decision-making there are many alternatives. It's not simply the case that one method suits all, and in many cases negotiation is not the best fit. The first step you must take is to understand whether or not negotiation is even a valid choice in your decision-making.

> *George, VP (Sales) at Xander Enterprises, was looking forward to his annual leave starting tomorrow afternoon. He had planned a three-week holiday in Italy with his wife and two children in a rented villa. It was a long overdue break after a frantic year working on a potential joint venture to build a business park with Phoenix Projects, a client company, on the edge of town. His CEO, Dan O'Reilly, came in to his office at lunchtime on Thursday and tasked George with checking over all the files before an important meeting with Phoenix on Tuesday next week.*
>
> *The contract documents were a total mess, with missing finance information and requiring many changes to specifications and drawings that needed to be analysed and prepared for discussion on Tuesday. This was not a 24-hour job. George would have to delay the start of his holiday until Monday evening at the latest. George would have to make a grovelling apology to his wife and kids, and assure them he would join them as soon as he could get away.*
>
> *George was very angry to be put in this position in the first place. The account was not one of his, but of the Contracts Manager, Sam, who was on sick leave and would not be back in time to help with the preparation or the meeting next week. This left George as the only suitable option to help out at such late notice. Though he noted it would be a feather in his cap to fix the problem and it would do his promotion prospects no harm at all, he was all too aware of the price he would have to pay domestically, as this was not the first time work had caused him to miss out on family events.*

Now, imagine yourself in George's position on Thursday afternoon when the boss calls on you to work over the first weekend of your annual leave. How do you feel about that? As annoyed as George? Well, we don't know what George said or did when he heard Dan's instructions; we only know that he worked through the weekend. If you had been faced with a similar instruction from your boss, how might you have reacted? What could you do to make yourself happier in this type of situation, both at work and domestically?

> **Exercise 1A**
>
> *What could you have done in this situation? Write down your answers on a separate sheet of paper, numbering them 1 to 10.*

My suggestions follow, in no particular order of priority. George could:
Tell Dan that his holiday was contractually sacrosanct and refuse the assignment.

> *Question*: What would this have done to his career prospects?

Suggest to Dan that somebody else should undertake the assignment and use good arguments to support his suggestion (perhaps appealing to Dan's sense of fair play?).

> *Question*: What happens if he fails to persuade Dan to change his mind?

Suggest that Dan assign somebody else along with George, with whom George would work until Friday evening, and thereafter the other person would complete the task over the weekend by himself. (Perhaps he could offer to work through Thursday night?)

> *Question*: What happens if there is nobody else qualified to undertake the work after George leaves?

Tell Dan that he did not want to break his holiday in this way, but that he was prepared to toss a coin with him to decide whether he should continue with his holiday plans or start work on the problem.

> *Question*: What happens if Dan has an aversion to a gamble and anyway sees no reason why he should put himself at a 50 per cent risk of doing without George's services?

Offer to do the work, provided that Dan paid his airfare to Bordeaux on Monday and extended his holiday by a week in compensation.

> *Question*: What happens if there is no pressure on Dan to negotiate with George?

Ask to see the company President to adjudicate whether Dan's assignment was a reasonable request just before his holiday.

> *Question*: What influence can George bring to bear on the company President before he makes his decision?

Threaten to resign and sue the company for constructive dismissal.

> *Question*: How credible is the threat and would Dan give in to it? How expensive is litigation and would he win?

Tell Dan he will consider it and let him know when he returns from holiday.

> *Question*: What happens when a decision cannot be postponed?

Instruct one of his own subordinates to undertake the assignment.

> *Question*: What happens if the junior refuses the instruction?

Undertake the assignment.

> *Question*: What does giving in cost him in a ruined holiday?

This chapter is about some of the options people can consider when their interests are in conflict with another's and how we might approach discussing these options.

Alternative methods of making decisions

People make decisions all the time and they use a variety of methods, mostly without thinking about the differences between the methods, to reach and implement their decisions. We can illustrate the variety of methods available to people by considering the suggestions you came up with for George in the introduction. Almost certainly you included some, if not all, of the ten in my list (and perhaps a few others?). Each of my ten suggestions is based on a different method of reaching a decision, and we can name each type of decision method as follows:

Say 'No'

To reject outright a proposal usually means having to live with the consequences, unless the proposer backs off. If a man puts a gun to your head and says: 'Sign the contract or I will blow your brains out', you would surely have to have a serious objection to the terms of the contract if you persisted in refusing and he was serious about his threat. Saying 'no' and meaning it is appropriate when you cannot endure the offer but you can endure the consequences.

Persuasion

All selling skills are based on persuasion. If you have ever attended a sales training course you will recognise the role of persuasion in the advice to sellers to 'sell the sizzle, not the steak'. This approach can persuade someone to say 'yes' because their imagination is more likely to be fired by the image of a sizzle than the unadorned image of a steak. The advice to sell benefits, not features, is another example of the talented use of persuasion skills. Persuasion is usually the first method we choose when we want something. When persuasion works it is a fine method, but when it does not work it often leads to tension and conflict:

> I tried to be reasonable and explained why Dan should choose somebody else, but he was not interested in my views, only in his own, which shows I was right to call him an idiot of a boss, and he proved this by sacking me.

Problem-solve

This is not as universally applicable a method as its proponents claim (in fact, no single decision method is a panacea for all conflict situations). Problem-solving methods require a high degree of trust between the decision-makers, who also have to agree that they share the problem. If either of these conditions is absent, problem-solving breaks down when individuals 'hold back' just in case their candour is ambushed by your denial that you share their problem.

Chance

This is not as silly as it sounds. Some large decisions are made by the toss of a coin. For example, in a choice between two otherwise identical projects for which there are funds for only one, tossing a coin might save a lot of acrimonious argument or indecisive dithering. If you are indifferent between two events (going to the football match or watching television), you have a 50 per cent chance of enjoying either event if you decide between them by tossing a coin. Kerry Packer, the Australian businessman, chose between his lower price and David Frost's higher price for the Australian television rights to Frost's interview with ex-President Nixon by tossing a coin. The interesting feature of Packer's decision is that he allowed Frost to call 'heads or tails' over the telephone line separating Frost in California from Packer in New South Wales, and he announced that Frost had won the toss! Whether Packer actually tossed a coin or not is an interesting speculation; if he did toss the coin and Frost's call won, this makes Packer a very honest man; if he tossed and Frost's call lost, or if he did not toss a coin at all, this makes Packer a very generous man.

Negotiate

This is a widely used option where conditions for it exist. These conditions normally include the mutual dependence of each decision-maker on the other. If the boss needs your consent for you to do something he wants and to which you cannot unilaterally say 'no', nor can he make you do it, it may be possible to negotiate something that meets both your own and your boss's concerns. This usually involves you getting something, tangible or intangible, in return for your consent. But if you have nothing to trade – he does not need anything you have, including your consent, nor does he have anything in his gift that would persuade you to consent – then negotiation is unlikely to be appropriate.

Arbitrate

When decision-makers cannot find a basis for agreeing, and provided they can at least agree on who is to be the arbitrator and that his decisions will be accepted, they can choose arbitration. The building and construction industry uses formal arbitration procedures to settle the many disputes that arise over increases in costs and variations in specifications after the contract price has been agreed. It is also used in commercial disputes between countries. Though widely used, arbitration is also abused, particularly when the parties reject the arbiter's award, or when one of them demands arbitration merely as a device to improve the other party's last offer by letting the arbiter split the difference. This abuse has been overcome by the Pendulum Arbitration system, which requires the arbiter to choose one or other of the party's claims, rather than award some compromise between them. The problem for George is how to appeal over Dan's head without compromising his own relationship with the company. Dan's boss might take a dim view of managers who do not work 'above and beyond' the call of duty and he might take just as dim a view of Dan for failing to manage his own people; the former inhibits George from going over his boss's head and the latter inhibits Dan from letting him. George also has the risk that the arbiter's decision would be the same as Dan's.

Coercion

Threats lie on a continuum from a gentle reminder that you have an option to a declared intention to use violent intimidation to get your own way. Various degrees of coercion are common in many conflict situations, for example: a union reminding the employer that its members voted unanimously for tougher action in support of their demand (adding: 'Only our authority is holding them back, so give us something to put to them to defuse the crisis'); or a supplier warning the buyer that continued late payments will result in delayed deliveries or even cancellation of the contract; or a government warning a neighbouring country that, unless it acts to stop terrorists getting onto flights, it will ban all flights from that country. Of course, using coercion to achieve desirable decisions risks retaliation ('We will not be pushed around or blackmailed').

Postpone

This is a relatively common practice. Countless organisations attempt to resolve internal disputes and isolate the traumas of disagreement by forming 'working parties' or 'subcommittees', which effectively postpones the decision long enough to secure agreement, or long enough for the parties to forget how passionately they felt about it when it was first raised. But where time is of the essence – the shipment has to leave by 4 p.m. to catch the last flight to New York – postponement may not be an option. Indeed, in some situations, an attempt to postpone a decision could be interpreted as a form of coercion, or simply as an underhanded refusal to agree.

Instruct

This is the appropriate choice when the person instructed is obliged and certain to carry out the instruction. Managers do not normally expect subordinates to question their instructions when their instructions are within the terms of their relationship. Telling the chauffeur to drive to a downtown restaurant at lunchtime ought not to provoke a conflict if that is what the chauffeur is paid to do and lunchtime is within his working hours. The efficacy of instruction rests entirely on the probability of the instruction being obeyed. If it is unlikely to be obeyed – we need their consent – we must switch to another method. For example, instructing children to go to bed is not always successful, and parents often resort to other methods – persuasion, negotiation or coercion – to overcome a challenge to their authority.

Give in

This is what we do when we accept an instruction. Giving in is not as weak an option as it sometimes seems (or as it is presented by people who perceive themselves to be 'tough guys'). I regularly give in when the odds are overwhelming (the man with the gun means business) or the costs of doing otherwise are excessive (to argue will take up more time than I have to spare on resisting doing what I am told). Every time you buy an item at the seller's asking price, you are giving in, and it makes sense to do so if you cannot abide the alternative of doing without the item. Supermarkets do not normally negotiate on the prices of their groceries, and if they were to do so, it would extend by hours the arduous chore of weekly shopping, with people waiting in checkout queues while those ahead of them completed their haggling over the prices of their trolley loads of groceries. Faced with this consequence, most people who shop regularly would give in and find a competing store that arranged its pricing system to minimise the time they had to spend waiting to go home.

Exercise 1B

Now go back to your list of options you decided were open to George. How would you classify each of your suggestions according to those in Table 1.1? For each entry you made, decide what type of decision it is and note its number alongside the corresponding entry in the table.

Your list almost certainly will have been written in an order different from mine (which does not matter because the order is irrelevant) and you may also have duplicated one or two of your suggestions by giving different examples of the same decision method. This too does not matter too much, as long as you can identify the method. The importance of this exercise is for you to recognise that there are at least ten methods of making decisions potentially available to you in conflict situations.

Each of them emphasises a different approach, each has strengths and weaknesses and each has different consequences. In your daily interactions, you switch between these alternatives to suit the circumstances as you see them. As an adult, you have considerable experience choosing between these methods and recognising which method is being used on you by somebody else. Not that you and the people you deal with always get it right! For example, you might attempt to instruct somebody and, in consequence, have your ears assaulted with the noise of their outrage at your insult, or you could arrive at the meeting willing to listen to reason but react angrily at their unnecessary attempts to coerce you into submission.

Observation shows that people are adept at choosing different approaches to conflict, but it also shows that their choices are not always appropriate to the

Table 1.1 Ten alternative decision-making methods

Number	Method	Corresponding number in your list
1	Say 'No'	
2	Persuasion	
3	Problem solve	
4	Chance	
5	Negotiate	
6	Arbitrate	
7	Coercion	
8	Postpone	
9	Instruct	
10	Give in	
Others not in list		

circumstances. They are not confined to using one form of decision-making in particular circumstances when switching to another might move things forward. A sales sequence could begin with persuasion (selling benefits, not features, and answering the buyer's objections). The sales pitch could confine itself to persuasion if persuasion were sufficient to win the order. It could as easily move into negotiation when buyer and seller discuss the terms under which the buyer's decision, in principle, to buy is matched to the seller's willingness to sell. It could also slip into a gentle form of coercion, as when a seller warns a buyer that, even though he does not need steel for the moment, unless he places an order immediately for the special steel he requires, he will miss the current production run at the rolling mill and will have to wait another three months before his order can be placed (and for good measure, he will face a price increase as well). Those skilled in persuasion are not immune to slipping into some degree of coercion. For example, many an attempt by credit control to collect money from debtors begins with gentle persuasion and ends in ungentle litigation.

Hence, some situations involve switching in and out of several alternative methods sequentially in a short space of time. This is important to negotiators because it helps if they can recognise which method is being used at a particular moment. For just as each method is appropriate in some circumstances and not in others, so some methods are not appropriate when they operate against each other. For example, if you rely stubbornly on persuasion to win over a meeting to your point of view, and your opponent switches into credible threats to intimidate the meeting into compliance with his wishes, you might find the meeting slipping away from its inclination to support you. Alternatively, you could decide to give in to a specific request from the other negotiator, only to find that this act of goodwill did not lead to a solution. Instead of reciprocating your offer to give in with some movement on his part, he might take your giving in as a sign of your weakness and promptly demand more! From similar mismatches of decision methods, more than one negotiation has collapsed.

What is negotiation?

Negotiation is one of the forms of decision-making. As with all of the decision-making methods, it is neither inferior nor superior to any of the others, it merely depends on the circumstances which one is preferred. So when is the right time to choose negotiation?

By definition, negotiation is the process by which we obtain something from somebody who wants something from us. At its most basic level, negotiation is the process of an exchange. It is how we manage that exchange, how we work towards getting a deal. So firstly, there needs to be a desire from both parties to want to make an exchange, and they must have discretion on whether or not they wish to make the exchange at all.

> **Learning point:**
>
> *Negotiation is trading; it's an exchange.*

Millions of exchanges are made each day. Workers exchange their labour for wages, which they then exchange for goods and services. Producers exchange their outputs for earnings. Governments exchange taxes for investment and services. There is a dependence on each side for the transaction, and many transactions require negotiation to set the 'price' of the exchange. Buyers and sellers are part of each of the exchanges, as there is always someone looking to buy a product, a service, your time, your skills, etc. For example, a worker sells their time and skills to an employer. A manufacturer buys raw materials and employees' time to make his output, which he then sells to his customers.

Prices vary and are set by market rates and individual requirements. Often, differences in prices are dependent on the buyer's need to buy or the seller's need to sell. In fact, the complex 'price' of any transaction is why negotiation is such a crucial part of everyday life. Values of the same product or service can vary hugely, and all negotiators value things differently (one of the inherent negotiation rules to remember!).

Buyers will often buy goods without challenging the terms and conditions (supermarket shopping, for example), but the propensity to challenge becomes ever greater with the price. Buying small goods, such as food, is not worth the time and effort involved in negotiating with the checkout staff (not that many would entertain it), but instead we might shop around for better prices in rival stores and take our business elsewhere. When we buy goods that cost us considerably more than a few pounds, we might be prepared to put more effort into the exchange. Price comparison will play a part again, but many of us will challenge or 'haggle' for higher-priced goods, such as washing machines or fridge-freezers. A car purchase is often seen as a game of high-stakes negotiation with the wily car salesperson. Once we move away from domestic transactions, the role of negotiation becomes more commonplace.

Negotiation develops as the process through which the activity of trading and exchanging tangible or intangible things between people is conducted. Its underlying principle is expressed in the statement: 'Give me some of what I want, and I will give you some of what you want'. It differs from instruction and coercion, precisely in the way that it employs the principle of voluntary exchange between two parties who cannot, for whatever reason, either take what they want or get what they want, unless they accommodate in some way to the wishes and desires of each other.

Individuals negotiate with family, friends, employers and producers. Producers negotiate with staff, suppliers and customers. The government and its agencies negotiate to buy and sell labour services (the civil service, the armed forces, the judiciary, etc.) and output (public infrastructure, medicines, school pencils, etc.) on much the same basis as private producers do in the market economy. They also negotiate in the political market, both internally and externally. Internally, government ministers might negotiate over party issues, overlapping jurisdiction or simply on policy. Externally, governments negotiate with other governments on all manner of issues (e.g. trade, foreign policy, immigration or relations), some having more success than others. Hugely complicated negotiations between governments have not only the ministers, themselves, to please, but also the people whom they represent. The most contentious negotiation in recent times for the British government is Brexit, which shows how a difficult negotiation can only be made worse when there are numerous parties, all with varying opinions on how to progress or even what is the preferred outcome.

Negotiations do not always end in an agreement. Those making a decision by negotiation usually have the option of choosing some other solution, of saying 'no', of walking away or of minding their own business. If their consent is required for an agreement to be reached and if they cannot agree, then no agreement is made. They cannot be forced to agree, for if one of them can force the other to agree, it would not be a negotiation (and anyway, why would a person negotiate with somebody who has no choice but to obey their instructions or to furnish them with what they want?).

Negotiation as a process

We have established that negotiation is the process of exchange, when both parties have the discretion to deal or not. But there is more than one way to negotiate. There are three main types of negotiation: distributive bargaining, integrative bargaining and rational bargaining (see Table 1.2). All three go through the process of getting to a deal – or at least attempting to, because it is always possible to 'say no' – but they go about it in very different ways.

No matter which type of bargaining you are using to manage the dealmaking process, there are several other factors that play a part in how the deal is done. Negotiations are done by humans, and humans are not 'one size fits all'. There are many types of people in the world and their background can make a huge difference to how they negotiate (see Figure 1.1). We all have experiences that have shaped our lives, but it can be much deeper than that. Where we were born can

Table 1.2 Three types of bargaining

Distributive bargaining	Single issue
	Zero-sum bargaining
Integrative bargaining	Multi-issue trading
	Practical
Rational bargaining	Highly theoretical
	Based on rational decision-making

```
                    ┌─────────────┐
                    │ Negotiation │
                    └──────┬──────┘
          ┌────────────────┼────────────────┐
    ┌─────┴─────┐    ┌─────┴─────┐    ┌─────┴──────┐
    │  Beliefs  │    │ Attitudes │    │ Behaviour  │
    └───────────┘    └───────────┘    └────────────┘
    Seldom change   Changed by events  Changed by training and
                                       experience
```

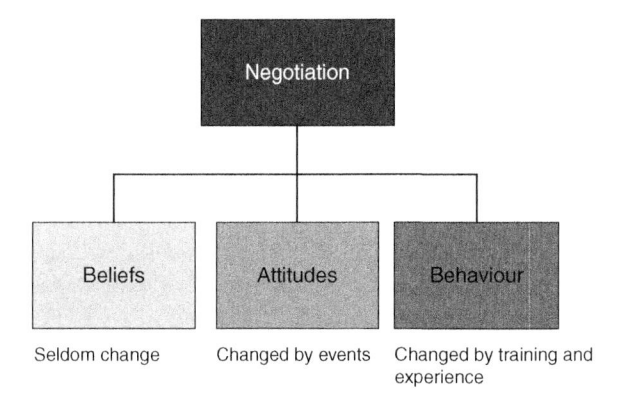

Figure 1.1 Negotiation.

shape our behaviour – from as general as what country, to a much more specific 'which part of town' can make a difference to perceptions, ideals and attitudes to life in general, which in turn can impact who we are and how we behave.

As we grow up, there will be other things that change us, from learning and education to life experiences, and these events will either challenge our beliefs or reinforce them. They can change how we behave or encourage us to stay the same. As negotiators, it is not enough to be good at the process of negotiation; we must be able to deal with different people in our negotiations. We need to be able to manage the behaviours we encounter while also making sure our own behaviours benefit the negotiation process.

In addition to the behaviours and styles of the negotiators, there are other influences on the negotiation process, which we will cover in later chapters. Ploys and tactics are common negotiation techniques used to manipulate the outcome of deals, and the role of culture in negotiations is also explored.

Conclusion

Some people think of a skilled negotiator as someone who can bluff and double bluff their way to whatever they want. The negotiator is a schemer, a manipulator of others and hardly to be trusted. Ice-cold blood runs through their veins and they have a heart made of stone. In politics, this individual's name would be Machiavelli; in personal relations, Casanova.

None of these images concur with our view of negotiation or of how effective negotiators approach their work. Everybody negotiates, sometimes for momentous issues, but mostly for trivial everyday things. We bring the same range of personality traits (and blood temperatures!) to our negotiations as we do to the other parts of our lives. If by nature you are a schemer, then no doubt you will continue to scheme when you negotiate, but most people you negotiate with will not be schemers, though they may suffer from other afflictions to their personality.

12   What is negotiation?

Negotiation is one among several options you have when you are attempting to make a decision with another person. You should think of negotiation simply as a decision process and not as a mysterious set of behaviours best left to those skilled in office politics or jungle fighting. You can become competent in negotiation without compromising your sense of ethical conduct.

We negotiate because our decisions affect others and their decisions affect us. Individuals do not wish to leave decisions that affect them to the whim and fancy, not to mention material benefit, of somebody else. In feudal times, everything was arranged by order of the monarch and enforced by his barons, and people knew their place (and were violently reminded if they momentarily forgot it). Church and State laid down their path through life from birth to death. Order prevailed and stability reigned at the price of personal liberty.

The liberal democracies have since inherited much of the Earth, or at least the richest part of it (yes, there is a connection!), and with their liberalism has come the demand to have one's interests accounted for in the decisions others take. This occurs in every family, every community and every area of activity from school to corporation. Where people insist that their consent be obtained before a decision is taken, the conflicting notions of what the decision is about must be reconciled. In politics, we call it democracy, in economics the free market, in justice the rule of law; in all its varying manifestations the most common process used to achieve voluntary consent is what we call negotiation.

Negotiation has a long history, perhaps even a pre-history, as the early humans found forms of cooperation that signalled the beginning of an ever-widening difference between them and the animals outside their caves, who knew of no alternative to fighting for what they wanted. But long as its history is, negotiation has only recently come into its own as an appropriate method with a potential for use in almost every sphere of human contact. It is no accident that the number of international agreements is growing each year, that commercial contracts are negotiated by the millions, that the new professions of mediators, conciliators, arbiters and consultant negotiators are growing in numbers across the globe, that more legal firms are turning to negotiating settlements rather than merely litigating their claims, and that there is a growing interest in the theory and practice of negotiation. The age of negotiation coincides with the spread of pluralistic democracy and growing international economic and political integration.

Because people are freer, they will not accept arbitrary instructions to the degree they did only a generation or two ago. Employees reject the heavy hand of misplaced managerial or union power as much as they reject the blind obedience their parents and grandparents conceded to authority in all its guises. Employees are no longer in a 'job for life', which gives them choice and free movement and with it the demand for more rights.

Consumers look for better deals, where again huge choices and options on where and how to spend their money all play a part in their decision-making process. Fixed-price buying is common, but bargain sales, 'Black Friday' events and constant competition from rival stores has led to almost permanent sales and discounting. The spread of discount stores across the UK in the last decade alone has been huge, with the 'big five' supermarkets having to rethink strategies to cope with the new entrants, Aldi and Lidl, who have taken a huge chunk of the market. Cheaper offers are made by online-only stores, who don't have to pay for expensive town premises, and huge internet shopping giants like Amazon, where you can buy anything and have it delivered in a day. The consumer's quest for a better deal is shaping the market.

To call this the age of negotiation risks underestimating the importance of other methods of decision-making that have also expanded in the first quarter of this century. For example, persuasion has enjoyed a substantial boost in the form of multi-billion-pound sales, social media influencers and marketing activities. The buyer is wooed – and not just over price. The take-it-or-leave-it indifference of the local monopolist (state or private) has succumbed to the competitive option afforded by the globalization of markets and the emergence of e-commerce. Total quality programmes that settle for nothing less than zero defects in output shipped to customers are a common corporate culture. Marketing techniques have dug deep into human psychology to find ways to persuade the buyer to want what the seller is offering. Persuasion through the, sometimes questionable, techniques of public relations management has enjoyed a boom and is now an essential component of corporate and political success, and of damage limitation when things go wrong, as in environmental disasters, political peccadilloes and legal embarrassments.

The swing has been away from people giving in to coercive methods and the acceptance of dictatorial instructions towards persuasion, problem-solving, mediation, arbitration and negotiation, which have in common varying degrees of voluntary consent. The spread of negotiation, therefore, should be seen in this broader context.

Checkpoint 1

1.1 When is negotiation an appropriate decision-making method?

1.2 What is the definition of negotiation?

1.3 What are the three types of bargaining?

2 Distributive bargaining

Introduction

> *Jenny wants to buy a second-hand car. She saw one advertised for sale for £9,000 and is satisfied that this is the car she wants. She also knows that she doesn't want to pay as much as £9,000 for it. The most she is prepared to pay is £8,500. She assumes that the seller, Rohan, will be willing to accept a lower offer, but she is not sure how much lower.*

Exercise 2A

Before reading on, what would you suggest that Jenny do? On the limited information that you have, should she:

(a) *Open close to her highest price of £8,500?*
(b) *Go in much lower than her highest price at, say, £7,500?*

Alternatives

Answer (a)

Suppose Jenny were to offer close to her highest price of £8,500, let's say at £8,400. What could happen? Rohan could compare her offer to his undisclosed lowest price, and if her offer of £8,400 was higher, then he would know that he will be doing better than his lowest expectations. This could encourage him to remain steadfast on his opening price – it's not that far away, and it would test Jenny's resolve if he were to push for £9,000, perhaps pushing her beyond her highest expectations.

Opening close to her highest price could also cause her additional problems. Jenny, by making a relatively high offer, might merely provoke Rohan into being more resolute in defence of his opening demand of £9,000. Or worse, if Jenny makes her offer before Rohan tells her that he is looking for £9,000, she might provoke him into believing that he can do much better than £9,000 and thereby motivate him to increase his opening demand to, say, £9,550. Jenny reasonably could react negatively to Rohan's response, though it was provoked by her own actions, and she could decide that, because Rohan has demanded £1,000 more than the highest price she is prepared to pay, there is little likelihood of an agreement. The result? She takes her business elsewhere, ending up without the car, and Rohan loses a prospective sale.

Answer (b)

Can Jenny do better, then, if she opens well below her highest price for the car? Ideally she would open just below Rohan's secret lowest price, but of course she has no way of knowing what that price is.

By going in very low, she risks Rohan walking away. If her opening is much lower than his maximum aspirations (in this case, £1,500 less), he could decide that the offer is derisory and simply not worth his time trying to discuss a better price. Alternatively, if Rohan decides to try to move her price towards his acceptable (but lowest) price, it could cause problems, as Jenny may not want to move that far forward. If she does move, repeatedly, towards an acceptable price for Rohan, she is weakening her position with every step, especially if she has a long way to travel. She could find herself giving up on the deal if Rohan doesn't make reciprocal movements towards her. Deadlock beckons.

Either way, Jenny will end up without the car, as her very low bid has caused difficulty for both her and Rohan to move to a comfortable position on price, even though she would have paid more for it than Rohan's lowest acceptable price.

The best strategy

In theory, Jenny's best strategy is to persuade Rohan to disclose how little he is prepared to accept, without her disclosing how much she is prepared to pay. But Rohan's best strategy is the reverse: to persuade Jenny to disclose how much she is prepared to pay without his having to disclose how little he is prepared to accept. However, can Jenny get Rohan to disclose his lowest price? Not without some difficulty, if Rohan is wary of making disclosures that undermine his negotiating position.

Jenny appears to be caught in a dilemma. If she opens too close to her highest price, she risks paying more than she needs to; if she opens too far below her highest price, she risks antagonising Rohan into a deadlock.

Experience shows that Jenny's dilemma, when it is a single-issue negotiation and no other considerations are involved, has no obvious solution. Having decided on an opening price, you must also move the other negotiator towards your price while you move towards his price, in the certain knowledge that what you gain in a lower price as he moves towards you, he loses in the higher price he might otherwise have secured. In these contests there is a 'winner' and a 'loser', and people do not like losing. Both negotiators could end up unhappy with the outcome, one because she paid more than she wanted, the other because he got less than he wanted (i.e. it is a lose–lose outcome). To avoid this outcome, both strive hard to make the other do the moving.

Fortunately for the used-car market, if not the self-fulfilment of buyers and sellers, people do agree on the prices they pay or receive for their cars. Otherwise, they would remain so paralysed with the dilemma of where to open that they would fail to complete the transaction. The dilemmas faced by Jenny are felt by negotiators around the world on issues large and small, but because negotiators have to open somewhere at some time to make progress, their dilemmas are overcome in practice.

This chapter is about distributive bargaining, the single-issue negotiation between two parties, such as a negotiation between you and your bank manager about the extent of your overdraft, or between you and your children about how much time they can spend on their tablet tonight, or between you and your neighbour about the decibel level of their house party. By starting off with the seemingly simple negotiation of two parties over a single issue, we can make a lot of progress quickly in our search for answers to practical questions, like: 'Where should I open my offer?', 'How long should I continue negotiating?' and 'When should I cut my losses and stop negotiating?'

Distributive bargaining

Distributive bargaining is a single-issue negotiation. There is only one variable, often price but not exclusively so, that the two negotiators need to agree upon. Movement is often difficult, as all you get in return for moving further away from your entry point is the 'hope' that you will come to an agreement before you have to move any further. It's a fixed pie from which both negotiators want the biggest slice.

Let's start by generalising about the single-issue haggle and its component parts. Whether that is the price of a used car or a line in a contract, we need a way to analyse what is happening in the negotiation. Each negotiation starts with two possible solutions to the deal – yours and mine. The objective of the negotiation is to search for only one solution, the one we can both agree on. Thinking back to the car sale, at the start there was Jenny's (lower) price she wanted to pay for the car and Rohan's (higher) price he wanted for the car. If the car is to be sold, there can only be one price for the car, on which both Jenny and Rohan must agree.

A negotiator opens the negotiation with his Entry point (see Figure 2.1). This is the price he would like to achieve in the negotiation and can be based on many things: experience or detailed knowledge of what the market will bear, costs plus a 'mark-up' for his efforts, some consideration of tactics, etc. Whatever the reason behind it, the Entry point is where the negotiation will start. Each negotiator will

```
Buyer's entry point                    Seller's entry point
       |                                      |
       |──────────────────────────────────────|
           ◄──── Total negotiating range ────►
```

Figure 2.1 Entry points.

have a different entry point, and the difference in value between both negotiators' entry points will be the Total Negotiating Range. In other words, somewhere in between those two starting positions, an agreement can be made on a price.

Entry and exit prices

How can they reach agreement if their entry prices are separated by a negotiating range? The negotiating range implies distance, and the need to come together implies movement. The image of a distance between them is echoed in the language you will hear negotiators use to explain the progress, or lack of it, in their negotiations. They say things like: 'After 12 hours of talks, we are still a long way apart'. The idea of movement is similarly highlighted in statements like: 'At our last meeting, considerable progress was made as the parties moved closer together on some issues but not on others'. Neither of these images implies that movement is inevitable; quite the contrary, movement in negotiation is often grudgingly undertaken and only after a great deal of effort. Negotiators are less like ice skaters and more like rock climbers!

Movement in negotiation from their entry prices is essential if the two parties are to agree on a common price. Hence, they do not open with their final price; they give themselves 'negotiating room'. They expect, or prefer, the other negotiator to move towards their entry price, but they accept that it is unlikely that the other negotiator will move all the way. Some reciprocal, though not necessarily equal, movement will be expected.

How far, or how fast, the negotiators will walk towards each other depends on many factors, but there is some limit beyond which they do not intend to go in the current circumstances. This point is what I call their Exit point. It normally lies somewhere in the negotiating range between the entry points of the negotiators.

In some cases (see Figure 2.2), the exit points of the negotiators do not overlap, so the highest price the buyer is prepared to pay before walking away is lower than the lowest amount the seller is prepared to accept before walking away. Trying to move each other towards or beyond their exit points while not being within their own acceptable range will cause difficulty to each side, and no further progress will be made. Unless one or the other of the negotiators revises their exit price, they will fail to reach an agreement.

18 *Distributive bargaining*

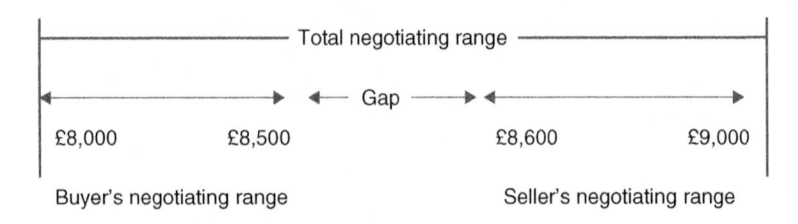

Figure 2.2 The gap between the negotiators' exit points.

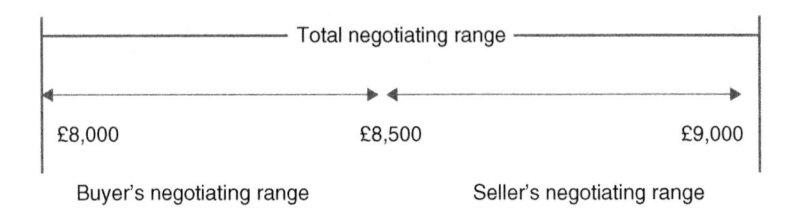

Figure 2.3 The negotiators' exit points meet.

Settlement range

So we have our first rule for single-issue negotiations: for an agreement to be possible, the exit points of the negotiators must, at the very least, meet, but preferably overlap. If they meet, it is possible that both negotiators will discover the price that is acceptable to both parties and come to an agreement (see Figure 2.3). So, if Jenny's highest possible acceptable price (her exit point) is £8,500, and Rohan's lowest acceptable price is £8,500, it is possible through movement from each other, that one of them will suggest this price and the other is able to accept.

When exit prices overlap (see Figure 2.4), the negotiators are much more likely to reach an agreement than when they simply meet. The overlap between the exit prices of each negotiator (i.e. between the prices of £8,250 and £8,500) is what I call the Settlement Range, because within this range a settlement is possible, though, as always, it is not assured.

Suppose the buyer (Jenny) offers to pay £8,251, which is within the settlement range and just above the seller's exit price of £8,250; would the seller (Rohan) accept this offer? Though it is possible that he might agree, we cannot say he will for sure. He might if he believes that the negotiation is likely to take up time that he would rather spend on something else, or if he believes that this is as far as the buyer will go. He might not if he thinks he has alternatives.

He could, for instance, decide to keep negotiating because, with an entry offer of £8,251 on the table, he knows now that he will settle higher than his exit price of £8,250. This could motivate him to keep trying to improve Jenny's price and see just how far she will go (unknown to the seller, the buyer is willing, in principle,

Distributive bargaining 19

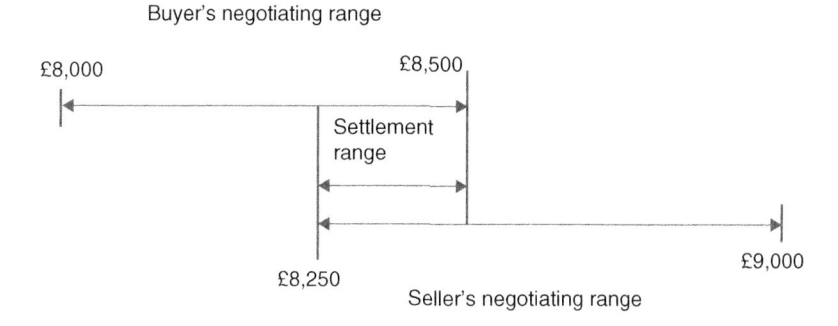

Figure 2.4 The negotiators' exit points overlap.

Figure 2.5 Negotiators with overlapping entry prices.

to go as high as £8,500). On the other hand, by delaying a settlement, he might fall foul of the buyer's impatience: perhaps the buyer only opted for a price of £8,251 to force the issue; perhaps she is less keen on buying now and has no wish to use up more time moving slowly towards her exit price of £8,500. Alternatively, she could feel that, as she made a 'generous' offer of £8,251, the next move should come from the seller and not from her. You can readily accept that, out of such misunderstandings, a lot of aggravation can be stimulated.

In general, as neither negotiator knows the exit prices of the other, they do not know whether the current offer is final or whether it is a prelude to a better price ('Does he mean "no", or is he merely testing my resolve?', thinks the wary negotiator). Moreover, when a negotiator discloses his entry price, he also implies something about his exit price which, in some circumstances, can be disadvantageous to him. Consider the situation in Figure 2.5.

Here, the negotiators have individual negotiating ranges of an unusual kind. First, think of the seller's point of view. He has an entry price of 115 and an exit price of 100. Suppose before he offers to sell at 115, the buyer cuts in and offers to buy at 120. What effect do you think this would have on the seller? Whatever else it does, it ought to cause him to pause before he responds. As the buyer's entry price of 120 is larger than the seller's entry price of 115, the seller now knows that the buyer is prepared to pay more than the maximum price he expected to receive. What would you do if somebody offered you more than you expected to receive? No doubt you would be inclined to accept this generous offer. (I hope, though, that you would hesitate before jumping in with a 'yes' to a buyer's first offer!)

> **Learning point:**
>
> *Negotiators think in ranges, not fixed positions. If someone opens with an appealing offer, how much further might they be prepared to go?*

Negotiators with overlapping entry prices

Because the seller knows that a buyer's exit price is bound to be larger than his entry price, he knows that the buyer is prepared to pay even more than his opening offer of 120, though he does not know by how much the buyer is prepared to increase his offer. In my view, the seller's best response here would be to reconsider his own, as yet undisclosed, entry price. This has the effect of moving his individual negotiating range to the right, as shown by the dotted line in Figure 2.5. His new exit price, in my view, should be at least 120 (the buyer's disclosed entry price) and he should consider just how far he should open above 120 to flush out the buyer's, hopefully, higher exit price.

It could be, however, that the buyer opened at 120 to force a quick decision and that he has no intention of spending any more time haggling over the price. For him, perhaps, 120 is a 'take-it-or-leave-it' offer. This still ought not to affect the seller's initial reaction (note my prescriptive advice). I am sure that you would agree that it would be silly for the seller to open at 115 after an offer of 120 from the buyer was on the table. Therefore, it seems sensible to advise him to test the buyer's resolve by opening with an entry price higher than 120. Most sellers would tend to do this, unless, of course, they are intimidated by the buyer's threat of 'take-it-or-leave-it' and steer clear of arousing their wrath. Despite this, however, I still recommend that you always challenge an allegedly firm price from anybody, even if you feel it necessary to disguise your challenge in the nicest of possible ways.

Buyers are unlikely to *knowingly* open at a higher price than the seller thinks they can get, though they might *unknowingly* do so. The price for anything depends on what it is worth to a buyer, and it is a wise seller who knows the value of everything to everybody else. When other negotiators disclose that they are prepared to pay more than you expect, it makes sense to revise your expectations. You might have missed something in your valuation; circumstances may be changing that

Distributive bargaining 21

you should be aware of; or you could be 'giving away the store' without realising it (if you don't know your business, you can be sure your rivals will teach you it!).

The 'run-down' hotel negotiation

The owners of a building in a run-down block in central Manchester were anxious about the state of their small hotel business. The profits from the business were not covering the monthly mortgage and operating costs of the hotel. In an attempt to save money, they made some staff redundant, which only served to reduce customer satisfaction, with the knock-on effect of reduced sales. The premises needed upgrading, with the local council pushing for an urgent upgrade to the toilet facilities in the bar/restaurant area, which were below standard and in need of disabled access. The building itself could do with some refurbishment and, at the very least, a lick of paint.

After much debate about how to finance their business, the owners decided to put the property on the market as a 'going concern'. They calculated that to pay off existing debt and cover any costs, they would need at least £400,000, though they conceded that they would be lucky to achieve £370,000. To test the market and see what offers they might receive, they decided to put the hotel business and building up for sale for £450,000.

While they received some interest, none of the potential buyers were willing to commit to an offer. The only real offer fell too far short of expectations to make negotiation worthwhile. The owners became more anxious to sell as their financial situation deteriorated, and as they were subsidising this business from the profits of their other operations, they became increasingly keen to release their capital and use it more profitably elsewhere.

A prospective buyer approached them, who clearly had little, if any, knowledge of the hotel trade. Having asked some questions, as well as nominally looking through their books and having the building surveyed, he made an offer to purchase for the asking price of £450,000. Meanwhile, the owners received an order from the city council for them to upgrade the kitchens at a cost of £70,000 or face the loss of their trading licence. This prompted them to accept the offer without further delay.

After buying the building, the first thing the buyer did was shut the hotel business down. The last thing he did was sell the building for redevelopment for £3 million. What was going on?

The owners of the hotel complex thought they were selling a hotel business to a naïve entrant to the hotel trade, when, in fact, they were naïvely exiting from the real estate business they did not know they were in.

Exercise 2B

From the story above, draw a diagram to represent the relationship of the entry and exit prices of the hotel sale.
You will find my answer in Appendix 2 checkpoint answers.

Distributive bargaining

The negotiators' surplus

If I am prepared to accept a price for my property between, say, £150,000 and £250,000, this defines my negotiating range. The existence of this negotiating range implies that I am effectively willing to accept as much as £100,000 less for my property if I sell it to you at £150,000 instead of my top price of £250,000. Conversely, if I achieve a price of £250,000, I have settled for £100,000 more than the least I would have accepted. All prices between £150,000 and £250,000 will divide the difference between us of £100,000 into the amount I give up by accepting less than £250,000 and the amount I keep by persuading you to pay more than £150,000. Naturally, I would prefer to keep as much of the £100,000 as possible (preferably all of it!), which is equivalent to saying that I prefer to settle at, or close to, my entry point.

This simple notion can be extended to give us a useful analytical tool by considering the arithmetic of the settlement range created by the overlapping negotiating ranges of the negotiators.

We can see the settlement range for the car sale between Jenny and Rohan in Figure 2.4. The range is between the buyer's highest (exit) point of £8,500 and the seller's lowest (exit) point of £8,250. As there is the overlap, any price suggested between (and including) £8,250 and £8,500 could lead to an agreement between both sides. If we call that price P*, we can see that represented in Figure 2.6.

Learning point:

The Surplus is, in effect, the amount the negotiator gets to keep from his negotiating range by not settling at his exit point.

The seller wants any price higher than £8,250, so the seller's surplus is represented by S, which is P*, less the seller's exit point.

S = P* − SEP

Seller's Exit
£8,250

Buyer's Exit
£8,500

P*
£8,400

◄─── Seller's surplus ───►│◄─── Buyer's surplus ───►

◄─────── Negotiators' surplus ───────►

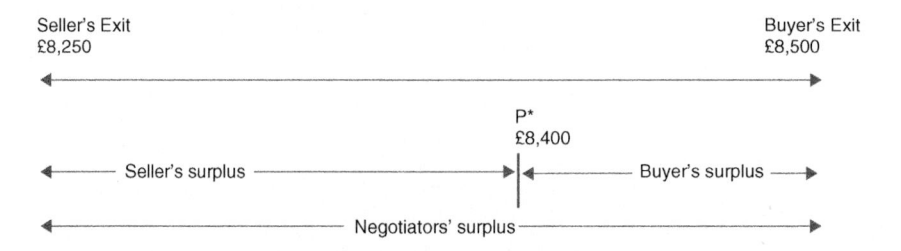

Figure 2.6 The negotiators' surplus when exit points overlap.

The buyer wants any price less than £8,500, so the buyer's surplus is represented by B, which is the buyer's exit point, less P*.

B = BEP − P*

The negotiators' surplus (represented as N) is the total available surplus in the negotiation, so the buyer's exit point, less the seller's exit point.

N = BEP − SEP

You could say that in a negotiation the seller and buyer are effectively seeking agreement upon the distribution between them of the available negotiators' surplus. Logically, it is necessary for the seller's exit price to be lower than the buyer's exit price (i.e. in symbols, SEB < BEP) for there to be a settlement range. The negotiators can only distribute the available surplus between them by agreeing to a common price, P*, within the settlement range. A failure to agree on the distribution of the available surplus leaves them both without any surplus from that negotiation. In these circumstances, they will have to search for another negotiator to realise the available surplus.

A point to note here is that there are many occasions where prices within the settlement range are not accepted; just because it is possible to do a deal within this range, does not mean the parties have to agree. There could be many reasons why what seem like perfectly reasonable proposals are rejected despite falling well within the range. These include the desire to not be the first to give in, a determination to move closer to your own entry point, a perception of power or just plain stubbornness. Whatever the reason, it's not uncommon to see deadlock in single-issue negotiations, even when a price 'should' be acceptable.

If we look at our car sale example, though, we can see how the surplus might look for Jenny and Rohan. If we assume that they agreed to a deal at £8,400, we can calculate that the Negotiators' Surplus is £8,500 − £8,250 = £250, the Buyer's Surplus is £8,500 − £8,400 = £100 and the Seller's Surplus is £8,400 − £8,250 = £150.

What can we learn from this? In practical terms, we could never make this calculation for a real negotiation as we never find out the other person's exit price. This can perhaps explain why negotiations can be fraught and tense, and we sometimes are reluctant to agree to a price even though it is within our own range. If we are close to, or even on, our exit point, are we creating more surplus for the other party? It is normal to question how much they are gaining compared to us, and that desire to not be the perceived 'loser' can cause us to question the validity of doing the deal. If both parties feel the same, it can increase the tension and likelihood of a deadlock, as neither party wants to have the smallest surplus.

Sometimes negative perceptions are self-fulfilling in that they cause one or both sides to apply sanctions (strikes and lock-outs) to coerce the other into agreement, or to warn them off from misinterpreting their willingness to agree as a sign of weakness. Alternatively, third-party mediation can be tried to unlock the apparent deadlock. In fact, mediation could be defined as a method of discovering whether or not there is an available surplus for the negotiators to distribute without jeopardising their longer-term interests.

How do you know if a negotiator is being truthful when he claims that his current offer is the best he can do? The best way to tackle this kind of question is to approach it from another angle: let us ask instead what happens if you believe that the other negotiator is pretending that his current offer is his exit price. You could express your doubts about the offer with statements like: 'I know you can do better than that', or, 'Nobody can realistically expect to offer so little with the profit levels you have attained this year'. More colourful expressions are also possible, such as: 'Are you kidding?', 'Can you be serious?', and 'Do you think I am stupid?' (the last being particularly inept, as it will only lead to argument).

Now think of the position the other negotiator could be in if, indeed, his last offer was close to, or at, his exit point, and you are pushing him to move but he cannot. The more the negotiator protests that his current price is his exit price, the more he convinces a negotiator who is predisposed to assume that he is lying that his suspicions of duplicity are justified. A perception, once it has a hold on you, requires quite a lot of convincing to dislodge it. The result is that the level of tension between the two negotiators rises. Frustration leads to anger and, in negotiation, it leads to deadlock.

Interestingly, the words, gestures and tone of a negotiator defending a current offer and the same negotiator defending an exit point are normally indistinguishable, and a moment's thought will reveal to you why this must be so. For if it were not – if in practice a negotiator had a different set of words, gestures and tones for an exit point to the ones he used for the other prices between his entry and exit points – it would make the negotiation process redundant – we would simply wait for the appropriate words, gestures and tone for an exit point to be used and ignore everything else before it.

But, you could interject, would it not benefit decision-makers if we could short-circuit the often lengthy negotiation process by the device of established words, gestures and tones that signify the true exit point of a negotiator? Surely this could save time and avoid misunderstandings? This would be true if – and it is a big if – we could be sure that the people we negotiate with do not artificially use the words, gestures and tones appropriate for revealing their true exit points to support offers that are not their true exit points. In short, we are vulnerable to their manipulation if they learn to act as if they were at an exit when in fact they are not. This brings us full circle.

You have no way of knowing for sure that any particular offer is as far as the other negotiator will go. You know yourself how often you are prepared to offer more, or accept less, in your negotiations, and you can take it that what is true for you is true for the other negotiator. This suggests that negotiators should always assume that the first offer is never an exit offer and you should, in consequence, refrain from treating a first offer as if it were (hence, my prescriptive advice above not to accept even generous first offers!). It follows that all offers should be treated as if there is another, last or exit, offer in reserve.

This brings us to our second rule for negotiators: negotiators think in ranges, so never accept a first offer, no matter how generous. Always negotiate.

The broad strategy for the seller is to move the settlement price, P*, to the right, as close to the buyer's exit point as possible; the buyer, meanwhile, is trying to move P* to the left, as close to the seller's exit point as possible. But normally neither of them knows each other's exit point and, therefore, they cannot be certain that the price they settle on within the presumed settlement range is the absolute best they can do. As a negotiator approaches his exit point, he will increase his resistance to further move towards it, and behaviours associated with increasing resistance (e.g. a firmness in his language, more aggressive assertions about what might happen if agreement is not reached, general irritation and bad temper, etc.) might be a sign that his exit point is looming; but how can you be certain that the observed behaviours normally associated with increasing resistance are nothing more than a ruse to bluff you into settling where he is, rather than an indication that he is approaching his exit point? The answer is that you cannot be certain of judging a negotiator's exit price from his behaviour – negotiators learn how to act as if they prefer deadlock to moving again.

A failure to settle is not proof that a settlement was impossible, merely that one did not occur on this occasion between these two negotiators over that issue. Neither is a settlement proof that the negotiators maximised their share of the available negotiators' surplus – though they may be relieved that they settled within their limits. Perhaps if they had handled the negotiation differently, by hanging on for a little more for a little longer, they might have increased their share of the available surplus.

Is there such a thing as the perfect negotiation, where we are confident that we have wrung out the very last amount of surplus available? Should we in fact keep negotiating until we feel we have reached this peak surplus? It is impossible to judge accurately how much surplus is available – remember, we only ever know three out of the four key pieces of information required to calculate the surplus: our entry and exit points and the other negotiator's entry point. The reality is that the perfect deal exists only if we leave our perceptions of surplus equality (or inequality) firmly behind us and focus only on the fact that both parties were happy to do the deal on those terms. That is the definition of a successful negotiation.

The perfect negotiation

Consider the story of Gavin, working in a hotel on the west coast of Scotland. In the public bar, where all the locals gather to drink, he was chatting to Jim. Jim was on cloud nine, ordering drinks for all his friends to celebrate. He had sold his boat. His boat had been unusable for three years, needed thousands spent on it to make it seaworthy again, and was costing him fees to keep in a nearby marina. The hole in its hull was the least of his problems, though, as his wife had had enough and threatened to leave him by the end of the month if he didn't get rid of the boat. He'd looked in to selling it, but the reality was he

> would have to pay £250 to get someone to pick it up and scrap it. Imagine his joy when a young girl from Glasgow turned up and offered him £1,000 for it.
>
> The young girl from Glasgow was Joanne, and she was sitting in the hotel restaurant eating steak when Gavin went through to deliver the bottle of champagne she had ordered. Gavin enquired if she was celebrating something, and she told him she was delighted that she had just bought a boat. She had been looking for a few weeks and finally agreed with a local man to buy his boat for £1,000.
>
> Gavin was concerned that she had done the worst deal ever, so he asked her if she knew much about boats. She replied that no, she had no clue about boats; she was a props manager for a television production company and had been tasked to find a boat to blow up in a tv show. She was delighted that she had managed to find the perfect-sized boat; ok, it had a hole in it, but with proper lighting, no one would notice. She was also delighted she had spent only £1,000 out of her £15,000 budget. She would be in her boss's good books for months for this great deal.

Could both parties have done much better in the negotiation? Yes, Jim could have received a few thousand pounds more, and Joanne could have paid much less, maybe even nothing, but they were both absolutely delighted with the outcome of the deal. Sometimes, when the deal is good, we should be happy to say yes and not worry about 'Could I have done better?'

Conclusion

The single-issue negotiation is common and is often based on one-off transactions where a good or service is being bought or sold. The trouble with the single issue is that it is tough to get movement. The fear of the unknown (the other negotiator's exit point) drives both negotiators to behave candidly, and often suspiciously, towards each other, constantly questioning the sense in moving further from your entry point and whether the other party might be making a fortune at your expense. What will you get for all your efforts? The same thing that you get if you agreed on a price nearer your entry point. It's this pressure that causes negotiators to suffer a form of 'psychic pain', as it is a battle within yourself every time you concede a little more to try to get agreement.

Whereas we often do not know what the other party's exit price was, it is possible to conceive of negotiating situations where both negotiators know each other's exit price, or where they can make a good guess at it. This is not as unusual as you might think. For example, we might be partners negotiating the distribution of a known commission we jointly earned from supplying a service, or we might be sharing a known prize in a lottery or even a windfall gain of a £20 note we found while walking along the street. In all these and similar cases, the amount to be distributed is the available negotiators' surplus, and this amount is known to both of us – it is the total commission, the amount of the prize, the amount of profit, or the £20 note. If we fail to agree on the distribution of the surplus, we get nothing until we do. Thus, our potential gain runs from zero to the total amount to be distributed.

Given we have a fixed sum to be divided, what do you think is the most likely division? In the absence of any other information that might indicate some special merit to our claims, it is likely that we would divide the sum in two equal shares. This conforms to notions of a 'fair' distribution. Indeed, so prevalent is the notion of fairness in this context that attempts by one negotiator to breach it by claiming more than 50 per cent, when no special merits support the claim, are likely to provoke strong resistance on the part of the other negotiator, even if the resultant deadlock means neither gets anything. This situation is not uncommon in bitterly contested claims of rival heirs to an estate. The contest can become so acrimonious that the competing heirs squander the whole estate in legal fees.

Fairness as a distribution principle operates most effectively where there are no asymmetries in the claims of the negotiators for their share of the sum available. Two people who put in the same amount of effort, the same amount of cash, took the same risks, and contributed equally to the idea that created the prospect of a yield, are going to be hard pressed to justify an extra share for themselves out of the fixed sum available. But if there are asymmetries in our respective claims to a share of the surplus, then we expect these to be acknowledged, particularly when each of us perceives our contribution to justify a share that is greater than half.

A concern for asymmetries in our entitlements lies behind the suggestion that, to prevent these asymmetries being overlooked by a one-sided manipulation of the negotiating process, we should arrange for each negotiator to declare their price in some honest manner at the start of the negotiation rather than leave it to be inferred, and perhaps misjudged, or even misrepresented, during the negotiation. If the joint disclosure shows that BEP<SEP, then no negotiation need be undertaken, and the negotiators can use their time for some other purpose, including seeking another negotiator with whom to do business.

What happens when disclosure shows that BEP>SEP? One obvious proposal could be to split the surplus in half (i.e. provide each negotiator with BEP + SEP/2). If we could rely on negotiators to always disclose their true exit price, it might be possible to take a shortcut through some of the seemingly interminable wrangling associated with negotiating. People in a hurry might value this system. But this system, like many others that are proposed to obviate the need for negotiating, has a fatal flaw: how do we know that the revealed exit price is the 'true' exit price?

If the buyer discloses that he will pay as much as 500, the seller has the choice of deciding that no deal is possible (his own exit price is genuinely more than 500), or of adjusting his genuine exit price, say, 450 (the least he would accept), to, say, 496. If he disclosed the truth, the resultant price, P*, would be (500 + 450)/2 = 950/2 = 475. By adjusting his exit price from 450 to a false one of 496, he raises P* to (500 + 496/2) = 996/2 = 498, an increase in his favour of 23. As he has an incentive to cheat, we must assume – and the other negotiator will certainly be inclined to do so – that he is likely to cheat. In these circumstances, the first negotiator to disclose his exit price might also feel it is prudent to cheat and reduce his genuine exit price of 500 to a false one and open at, say, 460, to counteract the possibility of cheating by the second negotiator. In the event of these suspicions being acted upon, the prospects of the attempt to curb the negotiation process succeeding will diminish, and the negotiators will be faced with resorting to the normal negotiating process.

Disclosing our exit prices simultaneously does not totally answer the objection. It certainly reduces the opportunity for a post-disclosure adjustment by the second exit price, but this does not prevent either negotiator writing down a false exit price with a view to gaining an advantage similar to those described above. Buyers will be inclined to minimise, sellers to maximise, their exit prices, each hoping that the resultant arithmetic moves the other into conceding more of the genuinely available surplus. Behaving in this way, without constraint, will provoke deadlocks as each overshoots the other's genuine exit price. Instead of time being saved, the negotiators will have taken the time to restart negotiations with others, or with each other.

Most negotiations involve no prior knowledge of the other negotiator's exit price; some involve no prior knowledge of the other negotiator's entry price, leaving you exposed to the danger of misjudging where you should enter if you are compelled to open first. Thinking in terms of entry and exit prices and of negotiation and settlement ranges helps to clarify the problem and to set out the negotiating tasks in specific cases. The strategic problem of uncertainty about the values and interests of the other negotiator can be addressed by looking for clues as to what determines where, and why, the other negotiator is likely to place his entry and exit points. People do not set their goals arbitrarily – they relate them, albeit often loosely if not remotely, to their perceptions of what they are entitled to in the situation they are in – and searching for the basis of their goals is essential if we are to prepare for what they might look for when they attempt to do business with us.

Do not underestimate the powerful background effect of the notion of equity in the distribution of a surplus between the negotiators. It pervades a great deal of the thinking people have about what is, and is not, a good deal for them. Bearing this in mind when you are analysing a distributive negotiating problem should prove fruitful. Let me give a short example of what I mean.

Usually we must decide on the distribution of a surplus *before* the activity that creates the surplus is undertaken. Here the relative keenness of the negotiators to undertake the activity that generates the surplus influences the outcome. For example, suppose you were a researcher, like Vassily, with no capital but with an idea for the commercial exploitation of a product he has developed. You might be persuaded by a venture fund with capital but no exploitable product to take a minority 40 per cent share (or even less) of the equity in your company you set up to produce and market your invention, the rest being retained by the fund. This unequal distribution is common in new projects that are widely treated as high-risk ventures by those with money to fund them. Vassily was so keen to get the project under way – he had spent several years working on it – that he preferred to forego an equal, or better, distribution of the equity because the alternative was to forego the project. The venture fund manager, on the other hand, was less keen than the researcher about the specific project because he had a choice of projects to invest in (or, at least, that is how he presented it to Vassily). He was solely concerned, he claimed, with the security of his investment, and to accept any distribution that does not leave him with the majority of the equity to 'protect my investment' would be inequitable.

It was at this point that Vassily asked for my advice. He was concerned about the deal he had been offered and was worried about his future. He had heard of a case, he told me, where an inventor agreed to a similar arrangement with another fund and, after a year or two of suffering various personal privations while he brought the product up to a marketable standard and could see the rewarding income stream on the horizon, he found one day that the fund had sold its majority share of the equity to an American firm already established in the business. The new owners put their own team into the plant, side-lined the inventor, and made a derisory offer for his small equity stake on a take-it-or-leave-it basis and went on to milk the profits from his invention. Vassily did not want something similar to happen to him (it was less a case of money than of personal pride).

I told Vassily that we had to find a distribution of the equity that met both negotiators' objectives, because if it did not meet their objectives, then one or both would refuse to consent to the distribution. Vassily wanted to borrow funds to develop a marketable product that he would own; the fund manager wanted to earn profits on his capital and protect his capital base. I suggested he propose a formula that changed the distribution of equity over time in step with the profits it earned.

The distribution of the equity could start off at 60:40 in favour of the venture fund. As the joint venture earned profits, Vassily could use some of his share of the profits to buy back equity from the venture capitalist for an agreed price. In the extreme, he could use all of his profits (perhaps topped up with borrowing from other sources) to buy back equity. This would meet the venture capitalist's concerns about the security of his investment and would provide him with a profit on his capital. The price of his equity at each successive round of purchase would rise with the increasing profitability of the joint venture, thus assuring him of a profit on his investment as well as of its security, and, in the absence of profits, but with a continuing desire of Vassily to acquire equity, would assure him of extracting his investment at its par value over time.

Clearly, the buy-back clauses in such an agreement would have to be drafted very carefully. So would the entry and exit points Vassily chose before the negotiation. If, strategically, he accepted the fund manager's argument about protecting his investment until it made profits, then Vassily would automatically have to accept a minority stake. He could open at 49 per cent and work downwards. His exit point could be established by considering how long, at his share of the projected profits, it would take him to buy back a majority stake. The higher the profits, the quicker he could buy back any given difference between his exit point (assuming he was pushed to that level) and 51 per cent. By narrowing the gap between his agreed share and 51 per cent, Vassily would make that task easier. He could also avoid the situation the other inventor got himself into by specifying that the fund manager could only sell his shares to Vassily at a price that related their value to the company's profits.

Setting out the negotiating problem in the form of distribution diagrams helped clarify what was at stake for Vassily. As we analyse increasingly complex negotiating situations involving several, and not just one, negotiable issue, we will find the basic structure of the single-issue diagram of great help in revealing the options open to us in our negotiations. Several negotiable issues, when linked, are the key to successful negotiation.

Checkpoint 2

2.1 What is the definition of distributive bargaining?

2.2 What is the surplus, and how is it calculated?

2.3 When should you stop negotiating in distributive bargaining?

2.4 You are considering selling your caravan for £12,000. While you are preparing to advertise the caravan, someone offers you £15,000 for it. Do you:

   a) Accept the offer?

   b) Tell them to wait until the caravan is advertised?

   c) Negotiate?

3 Integrative bargaining, part 1
Preparation

Introduction

As we saw in Chapter 2, distributive bargaining has its place in negotiation, but it has one major flaw – it is a single-issue negotiation. The majority of deals that we do have many issues, and that plethora of choices gives us much more scope to negotiate. Rather than the tough prospect of trying to move along the settlement range towards each other by guessing, and with every movement costing us more, integrative bargaining gives us the ability to make exchanges across different issues and, perhaps, add value rather than dilute it.

How do we manage the process of the multi-issue negotiation? There are four main phases in every negotiation, and by learning how each phase works, we can better manage our time in each phase and become more effective negotiators. The four phases are: Prepare, Debate, Propose and Bargain.

In this chapter, we look in detail at arguably the most important phase: Preparation. It's an area on which most of us spend far too little time. There are many valid reasons why we don't spend enough time preparing for negotiations: perhaps you have no time to prepare, as the negotiation has been sprung upon you; perhaps you have no time to spare to prepare, as you are very busy with all your other work, life, family, etc.; perhaps you are fairly confident you don't need to spend a lot of time preparing – after all, you know all about the elements of the deal and don't want to waste valuable time doing something that will not benefit you. However, you might want to think again about the importance of preparation; a little time spent now can save a great deal of time during the negotiation, and also make you a more effective, persuasive negotiator. Consider the following example:

> *Farmer Jones has a very restricted diet. He is a subsistence farmer who grows nothing but potatoes, which is his sole source of food. Hence, he has potato porridge for breakfast, boiled potatoes for lunch and roast potatoes for dinner. In between, for his morning break he has a potato sandwich with a mashed-potato filling, and for his afternoon break he has a plate of potato soup. In consequence, you can imagine, Farmer Jones is pretty fed up with potatoes.*

32 *Integrative bargaining, pt. 1: Preparation*

> *Farmer Jones considered his predicament and decided to do something about it. He filled a sack with some of his potatoes and, with considerable effort, he carried the sack on his back two miles along the road to his neighbour, Farmer Morgan. He offered Farmer Morgan a deal: 'Trade me something for my potatoes'. Farmer Morgan was most impressed with this offer and enthusiastically agreed to a trade. He told Farmer Jones: 'I will trade you your sack of potatoes for my sack of potatoes'.*

Exercise 3A

Is Farmer Jones likely to be as pleased with this deal as Farmer Morgan appears to be? Will he agree to the swap?

From the information you have been given, I hope you agree that it would be highly unlikely that the answer to these questions would be anything other than 'no'. But before you dismiss the issue as a trivial one, be assured that it is necessary to explore why Farmer Jones (or anybody else in similar circumstances) would be unlikely to agree to a trade. In the answer, obvious as it may be, lies the essence of negotiation.

Farmer Jones is unlikely to swap a sack of potatoes for another sack of potatoes because his motivation to trade arose precisely from his desire to eat something other than potatoes, of which he has plenty already. If the result of a trade with Farmer Morgan was to acquire another sack of potatoes, he might just as well have avoided the physical effort of transporting his potatoes. Why Farmer Morgan offered to trade his potatoes for Farmer Jones's is open to conjecture, though, except in the case where Farmer Morgan perceived there was a difference between his and Farmer Jones's potatoes; we might as well resort to Schiller's barb that, 'against stupidity, even the Gods battle in vain'.

Farmer Jones, however, is wasting his time and effort if he seeks to trade what he already has, and does not want, for more of the same from somebody else. Instead, he would be more likely to be looking for something entirely different, which in his case could conceivably be almost any other kind of food that Farmer Morgan has available for trade (such as cabbages, cauliflowers, parsnips, apples, bacon, beans, etc.). *The only decision the two farmers have to make is to agree on a rate of exchange of Farmer Jones's potatoes for whatever Farmer Morgan offers in trade.* But be absolutely clear: no trade will take place unless they exchange what each has for something different. (Would you trade an ordinary two-pound coin for another ordinary two-pound coin?)

Exercise 3B

Try some more questions with 'obvious' answers:
  Could Farmer Jones have avoided his wasted effort in attempting to trade with Farmer Morgan and still serve his original purpose of varying his diet:

a) *By hawking his potatoes round all of his neighbours until he found somebody with something to trade?*
b) *By asking Farmer Morgan what he would trade besides potatoes before he lifted the sack?*
c) *By checking with all his neighbours as to what they might offer in trade for a sack of potatoes?*
d) *By advertising his willingness to trade potatoes with anybody, providing the offered goods were suitable and the terms were right?*

Farmer Jones might still have wasted his time by hawking his sack of potatoes around his neighbours – perhaps they are all potato farmers – and this would leave him no better off in the exchange and worse off in the expenditure of his energy.

What are the differences in activities (b), (c) and (d) from (a)? All of them involve him in some form of **preparatory** activity before he commits himself to the physical effort of carrying his potatoes around in search of a customer.

Asking Farmer Morgan what he has for trade (b) enables Farmer Jones to decide whether to go ahead, and if so, to agree to terms, before he reaches for his potatoes; asking his neighbours what they might have for trade (c) gives Farmer Jones the opportunity to determine whether or not there is a wider range of options available than what Farmer Morgan is willing to offer; advertising his interest in a trade (d) widens even more the catchment area of people who might have even better deals on offer – in which case, he may prefer to deal with them – or introduces him to those who might have similar deals on offer – in which case, he knows that the local deals on offer are representative of the market price for potatoes. In short, the activity of preparation reduces wasted effort and time, identifies gaps in the information needed to make decisions by trading, and establishes the criteria for judging the merits of possible traded solutions.

Farmer Jones could have avoided much painful effort and, perhaps, not a little disappointment, by some pre-negotiation activity, or preparation. So could all those others who, despite the evidence to the contrary, continue to walk into negotiations comforted by the illusion that a commitment to 'hearing what they have to say' is a sufficient act of preparation. What if they ask you something? How will you answer? Will you give something away through being unprepared?

Preparation, of course, takes time, but invariably it is time well spent. In fact, I would go further and assert that much of the time spent in face-to-face negotiation is prolonged because negotiators, while ready to 'hear what the other side has got to say', are not able to respond sensibly to what they hear without doing the preparatory work they avoided before they met them.

Far from a negotiation being a carefully scripted exchange between people who know what they are doing, it is often a most confusing interaction in which the parties appear not to be sure of what they want or why they want it solely in the form they have asked for it. Moreover, life and negotiations are full of surprises. People often ask for things you do not have, on terms you cannot afford, and on time-scales that are impossible to meet. The usual reaction when we hear things that disturb us is to attack the source of the disturbance – which, in negotiation, risks a counter-attack – instead of setting to work professionally to secure what we want on terms that are satisfactory to both of us.

Preparation does not eliminate surprises, nor does it cause both parties to stick to the agenda, or even the topic under discussion. What it does is allow you to anticipate likely stances and demands, and to focus your attention on the potential for trade. If you are thinking about the potential for trade then you are thinking about the potential solution, and this alone increases your effectiveness as a negotiator. If we left preparation to our good intentions we would never get it done. Time for our other inclinations will always win out in a contest with our good intentions. Most of the time, most of us are just too busy to stop what we are doing, or to delay what we must do, to spend our precious time thinking about what might or might not happen, when and if the people we are about to see get to the point and start talking the numbers we want to hear.

What we need then is a method of preparation that is adaptable to various time pressures – nobody is always *that* busy! – and that is flexible as to the amount of detail we have time to consider. What follows is a version of the Negotek® Preparation Planner (see Figure 3.1), which was developed to handle complex negotiating problems, particularly where the outcome is highly prized and the parties have a fairly good idea of what they are about. On the basis that what works in the real world of professional negotiation should have value for you in your negotiations, the Negotek® preparation method should both elucidate the principles of preparation and provide you with a workable set of tools for any scale of negotiation for which you care to prepare more than half-heartedly.

Clearly, the more significant the outcome of the negotiation, the more detail (and time) required to make best use of your efforts, and, while I would not insist that you apply the entire Negotek® method to a routine purchase of a shirt, I would suggest that it is more than worth your while to apply it to a major deal. However, I should point out that even a routine purchase, if only by implication, involves the analytical considerations addressed by the Negotek® Planner.

The Negotiation Problem		
Interests		
Issues	Priorities	Negotiation Range
		Entry Exit
Tradables		
BATNA		

Figure 3.1 The Negotek® Preparation Phase Planner.

What do we need to do first?

> The Forth Agency is a very successful advertising agency based in London, with many high-profile clients. Over the years it has won many awards and is highly regarded for its work. Amanda is one of the directors at Forth and has been asked by the board to look at supplier contracts that are not working out and to find replacements where improvements cannot be made.
>
> Amanda's first supplier is PDQ, a small photographic agency, which is relatively new to the market. They started working with Forth 10 months ago after successfully bidding for the job. Their prices were very low compared to more established firms, and Forth decided to give their work a trial as their picture portfolio had been excellent. While the work they produced for Forth was of the highest standard, Amanda noticed that their cost to use them as a supplier was huge, not because of their work, but their paperwork. There were inaccuracies on a high percentage of invoices, which meant extra time spent by account staff checking and correcting errors. In effect, the money they were saving on the work was being eaten up by the costs incurred to use PDQ as a supplier.
>
> Speaking with her team, Amanda realized that she really didn't want to lose PDQ as a supplier (one of their photos had been used in a prize-winning advert), but unless they could fix the problem with bad paperwork, it wasn't going to be worth their while keeping them on. She tasked her project team with preparing a negotiating brief for her meeting with PDQ.

Exercise 3C

Where should the project team start? Which of these questions do you think they should ask first?

a) *Is PDQ liable for any poor performance issues?*
b) *What bargaining leverage does Forth have in the negotiations?*
c) *What data are available on the paperwork costs/time?*
d) *What demands can Forth make to PDQ on their performance issue?*
e) *What other suppliers can do the job?*

a) Is PDQ liable for any poor performance issues?

This may become an important task later in the team's preparation or if the negotiations falter or deadlock, but it is not the first thing the project team needs to know, particularly if it is looking for a negotiated, rather than a litigated, solution.

b) What bargaining leverage does Forth have in the negotiations?

Assessing bargaining leverage is also a task for later in the preparation phase. Too early a concern with leverage can lead to too early a reliance on leverage rather than trading.

c) What data are available on the paperwork costs/time?

'In God we trust; all others must use data' is excellent advice for all negotiators. The first task of a preparation session is to identify the data relevant to the negotiation and, before doing anything else, arrange to collect and analyse it. Good causes have been foiled by lack of data, or the sloppy collection and analysis of data, and even by the total incomprehension of the data.

Relying on general statements ('The paperwork is always late'; 'Your account staff are impossible to find when we need them'; 'The level of inaccuracies is woeful'; and so on) leaves the negotiator vulnerable to real data and to the question: 'What evidence do you have to support these complaints?' (in the absence of which, Forth's remarks are more likely to lead to an argument). If you can answer the question with supporting evidence, you are closer to a solution than if you cannot: 'Here is a record of the number of times your invoicing was incorrect'; 'The phone logs to your accounts department for the last 21 invoices show an average response time of two working days'; 'The average amount of problems with our other suppliers is 8%; your account amounts to 43%'. Without data, we are wasting our time, and worse, we are unlikely to get what we want.

d) What demands can Forth make to PDQ on their performance issue?

Forth cannot make demands until they know the extent of the problem and what form it has taken. This brings them back to data. Hunches are no substitute for proposals that address the actual problem they have and not the one they have chosen out of ignorance of the facts.

e) What other suppliers can do the job?

While this is interesting in general, and perhaps ultimately something we might need to know, it is hardly relevant in the immediate future, as Forth are unlikely to replace PDQ unless no other solution can be found; hence, for the immediate future, they are tied to finding a solution to the actual problem they have, with the paperwork they have, from the supplier they have. Suppose that upon investigation they discover that their own accounting procedures or their own demands on PDQ are the main cause of the problem? Until they know the facts, finding out about other sources of supply cannot be a priority.

It does not really matter what it is that you are planning to negotiate about; if you do not have data, you cannot do much but hope for the best. If you were planning to buy a car, you would be advised to check out prices for similar models from as many sources as is convenient (garages, newspaper advertisements, internet sales sites, television programmes, etc.) and to see what critics (and end-users) have said about the make and model you are considering. The process is similar if it is a house purchase or any relatively expensive item. We are seldom experts in the products we buy, and a lack of data only compounds our ignorance.

Large organisations require their purchasing procedures to include detailed reports on the market for the products they are contemplating buying and on the firms that are attempting to sell to them. This has implications, of course, for those trying to sell to large organisations.

The mere collection of data and its analysis does not give a negotiator a clear run at achieving his objectives. Data in negotiation is almost always controversial. Your data lead you (or are led by your selection of it!) to support your proposals; the other party is likely to place your data under close scrutiny to challenge your version of the most suitable or equitable solution.

The data required by the project team at Forth consist of the incorrect invoice rates and time spent by accounts correcting it for the relevant period. After all, it is the alleged failings of the PDQ accounts team that will be the focus of the negotiation. Without data, we are negotiating about impressions, feelings and assumptions, none of which provide a firm basis for effective decision-making.

Suppose that the data from the project team are shown in Table 3.1. Amanda can clearly see that, though some progress has been made in the last two months, the number of inaccuracies in the invoices from PDQ is, on average, 35 points higher than other suppliers, taking up an average of 30 extra hours – almost a week! – for the accounts staff each month.

What can Amanda offer to the photo producers by way of an incentive to motivate them to a sustained improvement in admin? This is the task she has set for the project team. Assuming that you were a member of the project team, you and your colleagues could approach your task in the following manner.

What are we negotiating about?

Having collected the data in Table 3.1 and considered its implications, you would have to prepare a workable proposal to the photographer and/or be ready to

Table 3.1 Data on invoice accuracy and time spent correcting those errors

Month	Invoice inaccuracy (%)	No. of hours correcting errors
1	31	20
2	46	34
3	59	39
4	38	27
5	41	29
Average	**43%**	**30 hours per month**

respond to one that might come from them. To do this, you would have to decide what you want to happen, and given the information you have to hand and the working assumptions you can make, you must decide what you can negotiate about to achieve what you want.

If you consider the outline Negotek® Planner in Figure 3.1 as a guide to your preparations, you will see all the aspects of preparation you need to think about before beginning your negotiation. Don't take my word for it, though; let's work through the example for Amanda's project team below.

The negotiators are guided to their wants by identifying their **Interests**, and from their Interests, selecting the **Issues** that will achieve those Interests; for all **Issues**, they would need to decide their **Positions**, or preferably the range of Positions that they will aim to achieve.

In Amanda's case, their interest arises from the data: because the reduction in cost from poor admin will make the supplier more valuable (their Interest), Forth wants to decrease errors on the accounts (the Issue), and the degree to which they want to decrease errors is their Position. Any negotiated solution would have to address their Interest; that is, implementing the agreed-upon solution would serve the desired Interest. Some solutions suggest themselves or arise from experience: for example, a need for higher margins through stemming avoidable losses is an Interest; the policy you choose to contribute to your Interest – reducing thefts from your warehouses – is an Issue; and the details of your anti-theft policy – you could propose a random-search policy for all personnel, for example – make up your Position. Likewise, to improve quality for competitive advantage is an Interest, a proposed preventative defects policy is an Issue and the details of policy form your Position. Finally, to increase provision for your retirement is your Interest, an increase in your annual salary is the Issue, and how much of an increase is your Position.

The distinction between Interests, Issues and Positions is of relevance when we are negotiating solutions because sometimes we can accept changes in our Positions or a switching of Issues to meet our Interests, and it is through this flexibility that we both seek to influence the expectations of the other negotiator and are influenced, in turn, by them. The ability to understand where you have flexibility in either the Issues or Positions is what separates a poor negotiator from an effective one.

What are Interests?

Interests are most conveniently found by asking 'why' you want something to happen. Issues are what you want, Interests are why you want them. If the negotiators keep their Interests in mind when considering solutions – even strange or unusual solutions that might be proposed by the photographer's negotiators – they will test the proposed solutions solely by their relevance to how they will improve profitability (their Interest) and not, for example, by who first proposed them, or whether it is a different solution to the one they had prepared. Interests themselves are not negotiable, but they do give an overall perspective on what needs to be achieved through the negotiation.

Many negotiators do not consider Interests; rather, they go straight to what they are there to negotiate – Issues and Positions. But they are missing a trick. Interests are not merely a headline or an arbitrary thought about the negotiation; they can be used to consider the bigger picture and provide some different thinking to solve awkward problems.

> *Consider a pay negotiation where Vikki is asking for a 3% increase from her boss. She has laid out all the information on why she deserves it, but during the meeting it becomes clear that there is no money in the pay budget this year for any increase. She walks away unhappy, with no extra funds. However, if Vikki instead was to consider the reasons WHY she wants more money in her monthly pay packet, it could open up the negotiation with her boss to get her what she wants. Vikki has been concerned about retirement (Interest), which is thankfully a long way off, but she is a sensible woman and wants to add to her private pension plan a little extra each month. Instead of just asking her boss for cash from a salary increase, Vikki could perhaps broach the subject of the company pension plan, or the company contributing to her pension plan, both of which might come from a different budget/department and remove the problem of no salary increase this year.*

Learning point:

Interests are the hopes, fears or concerns of the negotiator. They are what are motivating them to be in the negotiation. Interests are not negotiable, but they provide the Issues and Positions for the discussions, which are negotiable.

It is possible for there to be more than one Interest; as in this case with Forth, improving the relationship with PDQ could be seen as a second Interest. It is sometimes even possible for both parties to have a shared Interest, where they both consider the same thing to be driving the negotiation – perhaps increasing business together, maintaining relationships or improving performance.

What are the negotiable Issues?

Amanda, however, will want more from the project team than a declaration of what the team perceives to be Forth's Interests, important as it is to consider what these are. Reducing costs is all very well, but the vital question is what *specific* agreements are required to achieve this Interest, bearing in mind that whatever is proposed also has to achieve the support or consent of the photographer's negotiators by meeting *their* Interests. This distinction between our Interests and what we need to do to achieve them, usually expressed as the terms or conditions of the agreement, is not trivial. Many a negotiator identifies an overall Interest and then mistakenly believes that this is sufficient preparation to negotiate to achieve it.

For example, it is not unusual to find negotiators describing what they want to achieve from the negotiation with statements like 'maintain the business', 'make a profit', 'increase market share' or 'reduce costs'. Admirable as they are, these overall Interests are not negotiable in themselves. They represent the possible outcomes of a negotiation of the details by which their Interests might be achieved, and it is the details – the Issues and Positions and the so-called 'T&Cs' – that are negotiated in the main and not the Interest itself. This neither precludes the negotiators identifying another means of addressing an Interest, nor, by revealing an Interest, does it prevent the parties altering their perceptions of the importance of the Issues and Positions in respect of that Interest. Indeed, some Interests cannot even be disclosed in a negotiation without compromising the negotiator's credibility with the other negotiators. For instance, to declare to the other party that your overall Interest is to 'avoid bankruptcy' might prejudice a negotiation over the terms under which you disposed of a property to raise funds to avert a financial crisis: if they discover that you are close to insolvency, they might act to push you to the brink of financial ruin in search of a lower price (thus ensuring your bankruptcy!).

Negotiation is a means of making decisions on the basis of data; therefore, the next question we ought to address is: 'What Issues and Positions will deliver our Interest(s)?' Assessing the Issues and Positions to be addressed by a negotiation is analogous to the question sometimes asked by a business: 'What business are we in?' In the same manner as businesses can fail to address that question in good time (and go on to fail as businesses because the market changes but they don't), so too can negotiators fail to ask in good time what they are negotiating about (and then wonder why they are stuck with unsatisfactory deals or no deals at all).

What do we mean by the Issues and Positions (i.e. the content of a proposal) in a negotiation? It is anything that the parties have discretion over but that must still be decided jointly by both of them – in short, it is anything over which they can trade. And anything that a negotiator trades, or can trade, is an **Issue**. The trades they agree to (or not, as the case may be) on each Issue and Position are the output of the negotiation.

For many negotiations, the main Issues can be identified fairly easily. Hence, identifying the Issues should not prove too onerous. But even where it is easy and quickly completed, it is worth the effort because it is very easy to miss minor Issues rushing to settle what appear to be the most important Issues at that moment, only to find that it is the so-called minor Issues that later loom in importance. People, for example, often concentrate on the obviously important Issue of the price of something and neglect to cover themselves on seemingly unimportant Issues, such as warranty (who pays for repairing the appliance if it needs attention? how long is the warranty for? what exactly does it cover – parts and labour? labour only? parts only?).

For routine negotiations – those, for instance that you engage in on a regular basis – there is a tendency to narrow the focus of the Issues you negotiate and gradually to neglect what appear to be peripheral Issues, which if left uncovered in the negotiation can leave you without adequate protection. Discovering that you are not covered for an urgent call-out for an emergency repair could cost you dearly when the supplier invoices you for his shockingly high emergency call-out charge (when you need a plumber, you *need* a plumber!). This suggests that you should also prepare for routine negotiations by identifying the Issues that could be covered in the negotiation.

Let's consider Amanda's potential list of Issues, though we must bear in mind that any list of Issues is not exhaustive and should remain with some flexibility. What we can do when preparing is to list what we understand to be the Issues, and if, during the negotiation, some other Issues come up, we can add them to our plan and spend some time thinking about how they would affect our Position.

Some of the Issues will be fairly obvious, but others may require a little more thought. When preparing a list of things you wish to negotiate, detail can be important. Think about breaking some of the Issues down into options or different parts, for example, price can be as simple as a price, but also it could be broken down into deposit, final payment, payment dates, etc. The more detail you have, the easier it becomes to prepare effectively, making the rest of negotiation easier. Other things to consider are the less obvious Issues that may not seem worth adding to the list, but alternatives and Issues that we can use to get what we want are important to think about, even at this early stage.

The list of Issues in Table 3.2, which was written down as the individual items occurred to the team, describes the agenda as Forth sees it, but as neither side can unilaterally impose an agenda on the other, the negotiations could cover other Issues not yet listed.

What are the priorities for each Issue?

The next question for the Forth team is to decide on their priorities in respect of each Issue. This means they must decide on the relative importance of each Issue by its contribution to the decreasing error rate. Not everything contributes to the overall objective to the same extent, nor is everything wanted with the

Table 3.2 Forth's list of negotiable Issues

	Negotiable Issues
1	Minimum acceptable error limit
2	Incentive scheme
a	Incentive rate
b	Date of payment
c	Number of payments per month
d	Time frame for error count
3	Contract duration
4	Penalties for exceeding error limit
a	Rate of penalty
b	How penalty paid – credit/cash
c	When penalty applied
5	Admin support

same degree of urgency – if it were, we would have some difficulty negotiating a solution. We negotiate because we value things differently according to how they contribute to our wants (replacing a monotonous diet of potatoes with some delicious cabbage, for example). Asking about the relative value, or priority, we place on the Issues we can negotiate about is a first step to assessing what sort of agreement we value.

> **Learning point:**
>
> *Every negotiator values things differently; that is what makes exchanges possible.*

The Forth team must assign a notional priority to each of the Issues. It can do this by discussing 'Why is this Issue important to the achievement of our Interests?' or 'How important is this Issue to the achievement of our Interests?' In team negotiation, some sort of consensus in the team is essential, though it must never be assumed in your preparation. Different people have different perceptions about the importance of specific elements in an agreement. For example, accountants tend to prefer solutions that do not involve large amounts of work in progress because of the cost of the money they tie up; production personnel tend to prefer long runs of identical output with as few variations as possible because this optimises the learning effect on productivity and minimises downtime for resetting machines and moving personnel between jobs; sales departments tend to prefer large stocks of every conceivable variation in the product range because this facilitates their ability to sell output to customers who have 'awkward' needs. Outside these functionally based differences there are normal differences of opinion between people who bring to any decision process all sorts of perceptions, histories and views of the world and who are likely to clash over interpretations about the problem and expectations about the future. Team-based preparation will soon show that the negotiations actually begin within the team before they meet the people with whom they are preparing to negotiate.

The three categories of importance used in the Negotek® Preparation Planner are:

HIGH
MEDIUM
LOW

It should be stressed that these are organising, and not scientific, categories. You could just as easily run with a system marked A, B, C; or 1, 2, 3; or Crucial, Important, Desirable, etc. The important consideration is of the relative value to you of the Issues and not a fruitless discourse on the meaning of high versus low.

Broadly, those Issues considered to be of high importance to your assessment of the proposed agreement would be those that need to be obtained if there is to be an agreement at all, because, in their absence, the agreement would not serve – indeed, it might run counter to – your Interests. In short, the highs could become, ultimately, the 'walk-away' Issues that make agreement impossible. For this reason, you must be careful about what you designate as of high importance and therefore of high priority.

Too casual a designation of an Issue as of high priority leads to your overvaluing certain Issues, which increases the risk of an otherwise acceptable agreement. Your false sense of priority gets in the way of movement. Inexperienced negotiators tend to make almost everything of high importance and hardly anything is regarded as of lesser importance to them. This is reflected in their negotiating behaviour – they come across as too aggressive, for example – and in the difficulty with which they reach agreement. The fewer Issues you genuinely regard as of high priority, the better.

The medium category is for those Issues with which you expect to achieve your Positions but that would not cause you to walk away from an agreement if circumstances forced you to settle closer to your exit points. How well you do in negotiating the Issues you prioritise as of medium importance is a personal measure of your negotiating skills. Effective and well-prepared negotiators would want to have more Issues prioritised as of medium rather than of high importance.

Low is for all those Issues that are available in the negotiation but which, while you prefer to reach your Positions in each one of them, you are willing to trade them close to – or even beyond – your exit points, if by doing so they enable you to achieve your Positions with the Issues you have designated as medium or high. However, they are not 'give-aways' in the sense that you are willing to concede them unilaterally to the other negotiator merely because you place a relatively low value upon them (in negotiation, nothing is given away – it is always traded).

While we are presently considering what is the relative importance to you of the Issues, it is worth noting here that there are two parties in a negotiation and each of them has different value systems. What is high to you need not be high to them and, more significantly, what is merely low to you may have a much greater value to them. If it is of greater value to them than it is to you, it is hardly something you should 'give away', for that would only undermine your negotiating strengths. If you give away lows, you throw the whole burden of trading onto your medium and high Issues and, in consequence, you may have to go further towards your exit Positions on these relatively important Issues than you would otherwise have needed.

The Forth team would examine the Issues in Table 3.2 and allocate to each one of them an agreed-upon priority as, perhaps, set out in Table 3.3. Note that the list of Issues can often be re-examined at this stage or can be grouped as subheadings of others. This is to be expected, as the initial list of Issues is composed by noting them as they emerge from the discussion, whatever turns up in whatever order. We have no wish to restrict or artificially inhibit suggestions from team members of what is to be regarded as an Issue. After consideration,

Integrative bargaining, pt. 1: Preparation 45

Table 3.3 Forth's list of negotiable Issues and their priorities

	Negotiable Issues	Priorities
1	Minimum acceptable error limit	High
2	Incentive scheme	Medium
a	Incentive rate	Low
b	Date of payment	Low
c	Number of payments per month	Low
d	Time frame for error count	Low
3	Contract duration	Medium
4	Penalties for exceeding error limit	High
a	Rate of penalty	Medium
b	How penalty paid – credit/cash	Medium
c	When penalty applied	Medium
5	Admin support	Medium

some pruning or reorganisation is perfectly acceptable. The numbering used in this list is, however, set for the duration of the preparation session.

The allocation of priorities is purely notional on my part, but some discussion of my choices might elucidate the basic approach I have taken in this case. Consider the two high allocations:

1 Minimum acceptable error limit
4 The penalties for exceeding error limit

Why do I consider these to be high? Because if cost is a function of error rate, any solution that does not reduce the errors to a minimum acceptable level would fail to address Forth's main Interest. It follows that the minimum position that Forth can adopt is that any failure to reduce costs must carry with it a financial penalty that both deters the supplier from neglecting errors below this acceptable level *and* compensates Forth in some measure for the supplier's failure. Forth would be in favour of lower minimum acceptable levels of errors and stiffer penalties than the supplier, but within whatever limits Forth sets in preparation, it would work tenaciously to see that both these Issues were present in the final agreement.

In the case of the medium priorities, there are two main ones, in my view. First, the rate of penalty to be applied: this is medium but not high because the principle that there is a minimum acceptable error level is more important than the actual penalty, which at any level should be a deterrent for the supplier. Forth's negotiators would have some greater leeway over the level of penalty than they would on whether there was a minimum error level or not.

By similar reasoning, the details of the penalties that the supplier might attract – the amount of penalty, how the penalty is paid and when they are levied – are less important than his acceptance that there will be penalties of some kind for failing to maintain acceptable levels of errors. If, however, the supplier refuses all notions of penalties whatsoever, there seems to be little point in

46 *Integrative bargaining, pt. 1: Preparation*

Table 3.4 Forth's Issues prioritised

Priority	Entry	Exit
High		
1		
4		
Medium		
2		
3		
4a		
4b		
4c		
5		
Low		
2a		
2b		
2c		
2d		

making their details high, but if he agrees to the principle of penalties the details should be regarded as medium (i.e. within the expected achievable aims of the Forth team) and not regarded as being merely low and therefore of little significance to Forth's wants.

The low priorities include proposals for a change to the payment scheme. Forth would be pleased to achieve its minimum error levels without paying incentives; the photographer is likely to want an incentive to do so. It is neither of high nor medium importance to Forth that an incentive scheme is in place, but if such a scheme is the only way it can achieve its aims, then Forth would be willing to consider the scheme; hence, it is an Issue of low importance, as is the amount of the incentive, its rate, when it is paid and whether it is calculated on the average performance over the year or over individual weeks. This gives Forth some scope in proposing an incentive scheme and offering to trade it for agreement on Forth's high and medium Issues.

At this point, the team could set out the planner to reflect the priorities as follows in Table 3.4. This is a good idea where there are many Issues, as it helps to keep the high priorities together, etc., but with only a few Issues, it may not be as important to rearrange this way.

At this stage, the Forth team has a choice. They can go on to set out the ranges of the entry and exit points that they consider appropriate Positions for this negotiation, or they can postpone that detailed decision until they have had a preliminary look at what they estimate to be the priority rankings of the photographer. The choice is more one of convenience in particular preparation sessions – sometimes it is down to which members of the team are present – than any fixed advantage from either approach. For continuity here, we shall estimate the photographer's rankings before considering our entry and exit points for each Issue.

Integrative bargaining, pt. 1: Preparation 47

In practice, we would know something about the likely stances of the other negotiator on some of these Issues from our past experience of them or from similar negotiations with others. But clearly we are always likely to know more about ourselves and less about the other negotiators, and this will be reflected in the degree of certainty with which we allocate the other negotiator's ranking of priorities to the Issues we have selected for negotiation. At this stage, too, we have little idea what different Issues, if any, they might raise for negotiation.

While it is perfectly acceptable to spend time thinking about the other team's priorities and Positions on the Issue to hand, please let me indulge in a warning. **Nothing you put in the plan at this stage about the other party is to be treated as anything other than conjecture.** All information you add about their 'side' is based on assumptions that you have made, and are not based on any interaction with the other team. It is imperative that you remember this when planning your negotiation, and you must not act upon anything you assume until you have backed it up with facts from the debate phase with the other party.

Learning point:

The Preparation Planner is not set in stone; it is a flexible planning tool, and nothing in it must be used to propose a solution until you have discussed and confirmed any assumptions in the Debate Phase.

For presentational simplicity, in this case we shall assume that each team has selected similar Issues for negotiation, and from that estimate, we assume the photographer's ranking of those as listed in Table 3.4. How might we allocate priorities to them from the photographer's point of view?

Assuming that the photographers at PDQ need this revenue stream, it would seem sensible to suppose that the continuation of the revenue from that contract is one of his main interests. Of course, to continue the revenue he will have to meet Forth's proposal to reach some maximum admin error levels. His objective would be to negotiate with Forth some agreed but low maximum level of error – the lower the agreed level, the easier it is for him to avoid penalties and to earn incentives. The photographer's priorities would therefore be allocated as in Table 3.5.

The conclusions can be set out in the preparation planner as in Table 3.5. Briefly, the high priorities for the photographer are to agree to a (low) maximum acceptable error level in case Forth sets too high a target, and for meeting this target the photographer requires an incentive for achieving the acceptable error level over the shortest minimum duration. It is also of high importance that the photographer establishes whether coverage is to be calculated across whole months or by individual weeks according to whichever provides him with the best chance of earning an incentive (he will need, of course, data to make the choice).

48 *Integrative bargaining, pt. 1: Preparation*

Table 3.5 PDQ's Issues prioritised

Entry	Exit	Priority
		High
		2
		1
		3
		Medium
		2a
		2b
		2c
		2d
		4
		5
		Low
		4a
		4b
		4c

We now have two tables (3.4 and 3.5), and these can be brought together (figuratively) in Table 3.6. This is the first cut at assessing the relative priorities each side is likely to place on the Issues so far identified.

Exercise 3D

Looking at Table 3.6, can you see where there might be some trading possibilities?

Surely, each side could consider trading what is of low value to itself for what is of high value to the other negotiator? That, after all, is what negotiation is about. Think back to Farmer Jones and his disaffection with a potato-only diet. In a potential exchange of his surplus potatoes for somebody else's surplus of cabbage, the High-Medium-Low layout would appear as in Table 3.7.

Is it not obvious that Farmer Jones would be willing to trade potatoes for cabbages and that Farmer Morgan would be willing to trade cabbages for potatoes? What they must decide is the rate of exchange (their Positions on the Issue).

In Forth's case, the planner has identified a potential trade across the different valuations each has put on the common set of Issues. Forth regards a penalty scheme as high, its details as medium, while the photographer regards penalties as only medium with its details low (in the sense that he prefers *not* to have a penalty scheme, but would not go to the wall to resist one if it got him an incentive scheme with easy-to-reach targets). The photographer regards an incentive scheme as high and its details as medium, in contrast to Forth, who regards it as only medium,

Integrative bargaining, pt. 1: Preparation 49

Table 3.6 Forth's and PDQ's Issues prioritised

FORTH			PDQ	
Priority	*Entry*	*Exit*	*Entry*	*Priority*
High				*High*
1				2
4				2b
				3
Medium				**Medium**
2				1
3				2a
4a				2c
4b				2d
4c				4
5				5
Low				**Low**
2a				4a
2b				

Table 3.7 Farmer Jones's and Farmer Morgan's Issues prioritised

Farmer Jones	*Farmer Morgan*
High	**High**
Acquire cabbages	Acquire potatoes
Medium	**Medium**
Sell potatoes	Sell cabbages

with the details low (in the sense that, for Forth, they prefer a solution that does *not* include an incentive scheme, but they would not go to the wall resisting one if it got them a definite improvement in profitability from fewer errors).

Interestingly, Forth and the photographer appear to have similar valuations of two of the Issues. Each values a maximum error rate (1) as high and the inclusion of a new admin person (4) as medium. Does this mean an automatic deadlock? Not at all. It indicates that much of the negotiation is going to concentrate on the details of their respective Positions on these Issues: what will constitute an error, and how are those data collected? Noting this, the Forth team is forewarned to prepare their stance on these Issues with great care. If they are not ready with sensible reasons for their Positions on these Issues, and do not have robust proposals to deal with them, they risk creating avoidable difficulties for themselves.

Comparing the valuations of each side could show a situation similar to Figure 3.2 The sloping lines show that what is high to us is only medium to them; what is medium to us is low to them, and what is high to them is only low to us.

50 *Integrative bargaining, pt. 1: Preparation*

```
  Our Priorities      Their Priorities
       H                    H

       M                    M

       L                    L
```

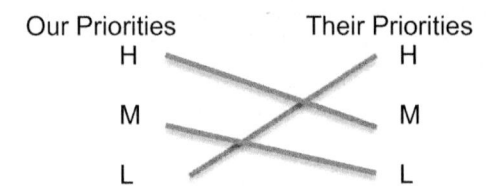

Figure 3.2 Comparative priorities – differing.

```
  Our Priorities      Their Priorities
       H  ──────────────  H

       M  ──────────────  M

       L  ──────────────  L
```

Figure 3.3 Comparative priorities – similar.

```
  Our Priorities      Their Priorities
       H  ──────────────  H

       M                    M

       L                    L
```

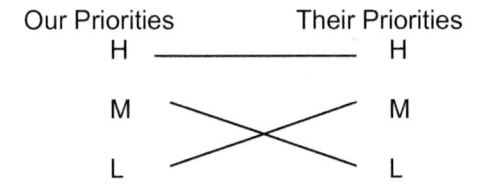

Figure 3.4 Comparative priorities – mixed.

In Figure 3.3, a different configuration of the valuations is shown. Here, what is high to us is also high to them; what is medium to us is also medium to them; and what is low to us is also low to them.

In Figure 3.4, another possible comparison of valuations is shown. This is more complex than the other two because it shows some valuations that are identically valued and others that are differently valued: our high is high to them, our medium is low to them, and our low is medium to them.

But what does this all mean in terms of trading? In Figure 3.2, the differences in valuation make trading across Issues a possibility. We could trade our high for their medium, our medium for their low and our low for their high.

In Figure 3.3, the identical valuations do not make negotiation easier, but they are not such an impassable barrier as they seem. A negotiated solution would depend on two aspects of the identical valuations. First, is there an overlap in the ranges for each of the Issues between each negotiator's entry and exit points? If yes, we can trade across the overlaps. Second, is it possible that movement on one or two of the identically valued Issues would ensure movement by the negotiators on the third Issue? If yes, we can trade compensatory movement in one or more Issues for movement in one or more of the remainder.

Figure 3.4 is more representative of the real world – valuations tend to be mixed. Here we could trade movement between our medium and their low and their medium and our low for compensatory movement between our high and their identical high.

What are the negotiable ranges for each Issue?

Negotiators prefer to give themselves a range of Positions in which to settle rather than attempt to secure a fixed position. The latter almost always requires the other side to give in, and this alone is difficult to carry through in the context of a negotiation. If they must give in to our position, why are we bothering to negotiate? Moreover, if it is a negotiation, why do we expect them to give in to our fixed position? For reasons elaborated in Chapter 2 on distributive bargaining, negotiators are more likely to decide upon entry and exit points for each of the Issues, and it is to this preparation task that we now turn.

Positions – setting entry and exit points

As with the allocation of each Issue to a specific priority, nothing decided in preparation about each Issue's entry or exit position can be set in concrete. We can never be certain that our pre-prepared Positions have any substance in reality until we meet the other negotiators and listen to what they have to say and propose. But this does not excuse us from preparation. The contact phase of negotiation is not scripted. We do not know for certain what will unfold once we meet with them. If we have to open first, we ought to be ready with something realistic and credible to say about each of the negotiable Issues that the sides share.

The Forth team should set the entry and exit point for each of the Issues in Table 3.6, and for illustrative purposes, I have suggested they might do this as laid out in Table 3.8.

Clearly, Forth cannot be sure of what the photographer's negotiators will propose, and its assessments are bound to be unreliable. In practice, it would be expected that some, if not all, of the photographer's entry points would be left blank – providing an agenda for information-seeking in the early stages of the negotiation – and those that were assessed with some confidence would still be open to confirmation. For these reasons, it is highly unlikely that the Forth negotiators would know anything at all about the photographer's exit points, and these must be left with a question mark.

The arguments for particular entry and exit points would depend greatly on the circumstances of the case. Those shown in Table 3.8 are my own interpolations from the details I know of the real-world negotiation upon which the case is based. A brief explanation of my choices might help.

52 Integrative bargaining, pt. 1: Preparation

Table 3.8 Forth's and PDQ's Issues with entry and exit points

	FORTH		PDQ		
Issue	Entry	Exit	Exit	Entry	Priority
1	5%	15%	?	25%	H
2	5%	10%	?	15%	H
2a	20% per 50	5% per 50	?	1% per 50	M
2b	60 days	35 days	?	40 days	H
2c	1	2	?	4	M
2d	Annual	Monthly	?	Weekly	M
3	60 days	35 days	?	40 days	H
4	Unlimited	Capped	?	No	M
4a	50%	Max £400	?	Max £50	L
4b	Cash	Credit	?	Credit	L
4c	Immediately	60 days	?	90 days	L
5	New team from PDQ	Provide one of our staff	?	Extra person part time	M

Forth would probably open with a proposal that sought for them an almost perfect admin performance. The average admin level of errors from other suppliers is 8%, but since PDQ are a relatively small supplier, there could be a little more leeway; their entry point of 5 per cent error rate is a ranging shot to demonstrate their earnestness about improving performance. On the other hand, the photographer would probably accept that 25 per cent represented a reasonable attainable performance, given the data, and he would be likely to open here, indicating a willingness to move upwards if conditions were right. Forth would press for high penalties for failing to meet targets and they could safely assume that the photographer would prefer low, if any, penalties. The photographer might prefer a scheme based on the performance over shorter time frames, on the grounds that some weeks would provide much fewer errors, with only complicated jobs creating the problem over short periods, so lowering his likelihood of repeated penalties over every month. Forth is unlikely to be concerned too much about which way the calculation went (it is only a low) but would be likely to open with an all-month proposal, but ready, if conditions were right, to accept an individual-week performance system.

The time frame to count the errors presents Forth with a difficult choice. Initially, the team might go for an annual measure – all submissions have to achieve low error ratios for a year before incentives are earned – but this is vulnerable on two counts. First, on grounds of equity, the photographer might argue for an annual measure before penalties are imposed, and secondly, remembering Forth's main aim – to achieve a lower error rate – an annual measure could work contrary to its interests. For instance, the photographer for much of the year could be performing below an acceptable level and is therefore protected from penalties until the year end. Worse, at some point during the year, it will be impossible for performance to be improved sufficiently to raise the annual average and, deprived of the possibility of earning incentives, the photographer has no incentive to make the effort! This misreading of your interests is not uncommon in preparation. It comes from forgetting that you are negotiating to achieve your interests and not to devise schemes that 'punish' the other side by making it difficult for them to work towards your ends. In this case, a review of this entry point when negotiations are under way – and the other side often can be relied upon to point out defects in Forth's proposals – would be advised.

The details of the two schemes for incentives and penalties broadly follow the principle that Forth prefers higher to lower penalties, and the photographer prefers higher to lower incentives. Forth has some room to manoeuvre here because it can afford any incentive scheme that is self-financing – the gains in profitability from lower errors greatly exceed the cost of the incentives. The photographer has some room for manoeuvring on penalties if the reliability of the admin can be assured to exceed the level at which penalties, even draconian ones, come into effect.

From the assumed data in Table 3.8, it is clear that there is some overlap on the details of the two schemes. The face-to-face negotiations will confirm or challenge the prepared entry and exit points of each party. But the preparatory exercise has not wasted the negotiator's time. For one thing, it has clarified the Issues, sorted out the Positions and provisionally related them to the basic aims of Forth. Second, it has given the Forth team command of the details of what Issues must be addressed and what is at stake. Few alternative systems provide such an economical way of surveying the detailed content of proposals.

Negotiators who have command of the details usually gain a psychological edge in terms of confidence over those who are poorly prepared. Last, it has highlighted the possibilities for a negotiated solution based on trading both across different valuations ('We will accept some form of penalty scheme if you agree to some form of incentive scheme') and within the available ranges of each Issue ('Taking averages over a year is too long; we would be prepared to consider averages over each quarter').

Tradables

Next, on the Preparation Planner, there is a section for Tradables. Tradables are items over which you have discretion, but perhaps they are not directly related to the negotiation. They are not something you are here to negotiate about, but they can be useful to consider to add movement later in the negotiation.

It is not strictly something that you have to consider at this point – though some companies will have lists of these to hand for every negotiator before they even start – but it is always a great time to think about what is available to you to use in the negotiation, should you need it. The Tradable list might be added to (or subtracted from) throughout the negotiation, and will come in to play in earnest in the Bargaining stage later on (see Chapter 6). Some Tradables for Amanda could be listed as in Table 3.9.

54 *Integrative bargaining, pt. 1: Preparation*

Table 3.9 List of potential Tradables for Forth

Number	Tradable
1	Early access to project plans
2	Priority payments on correct invoices
3	Better accreditation for photos used
4	Integrated IT and accounts system
5	Write formal recommendation
6	Put PDQ on Forth website/sales materials

BATNA

While this is not an *essential* part of any preparation, understanding your BATNA (Best Alternative to No Agreement – see Chapter 8) can be helpful, especially at this stage in the negotiation. Simply put, what are your alternatives if this deal fails to be agreed? Do you have another option? If you do, how does that option compare to this current deal?

The BATNA provides you with a very easy way to decide whether the deal on the table is worth agreeing to, or whether you should walk away from it. If the current deal is better than your alternative, then it gives you the green light to agree. If the current deal is less suitable than your alternative, it gives you the confidence to perhaps push for more from the current deal, or simply walk away and take up the alternative.

> *Consider Elaine, who placed her house on the market for offers over £120,000. She received an offer within the first week for £115,000 but rejected it instantly, as this was an 'insult' to her beautiful home (people tend to get very sensitive about their homes and cars when the market places a price on them). The fact that it was now mid-June, and the buying season was ending until it reopened in late August, ought to have led her to consider her BATNA. If she had done so, she might have calculated that the best alternative to the sole offer of £115,000 was a diminishing chance of getting £120,000 until mid-August, minus the cost of the bridging loan from her bank of around £5,000 on her new house. Her BATNA would have told her to take the £115,000 now rather than fork out £5,000 on bridging finance and have to deduct this from whatever she could get in August. As it was, she received the same offer of £115,000 in August, against which she had to net the monetary cost of £5,000 for bridging, and the psychological cost of her stress and strain at her problem throughout the summer months (not to mention the stress she caused among her friends who were compelled to suffer the retelling of her woes every time they met her).*

Your BATNA is an indicator of your bargaining power. This principle has application throughout negotiation. Not knowing your BATNA could unsettle your judgement when you are in the proposal or the bargaining phases and lead you back to the debate phase, and almost certainly into emotional, even threatening, argument.

Conclusion

Negotiators who concentrate on developing a traded solution are going to waste less time in posturing than those who switch in and out of intimidation and surrender in an attempt to get what they want. Preparation enables the negotiator to formulate a solution based on his real wants, rather than prejudices or emotional reaction to the other party. To discover real wants, we must begin with the data and analyse what will meet our best interests, given that our best interests are often constrained by the need to secure the consent of the other negotiators (just as their wish to meet their best interests is constrained by their need to secure our consent).

Neither Farmer Jones nor Farmer Morgan need be at war with each other to vary their diets: if they see each other as mortal enemies, then they will have to endure a monotonous diet of potatoes or cabbage and forego the opportunity to have a much more pleasurable and varied diet of both. Preparation, rather than reaction, forces the negotiator to consider solutions that are best for each party. It turns attention from the limited benefits of competing with the person you are negotiating with to the far more fruitful benefits of engaging them in cooperation. Such thoughts do not mean that you must give up all of your Interests or that you should deny yourself your Positions. Far from it. Preparation helps decide whether a negotiated solution is possible, and, if it is not, you will have to secure your Interests by some means other than negotiation, or through negotiation with some other person, or revise your Interests and your Positions on the Issues.

If the data show that the other negotiator has no influence upon, nor responsibility for, the situation we wish to change, it is hopeless conceiving of a negotiation with them. Amanda cannot expect the photographer to negotiate an error reduction agreement if he has been under pressure from the end user at Forth to make hundreds of last-minute changes to briefs resulting in confused invoicing deviating from their agreement. It is also hopeless to attempt to negotiate without any preliminary collection and study of the data – perhaps the problem is not what is happening but what we think is happening.

Suppose we have perceived that there is a problem and that we have collected and analysed the data and that we have some idea of what we want to happen. Our thoughts must turn to two areas: what is negotiable in the situation (identify the Issues), and what we want most to happen if we are to secure our objectives (prioritise what we value into high, medium and low).

We can choose now to take a look at what we think might be the priorities of the other negotiator. How does he value the Issues? What is he likely to be looking for? This preliminary assessment might throw out some interesting possibilities, for it is in the differing valuations that we find the possibility of negotiating a solution.

Checkpoint 3

Note the answers you think are correct, and why, before checking my answers in the back of the book.

3.1 In a dispute with a supplier over his failure to perform his contract, the buyer should:

   a) Check the contract carefully for evidence

   b) Assess who is to blame

   c) Collect data on failure to perform

   d) Arrange for a quotation from another supplier

3.2 Negotiators have Interests because:

   a) Some Issues are more interesting than others

   b) They are motivated by different factors to prefer some outcomes to others

   c) They prefer some Issues to others

   d) Their Positions are negotiated but their Interests are not

3.3 An Issue is:

   a) A topic for discussion

   b) A collection of Positions

   c) An item on a negotiator's agenda

   d) A decision for negotiators

3.4 Which of the following is correct?

   a) Negotiators cannot move from Positions with high priorities

   b) Negotiators can only trade on Issues with medium and low priorities

   c) Negotiators can use low priorities as 'giveaways'

   d) Negotiators can move from any Position on any Issue if it suits their Interests

4 Integrative bargaining, part 2
Debate

Introduction

Jackie was the office manager for AppItAll, a software company specialising in app development for smartphones and tablets. She was responsible for all contracts with suppliers, from stationary and office furniture to catering services, facilities management and energy providers. One of her suppliers, Admin Xpress, had been giving her a lot of trouble lately. In the last six months, there had been numerous occasions when she had been let down, including missed appointments for emergency call-outs on serviced photocopiers (with one in five missing their agreed-upon 24-hour service), poor-quality products and inaccurate billing. The last straw was a recent direct debit, which was for more than triple the monthly payment due. Jackie immediately e-mailed the sales manager from Admin Xpress to demand a meeting to discuss the service issues.

The customer service team at Admin Xpress had been unhelpful, and on one occasion was rude when Jackie tried to complain about late/missed appointments. Jackie had switched to Admin Xpress after a previous supplier had gone out of business, but the poor service was making her think about another switch. Unfortunately, she was only eight months in to a two-year contract with Admin Xpress, and there would be a charge to terminate the contract. The charge would be a factor, but realistically Jackie knew that changing was only going to cause much more work in finding a new supplier and then negotiating the contract, so it would be better if a deal could be reached with Admin Xpress to resolve the service issues and get back on track. If she could get some guarantees on call-out times, perhaps with a penalty for missed appointments, along with an improved billing system, she would be happy to remain a customer. There was also the issue of the overpayment last month, which would need to be returned immediately.

Ben Jones, Sales Manager at Admin Xpress, was surprised to receive the (in his opinion) rather abrupt e-mail from Jackie demanding he call her immediately to discuss 'the woeful service from your company'. He had been unaware of any issues from his team, but knew only too well that AppItAll had been a very demanding customer, with more call-outs per month than any other. In fact, he was sure that the office team were damaging the equipment through complete lack of care and costing his business money by having to make unnecessary repairs. The contract was barely worth the effort from such a difficult customer, but it was giving them a foothold in the Business Park where AppItAll was based, and Ben hoped this would give them access to the 40 or so other businesses in the area. By gaining the extra business there, Ben could save a great deal of money by basing an engineering team there, cutting travel times and costs and making the contract run much smoother.

Exercise 4A

From what has been revealed to you about the situation, what do you think Jackie could say that would worsen the chances of a settlement during her phone call to Ben? Make a list of the sort of mistakes she could make before reading on.

Your list could include some of the following possibilities: Jackie could argue instead of listen. She could assume that lack of service was solely down to Admin Xpress's poor planning. She could blame everybody else besides AppItAll. She could justify AppItAll's good record. She could introduce irrelevances. She could make assertions about Admin Xpress. She could abuse Ben. She could mock or be sarcastic. She could score cheap points. She could irritate Ben. She could make personal attacks and tactless criticism. She could make wild and unsubstantiated allegations. She could threaten or otherwise challenge Admin Xpress. This last would probably terminate the phone call.

Let me reveal what actually happened when Ben made a call to Jackie (I only heard Ben's version, so make allowances for his own bias):

The call was a disgrace. Jackie had no intention of listening to our case at all. All she did was rubbish our position ('dreamed up by some under-employed whiz kid in your department'); denied all responsibility ('our staff know how to use a photocopier'); told me I was daft to think that a firm the size of AppItAll would put up with such unprofessional service (there are plenty of other suppliers); said she wasn't prepared to cover up the inabilities of the engineering teams to keep up with the pace of their business (if they can't fix things on time, what use are they?); stated that the removal of such a large sum of money from her account was tantamount to theft, and we would be 'hearing from her lawyers if it wasn't put back immediately'; demanded compensation for all the poor service; and flatly refused to consider the issue further (until we hear back from your management team with an apology and a compensation plan).

Integrative bargaining, pt. 2: Debate 59

Exercise 4B

What could Ben do to make the situation above worse?

The short answer is that Ben could reply in kind to all of Jackie's misbehaviours. However, Ben vigorously denied that he behaved other than impeccably in the face of the verbal assault from Jackie. He claimed he was a paragon of virtue. If true, Ben was displaying a strength of character not commonly found when people receive Jackie's reported treatment. Most people would find it hard to resist responding in a similar vein to what Jackie said, particularly when they felt strongly about the issues.

Let us assume that Ben did rise to Jackie's bait. What might he have said in reply? I have interpolated likely remarks from Ben as might have been reported by Jackie if we had interviewed her after the call:

> *The call was a waste of time. Ben did not listen to a word I said. All he did was rubbish our genuine concerns ('put up to them by some smart-ass whiz kid in your company'); denied all responsibility ('our service record in this affair is beyond reproach'); told me I was daft to think that a minor customer such as AppItAll would get away with ruining his company's profitability ('your business is sometimes more trouble than it's worth'); said he was not going to cover up for our failings as customers ('your staff's inability to use the photocopiers and printers properly is not our problem; maybe you need to hire better staff'); stated that abusing their staff on the telephone was no way to behave ('perhaps you need some training on how to speak to people professionally; I can send over a training leaflet'); and flatly refused to discuss the issue further ('pay up, shut up, or we will see you in court').*

Little imagination is required to predict the likely results of this exchange, or the likely perceptions of who was the victim of the other's uncompromising behaviour. Ask either Jackie or Ben which of them is being unreasonable and you would get the same answer: the other one!

Consider a different phone call between Jackie and Ben. This time, there is no name-calling, abuse or threats. This time, Ben reacts in an altogether different fashion:

> *Jackie, I just received your e-mail. You seem to be experiencing all sorts of problems with our service. Rather than messing you about, can I suggest an immediate upgrade to our Gold Service Level, which will cover you for more callouts and speedier servicing times (12-hour guaranteed, rather than the current 24-hour time frame)? I'll also add in free delivery on all orders for the next three months, and I'll give you free copier paper for the rest of the month.*

Is this a better approach to the problem? It's certainly less antagonistic, but is it any more helpful? Ben has bypassed the debate phase altogether, and in failing to discuss the issues with Jackie has put down an offer with a value much higher than Jackie was expecting. Will this mean Jackie will simply accept and move forward? Jackie has three possible options:

1) Be outraged that Ben has not listened to any of her concerns, and if he doesn't listen to them, how can he fix the problems she has? She will take her business to someone who does listen to what she wants.
2) Accept his proposal, but realize soon after that the Gold Service Level doesn't come with the guarantees or penalties she was looking for, and the freebies don't recompense her for all the trouble she is still having with the company. They will be back to square one before the month is out.
3) Seeing as Ben has offered so much so soon, she could be tempted to demand a great deal more, putting them back in the position of arguing.

Debate is not something you can avoid, and any negotiator who doesn't spend enough time debating effectively will not come out of the deal in good shape. This chapter is about the all-important activity of debate in negotiation and what we can do to improve our chances of a settlement and, if we are not careful, what we can do to worsen our chances.

What is debate?

Negotiation requires communication. If the parties do not communicate in some way, it is difficult to see how they could negotiate. Communication need not be oral – it could be written; it could be via third or fourth parties; it could be by gesture or bodily posture.

In some circumstances, communication can be implied by the actions rather than the words of the parties. For example, the act of firing a shell ostensibly at the enemy but at the same time each day could be an attempt to communicate that the shell is not fired in earnest but purely for form. The soldiers receiving the regular and predictable shell fire can take elementary precautions, such as keeping under cover at the same time each day, and thereby avoid casualties. In return, they could recognise the implicit communication and conduct their patrols along the same routes each night, thus warning rival patrols from the 'helpful' shell firers not to stray into areas where they would have to be taken prisoner or, worse, shot at. Both sides, by their actions, have informally 'negotiated' a mutual non-aggression pact under the noses of the more conventionally belligerent of their safely distant commanders. Such local pacts were in fact 'negotiated' during the static trench warfare of the First World War without the soldiers involved acting treasonably by direct communication with the enemy.

What we say or do communicates some message to the other party. Whether the message that is received is identical to the one we intended to send is another matter. In discourse, there is considerable scope for misunderstanding as well as for outright duplicity. Once your message is sent and is interpreted by the receiver according to whatever perceptions of the world to which they subscribe, the effect is certain, and often no amount of assurance or explanation is successful in shifting their perceptions of your intentions, even when their impressions of you are genuinely contrary to your true nature. Hence, in communication we ought to be careful rather than casual.

Debate is the act of two-way communication. We send and receive messages and confirm or revise our perceptions of the other party. In the unscripted interaction of debate, we decide the fate of our negotiation. What form a settlement might take is decided by the activities of proposing and bargaining, but whether there will or will not be a chance to propose or bargain is decided by our behaviour in debate.

Debate shapes the tone of the negotiation. It removes or creates obstacles to agreement. It conditions the expectations of the negotiators. It confirms their prejudices or overthrows them. It opens up possibilities or shuts them down. It reveals or camouflages what the negotiators want. And once the dogs of argument are set loose, it is very difficult to rein them in again. It is much better, therefore, to understand the role of debate and to develop techniques for avoiding excesses of temperament when faced with an apparent unwillingness to give in to our demands.

Learning point:

Debate gives us the opportunity to understand what the other party wants from the negotiation. By understanding each other, we can make more effective trades and better deals.

Debate takes up the greater part of the face-to-face interaction of negotiators. On the basis of observation of many negotiations, I estimate that the activity of proposing takes up about 10 per cent, and bargaining less than 5 per cent, of the time spent in direct contact between negotiators. Debate takes up the rest (over 80 per cent) and covers all aspects of interaction that are not specifically those of proposing and bargaining: whenever we ask or answer a question, we are engaged in debate; whenever we make a statement of any kind, we are engaged in debate. In fact, debate covers such a huge proportion of the time used up in direct contact between the negotiators, and covers such a wide range of functions, that the contribution of its individual components is often obscured – truly a case of the wood getting in the way of the trees. If we can organise and discipline our debate behaviour, we have a very good chance of dramatically improving our negotiating effectiveness.

62 *Integrative bargaining, pt. 2: Debate*

Types of destructive debate

In debate we can be either constructive or destructive. Constructive debate moves us towards a solution or an acceptable decision; destructive debate has the opposite effect of moving us away from these desirable outcomes. Thus, debate is characterised by how it serves our intentions and not just by how it might be assessed by a neutral observer, or how it might conform to some pre-set criteria. We are not critical of destructive debate because of the offence it might provoke, or whether it is good- or bad-mannered to behave in that way (relevant though these factors might be in the normal courtesies of interpersonal interaction), but by whether this or that behaviour contributes to the negotiated outcome we seek.

Thinking back to the debate between Jackie and Ben over the claim for guarantees and penalties, we can identify several behaviours that commonly would have a destructive impact on the chances of their negotiating a settlement. In so far as Jackie might have concluded that she did not want to negotiate with Ben at all, his telephone behaviour is understandable, but this would merely force the resolution of the problem of poor service onto some other method of deciding, such as litigation, or, through Jackie's intimidation of Ben, to Ben's giving in on this occasion.

One way of highlighting the destructive range of behaviour is to monitor what happens in the debate using a simple chart, as set out in Table 4.1. This can be used to observe behaviours in negotiations and is an effective way of noting all types of behaviours in the fast-paced discussions found in any negotiation.

The left-hand column, time, is divided by rows representing each minute of negotiation. The columns to the right are labelled for different types of destructive debate, or what I shall call argument, running from threats through to irritation.

Table 4.1 Time sheet: argument behaviour

Argument

Time	Threat	Attack/blame	Point-score	Interrupt/block	Assert/assume	Irritate
11:00					x	x
11:01				x x		x x
11:02		x	x		x x	
11:03		x x			x	
11:04		xx xx		x		x
11:05				x		x
11:06		x x				
11:07		x				
11:08	x	xx x				
11:09	xx xx					

Note: Jackie and Ben's 8 February phone call commenced at 11:00 a.m.

Integrative bargaining, pt. 2: Debate 63

The observer of the interaction between the parties would mark with a tick any examples of the behaviours in the columns evidenced by either or both sides for each minute of the interaction. In Table 4.1 only a few minutes are shown, though in principle the observation could last as long as is necessary. For convenience, the observer uses the left hand of a column for noting behaviours of, say, Jackie, and the right hand for Ben. Thus, at a glance the trail of destructive behaviours, should they manifest themselves in the interaction, can be noted. For illustration, Table 4.1 shows the interaction between Jackie and Ben.

The striking thing about the interaction illustrated in Table 4.1 is the south-westerly drift down the observer's report. Jackie opens with **irritating** remarks ('This nonsensical e-mail you've sent . . .'; 'You can't expect me to take this seriously . . .') and rapidly runs through the entire range of destructive things she could say: 'Which under-employed legal whiz-kid put you up to this?' (**assert**); 'Don't give me that rubbish about your lost profit'(**interrupt**); 'Look, Ben, your engineers wouldn't know how to fix a photocopier better than my Gran' (**attack**); 'You should have managed your team better' (**blame**). Within eight minutes, Jackie is resorting to **threats** ('We won't use your company for anything until you agree to compensation').

After threats there is usually only one place to go – **deadlock**. The negotiation, such as it was, usually ends here before it begins. Both sides are not only further apart than they were to start, they are also angry and emotional. Wherever their relationship goes from here, it is more often characterised by resentment than by sweetness and light.

Irritation

The problem with destructive argument is that it generates a negative response. Negotiators who are irritated by what you say are put off from exerting themselves positively on your behalf. Your 'fair and generous offer' may be totally inadequate in the view of the other negotiator. To assert that your minimal movement towards them is 'generous' or 'reasonable' serves only to irritate them. While we can all recover from slight irritations of this nature, we soon get annoyed if they are continually repeated. If we are annoyed by what somebody says to us, we are seldom inclined to assist them in achieving their goals. Why irritate somebody with whom we want to do business? Is it necessary to make controversial claims for what are minimal moves on our part? If our first offer is 'generous', what does this imply about our last offer? Negotiators, therefore, should avoid irritating each other. It only reduces the chances of reaching our desired goals.

This has particular relevance to the use of sexist or ageist remarks. A young woman surveyor, entering the office of the senior male surveyor who is handling the sale of a property that she has been retained by her client to purchase, is likely to be very irritated if the man asks her: 'When is your boss coming to this meeting?' Sexist or ageist put-downs, and so-called milder put-downs about a person's origins, accent or appearance, can be extremely damaging because they deeply irritate the other negotiator.

Assertions and assumptions

Assertions and assumptions about somebody else's position or motivation are exceptionally dangerous for negotiators. Not only do they risk being exceedingly irritating for the person listening (to which the remarks on irritation apply, only more so), but they can lead to a great waste of time while they are corrected, or worse, they can destroy the chances of a settlement if the assertion itself impedes a fruitful debate and leads to a breakdown in communication.

Ben might genuinely believe that Jackie has invented the issue of late or problem call-outs to demand a change in terms more suitable to her business, but to assert that this was Jackie's motivation in asking for compensation for the servicing would raise more problems than it would solve, even if it were true. First of all, Jackie would be unlikely to admit that she was so motivated – in fact, she would almost certainly hotly contest the suggestion, whatever its basis in fact or fiction – and second, whatever Jackie's alleged motivation, her case for compensation would best be treated on its own merits if AppItAll and Admin Xpress are to continue their mutually profitable relationship.

When we make assertions about people's motivations, we are normally less than careful in our suspicions. People seldom suspect good intentions in suggestions that threaten their interests. For example, Ben feels threatened by the principle of penalties for lateness because AppItAll's claim means that he is being asked to pay for consequences beyond the control of his company (excessive call-outs are caused by inappropriate usage). If AppItAll makes their claim stick, then Admin Xpress will lose revenue, and the penalty clause would set a precedent for all their customers.

Sometimes our anger at suggestions that make us worse off spreads over into our verbalizing our suspicions as to why the proposers are making their suggestions. Our assumptions are likely to be without foundation. Best to keep our assumptions to ourselves and not to make assertions for which our evidence is prejudiced.

Interruption

Exercise 4C

It is appropriate to interrupt somebody who is clearly factually incorrect in their statements. Consider whether this statement is true or false before reading on.

Many negotiators, when asked to choose, claim that this statement is true. They argue that a 'clearly factually incorrect' statement should be corrected as soon as possible, though this is not what the statement says, in fact. It states that you should **interrupt** someone when they make (what you believe to be) a clearly factually incorrect statement. The truth or falseness of the statement turns on the act of interruption.

Now, I have asked audiences, sometimes of several hundred negotiators at a convention, how many of them like to be interrupted. I have never (yet!) had a single person raise his or her hand in favour of being interrupted. When I ask the same audience how many of them have never interrupted anybody, I still get no takers. Is that so strange? Yes, when you consider that about 30 per cent of the same audience will consider the statement in Exercise 4C to be true. Is there an inconsistency here? Only if we forget that we often divide what we like (or do not like) from what we do (or do not do). We do not like being interrupted, but we regularly interrupt each other. Yet what is true for us – we do not like to be interrupted – is also true for others – they do not like being interrupted either.

Perhaps it could be argued that we do not normally interrupt someone for the obvious reason that it is impolite to do so, but when they are 'clearly factually incorrect', that is a different situation. I find this unconvincing. According to my somewhat informal survey, people do not like to be interrupted – without qualification of circumstance (I certainly do not qualify my question in any way). And I have deliberately loaded the statement with the assertion that the person we are considering interrupting is 'clearly factually incorrect'. This is to tempt the negotiator into justifying behaviour that, on reflection, he would avoid. Who says that they are 'clearly factually incorrect'? That could be your honest opinion, but your opinion could also have no basis in fact.

Memory and confusion can, of course, cause many to wrongly believe they are correct about the 'facts', and it's not uncommon to have two very different opinions on what happened, even though the two people witnessed the same event. Take a court case, for example; if you have ever had the opportunity to sit on a jury, you will know that the same event can be recalled very differently by different people. That is not to say that one is not lying to protect themselves or others, but in some cases it's simply the perspective or the memory that makes it seem very different. I find it incomprehensible that my husband can confuse dates and events that happened only a few weeks ago, yet he is convinced he is factually correct when he says he was at a hospital appointment last Monday – it was, in fact, Wednesday. Until I show him the appointment card, he is intractable. Without evidence to the contrary, it can be difficult to bring the other party to correct themselves, though we should consider whether or not it is even worth our while trying to correct them.

There are few facts that are not controversial to somebody. In debate, there are 'my' facts and 'your' facts. It is good to remember that we do not need to agree with the 'facts' to move forward with a solution. Therefore, beware of interrupting in general, and particularly when you hear their version of the facts. If they are erecting a case on the basis of spurious facts, there are other more effective ways of assisting them in demolishing their own case. In few circumstances will interruption prove to be one of them. As with irritation, we can survive the occasional interruption, but when it becomes a habit and gets out of control, we should be aware as negotiators that we are making it more difficult to achieve our objectives by constant interruption of the other negotiator.

Blocking

We shall explore later the most effective ways of responding to a proposal, including those we disagree with, but we ought to note here the entirely futile activity of blocking a suggested solution or a statement on the grounds that we do not wish to go down that route at all. Negotiators are often interrupted, not just because, in our view, they are factually incorrect, but because they are talking about something we instinctively reject or have decided to reject in our preparation. Sometimes we justify blocking on the grounds that, if we did not, then their suggestion would gain credibility by being unchallenged. This is altogether unhelpful. If we know little of the views and thinking of the other negotiator, we will know even less if we interrupt them to block off statements that might lead to areas we are sensitive about for one reason or another.

Sometimes our sensitivity is provoked merely because we have not considered what they are suggesting and we react aggressively without thinking through what the suggestion might do for our objectives. To block negotiators is to waste opportunities to assess what they are thinking about. When negotiators express themselves, they reveal their case for their positions, often unintentionally. We need information about, and confirmation of, their approach to the problem under debate. Blocking denies them the opportunity to reveal more about themselves and denies us the opportunity of learning from their revelations. By permitting negotiators to elaborate upon a theme they have introduced, we do not necessarily legitimise their suggestions. Listening to a viewpoint is not an endorsement of it, for nothing is agreed unless and until we explicitly state our agreement.

Point-scoring

Scoring cheap points is a temptation most people find hard to resist.

> *Imagine a terse exchange between Frank, the owner of a small garage, and Alex, a very disappointed customer. Only a week after the annual service on his family car, the car broke down and cost Alex over £150 in roadside assistance and an even bigger dent in his family's happiness, as he missed watching his son play in the football under-10s semi-final. Alex had been informed by the roadside assistance engineer that one of Frank's team had missed a loose spring, which caused the breakdown.*
>
> *Frank insists, 'We bend over backwards for all our customers here at Frank's Motors and always have the highest of standards.' Alex retorts, in top point-scoring mode, 'Then I suggest that you try bending forwards; you might be able to see what is under the bonnet.'*
>
> *The impact of the remark on Alex's debate with Frank, as you can imagine, is catastrophic. A few more angry exchanges, and he walks out in a temper.*

Point-scoring is an all-too-easy trap to fall into. We do so because we find our quick repartee devilishly funny. We almost cannot help ourselves. We score by wounding the person we are trying to do business with. To put this bluntly, it is clear that point-scoring at somebody else's expense is self-defeating, but I have seldom noticed negotiators sidestepping an opportunity to wound, or wind up, each other.

Attacking/blaming

Not surprisingly, point-scoring almost inevitably leads to one negotiator attacking or blaming the other. If you attack people, they are almost certain to defend themselves; if you blame people, they will justify themselves. They will also counter-attack you, provoking you into defence and justification. Within a few sentences, a first-class row will be under way, each vehemently attacking the other and widening the disagreement for good measure. Attack and blame spirals seldom remain contained. Before long, the entire relationship between the negotiators and its history is a subject of contention.

As the heat rises, each says things that calmer counsels would foreswear. Ben, for example, broadens his attack from who was to blame for the equipment failures to the allegedly rude telephone behaviour and asserts that Admin Xpress is dealing with people 'who are more trouble than they are worth' (a point of view with which the holder is hardly likely to endear himself to Jackie). Most attacks are taken personally, and personal attacks are doubly tactless. A relationship may never recover from deeply wounding or offensive personal attacks. But even if the damage done by an attack is not permanent, it is almost certainly obstructive of a negotiated settlement in its immediate aftermath, and anything that obstructs progress towards a settlement is a serious impediment to a negotiator.

I have heard it argued by some negotiators that there is some tactical advantage to be gained by indulging in some 'controlled' attack or blame behaviour. When handled carefully, they assert, a few well-placed attacks can 'soften up' the other side and make them more willing to compromise. As with most aspects of human interaction, there is no doubt room for experimenting with every form of behaviour across all the circumstances you will experience in a short lifetime. However, I suspect that those who believe in 'softening up' the opposition by attacking them have exaggerated the incidence of the circumstances where judicious attacks have produced the kind of results they claim. In effect, I suspect that they are spuriously justifying behaviour that, while they are honest enough to admit to it, they are not objective enough to question. In the main, and for most occasions, I think you will find that attacks are seldom controllable and even less frequently are they beneficial to your interests.

Threats

In the drift of argument towards deadlock, threats constitute the final step. It follows that to open with threats is one of the crassest of negotiating mistakes. It always makes a bad situation worse and a worse situation hopeless. Consider the case where a developer wanted to extinguish a private right of way across some land upon which he wanted to erect some high-technology offices. The owner of the right of way, a local farmer, was not inclined to sell at any price that had so far been mentioned in previous meetings. At the meeting I attended, I was astonished (the farmer was furious) to hear the agents for the developer open with a series of threats as to what they intended to do unless the issue was settled quickly and in their favour. The threats ranged from the credible – applying for Compulsory Purchase Orders, not just for the right of way across their land, but for the farmer's house and land adjacent to it – to the incredible – having his business investigated for tax fraud and his medical procedures for TB testing. Predictably, not much progress was made that morning!

There are all kinds of reasons given for making threats. Few of them apply to negotiating, for the case against making them in a negotiation rests on a single premise: they seldom if ever have the desired effect (namely, to get somebody to comply with our wishes) and almost always have the opposite effect (they provoke them to dig in). Among the reasons advanced for making threats, the most common is an attempt to make the other side aware of the consequences of its failure to agree with what we are proposing. It is also the least successful thing we can do when faced with opposition to a proposal.

Threats produce their own counter, either in the form of a direct counter-threat or of some sort of demonstration that 'we are undeterred by the threat and can joyfully live with the consequences'. For example, you threaten litigation, and I counter-threat with a counter-suit; you threaten to cut off my water supplies, and I respond with a declaration that doing without water would be one of the great aesthetic experiences of my life. However serious or otherwise the threat and its counters are, we are no longer negotiating a solution. We are rapidly speeding towards some other means of arriving at a decision. Meanwhile, in the development case mentioned above, the right of way has stayed in the developer's way to this day, and the only people to gain from this sort of stand-off are those who do well out of litigation.

Threats made in anger are doubly destructive. Frustration produces more threats than anything else and often arises because we are stuck in destructive argument. Attacks lead to threats as water runs downhill. Once committed to a threat, we feel the need to go through with it even when its costs exceed its benefits. A union making little headway with management might threaten a strike and then be under pressure to mount one to show management that it cannot be taken lightly. The strike costs the employees their wages and the management its output. This weakens the business financially and reduces its ability to fund pay raises.

Constructive debate behaviours

A valid question at this juncture would be: 'Assuming we were inclined to behave impeccably, how do we deal with somebody else who is behaving destructively?' The alternative to destructive argument is **constructive** debate. This is

Table 4.2 Time sheet: constructive debate behaviour

Constructive debate						
Time	Neutral statement	Assurance	Question	Summaries	Signals	Listening

characterised by behaviour that serves our goal of seeking a solution agreeable to our interests. If it moves the negotiation towards an acceptable solution, then we are prepared to engage in constructive debate irrespective of the provocation to do otherwise. Indeed, there is no alternative to a constructive approach, *whatever the behaviour of the other negotiator*. To retaliate in kind to destructive argument is a certain recipe for deadlock and, *in extremis*, for a breakdown in the relationship. This is not to say that a constructive approach will necessarily produce the result you want, but it does have the best chance of doing so, whereas an argument has little or none.

What are the elements of a constructive debate? They are remarkably few in number and, for this reason alone, they are easy to recognise and practise. They can be illustrated by extending the time sheet for the incidence of destructive argument in Table 4.1 to the incidence of constructive debate in Table 4.2.

As before, the observer would tick each occurrence of the respective behaviour during each minute of the negotiation, using the left-hand side of a column consistently for one of the negotiators and the right-hand side for the other. This way, a trail of the negotiating interactions is produced, hopefully showing, as time elapses, a drift south-easterly towards agreement.

Neutral statements

The making of neutral statements is the most common activity in debate. These cover any statement by one negotiator that informs the other negotiator as to his views, opinions, attitudes and approach, or is in answer to a question on whatever is under discussion. The qualification that these statements are neutral distinguishes them from attacks, assertions and threats and from the destructive argument range of behaviours. For example, to tell the other negotiator that you have collected the data on the alleged incident and that your findings suggest that a delay of six weeks occurred, is a neutral statement if your tone is not accusative and your manner is not aggressive. To have used the words 'avoidable delay' might be construed as an attack and not as a neutral statement. If the tone or manner changes, the observer would classify the behaviour according to whether it moved the statement away from or towards neutrality.

In the course of a negotiation, it is common for short speeches to be made by each side as to their views on the subject matter of the meeting. In the main, these are neutral statements, and my experience of observation is that this column attracts the most ticks for much of the time. Communication in negotiation is essential, and the making of neutral statements appears to be the most common manifestation of communication – negotiators must inform each other of what they are about and explain why they have adopted the views they hold. Even answering a question requires information and explanation, as does the making of, or the response to, a proposal. The interaction of the parties to what each other says involves sometimes prolonged exchanges of neutral statements. These can also be repetitive.

Negotiators disclose information to each other (though how much they disclose could be of tactical importance). We might volunteer information ('I had a meeting yesterday with the site engineer, and he told me that the carpenters are running about three shifts behind in the shuttering work'), or we might give it out in response to a question ('I have no idea just yet as to why they are behind, but I can tell you the effect it is having on the completion bonus').

Information is the lifeblood of a negotiation. If we have not got accurate and timely information, we cannot make sensible proposals. We make assumptions but must test them with information. Our pre-meeting assumption might be that they are interested only in saving time, not money; when we meet with them, we must validate this assumption by listening to their statements, perhaps by asking questions, before we suggest a solution. If our assumption is wrong and untested, we might propose a solution that saves time when, in fact, they want to hear a solution that saves money.

> *Daniel, the owner of a double glazing plant, wanted to improve the efficiency of the glass-cutting and framing operations. He decided to computerise the system so that orders for similar sizes could be batched throughout the day to save setting and re-setting downtimes. In conversation with him about this, I asked from whom he was going to buy his computers. 'Apple', he replied. 'Why Apple?' I asked. 'That's easy. I was looking out of my window one morning and spotted our apple tree, full of fruit, ready to pick', he said (he always said apples were his favourite fruit!), 'and I thought that as Apple was the world's largest computer company, they must be doing something right.' The logic was impeccable, but it occurred to me that if a rather keen computer salesperson were to walk into Daniel's office that morning and, on the assumption that most businesses were cost conscious, were to offer him a system costing 40 per cent less than Apple (a not impossible proposal), he could be wasting his and Daniel's time. It was not the price that motivated Daniel's choice of system, but the security in knowing that the system would work.*

When people speak, they inform us of their priorities, though not necessarily directly or with candour; by listening, we learn about their priorities and their values. They also reveal their inhibitions – the factors that motivate them to say 'no' to our suggested solutions – and this information is of direct benefit to us. By elaborating on their inhibitions – perhaps they do not trust our intentions – we can make helpful statements that address these inhibitions. In any event, understanding what is inhibiting a solution must be beneficial to our interests because, unless and until we remove or meet the inhibition, we are unlikely to make progress.

Much of the time spent in debate is in an effort to persuade the other negotiators to see our point of view. We try to influence their perceptions of the possible outcomes and persuade them to modify their expectations. Hence, we make statements to these ends, though not always consciously. We marshal whatever arguments we can think of that present our views in the best possible light and try to counter their arguments that contradict our own. Put this way, you can see why carelessness in the debate phase can undo a great deal of our effort to influence their thinking. It certainly never ceases to amaze me the number of times that I see negotiators browbeating the very people they are supposed to be influencing. Careless behaviour of the argumentative kind works directly contrary to the tactical necessity of persuading them to work towards our objectives.

Questions

Given the importance of the task of establishing what the other negotiator wants, how badly he wants it and what he is prepared to trade to get it, the role of questions is overwhelmingly important. Yet negotiators can have difficulty achieving a questioning rate of one per hour – most of the time they are talking, usually argumentatively, and to no good purpose. Questions are always a sign of effective negotiating behaviour – a rate of four questions per 15 minutes is a welcome sign that the negotiators understand the key role of the debate phase in establishing what each of them wants. Of course, the kind of questions you ask can make a difference, as can whether or not you are listening to their answers.

Broadly, there are two main types of questions: **closed** and **open**. A negotiator should know the difference between them. Consider this: a closed question can sensibly be answered with a 'yes' or 'no'; an open question invites a more general and detailed response. For example:

Closed questions:

Do you carry out safety inspections?

Was this consignment checked?

Did you sign off the paperwork?

Are you having difficulty clearing the site?

Will you accept late delivery?

Open questions:

When was the last safety inspection?

What is the procedure for checking consignments?

Why did you sign off the paperwork?

How difficult is it to clear the site?

When is the latest we can deliver by?

In practice, in normal interaction, though not necessarily in the formal circumstances of a court of law, the answers to questions can vary beyond the confines of the differences between closed and open questions. Some people answer a closed question with a long elaboration (for example, in reply to the first question above, 'Do you have a safety policy?', one could answer, 'Yes, and a very good one it is too. It was praised by the Department of Energy . . .'), and some people answer an open question with a single word (for example, in reply to the last question above, 'When is the latest we can deliver by?', one might say, 'Can't!'). However, in the main, the closed question shuts off dialogue and the open question invites it. In negotiation we want to avoid the former and encourage the latter. Hence, increase your question rate and formulate more of your questions as open questions.

Listening skills

There is very little point in asking any questions if you are not properly listening to the answers. In truth, we are very poor listeners, as we are easily distracted by our thoughts. These thoughts can be related to the discussion or completely unrelated; neither is helpful because the second we start thinking about something, we are no longer listening to what is being said. We could miss something important, miss the point or even just misunderstand the message.

When we hear something that is of interest to our position, we can start to think how to formulate a response or consider how it fits our wants, and if the other person is still speaking, we miss what they are saying to us. They could be offering a solution, offering more, asking for something, qualifying their position or giving us some vital information. We often allow our over-active brains to take charge; instead, try to engage in some active listening.

Of course, even when we are listening, we often hear what we want to hear. We skew what we hear into what we expect, what means more to us or what part matters to us. We make assumptions. Making assumptions themselves isn't a big problem, but it will affect your negotiation outcome if you act upon those assumptions. You are setting yourself up for more disagreement or mistakes.

How can we do better at listening? You need to make sure not only that you have heard everything they have said, but that you have understood it correctly. Making notes while listening can train your brain not to 'think' – you can listen and write, but you can't listen, write *and* think about what is being said. Once you have listened, check for understanding by asking clarifying questions and making summaries.

Summaries

Some people merely want to have their point of view listened to and understood. They react negatively to people who do not listen, who make it obvious they do not want to listen and who, having gone through the motions of listening, still do not understand what they were told. If this reaction is provoked, it slows progress and can sometimes reverse it. The person who feels that they are not being listened to slips into the argument range, and the inevitable deadlock ensues.

Negotiators can avoid this happening by listening and demonstrating that they are listening. This illustrates two of the three roles of a summary. It informs the other negotiators that you have listened to what they have said and that you have understood them. Sentences such as the following provide the verbal mechanism for testing your understanding and demonstrating that you have been listening.

> 'Let me see if I understand what you are saying . . .'
> 'Correct me if I am wrong, but as I understand it, you want . . .'
> 'OK, let me summarise what you want . . .'

If your summary is correct, they have proof positive that you are listening and understand them; if it is incorrect, they have the opportunity to clarify the points on which you misunderstand them. On either count, they are happier than they would be in the absence of such opportunities.

A minor problem sometimes arises when negotiators mistakenly believe that, because you have listened to them and have demonstrated that you understand them, that it necessarily follows or implies that you agree with them. This, of course, does not follow at all, and you may need to make this clear in certain circumstances. For instance, you could insert the comment: 'Before responding in detail with my views on your position, I think it would be useful if I attempted to summarise what you have said to ensure that I understand it'. Merely repeating what someone says does not imply agreement with them and it does you no harm to make this clear occasionally. 'Nothing is agreed until everything is agreed' is a valuable verbal device to insert into the debate phase at key points.

The third role of a summary, beyond conveying proof that you have been listening and that you understand what they have said, is to redirect the attention of the negotiation onto the central theme of the debate. It is not uncommon in an unscripted interaction for the participants in the debate to wander off the topic, or to become repetitive, or to move into dangerous and contentious areas. A judicious summary of what has been said in respect of the topic has the useful role of bringing the debate back onto the main track you wish to go along:

> Let me summarise where we are. You have outlined your views along the following lines . . . . I shall explain to you how we see the problem by briefly outlining the following points . . . . Now, how can we move forward from here?

Assurance

The simplest verbal device can be used to motivate somebody to work towards your objectives. It does not necessarily evangelically switch them over to your views, but it certainly contributes towards their doing so. I refer to a category of influencing skills called **assurance behaviour**. These can be as simple as saying positive things about the relationship between you (past, present or future). For example:

I am sure that we can sort this problem out.

We value the business we have done so far together, and we look forward to continuing to do more business with you in the future.

The fact that we let you down causes me even more pain than it evidently caused you.

These or similar statements are directed at assuring the other negotiator that you have positive rather than negative – or neutral – feelings about your relationship. You acknowledge that they are special and, by implication, that the matter under discussion is manageable within the positive range of your relationship. For example, faced with a very difficult negotiation – over a serious breach of ethical conduct by a firm of solicitors – the negotiator for the aggrieved party fully understood the concerns of the solicitors (fears of professional misconduct litigation, consequent loss of reputation, etc.) and knew that such concerns could block progress in the negotiations if the solicitors decided to fall behind a preliminary defence line of saying little, admitting nothing and dragging it all out for as long as possible, bankrolled by professional indemnity funding. His opening assurance remark, 'Gentlemen, I am in the solution, not the retribution, business', had a plainly visible positive effect on the somewhat overly defensive solicitors. An agreement was worked out in a couple of hours to the relief of the solicitors and the satisfaction of the negotiator's clients.

Another good example of excellent assurance behaviour comes from a recent experience with some rather poor service with a UK retailer. I had ordered a new sofa and chairs, but on delivery one of the chairs was damaged. The company reordered it, but there were delays upon delays, and after four months I still didn't have a complete living room set. After much complaining getting me nowhere – except angrier – I was put through to the 'escalation team'. The lady was utterly charming and assured me that she would 'listen to all your issues, fix the problem and make sure you are 100 per cent satisfied'. At first I was still a little sceptical (it was my tenth call to the customer services team by this point), but over the course of the 20-minute call she listened to me, agreed with all my arguments and even went as far as to appear to be on my side. I felt my anger dissipating with every minute that passed. Even though I was totally aware of what she was doing, I couldn't remain angry with her, as she was agreeing with me. I came off the phone and was completely happy and convinced that it would be sorted. She went on to follow through with her promises, and although it still took some time, she fixed all my issues, and we agreed upon a fair amount of compensation. I came away a much happier customer. The lesson is clear: assurance behaviour helps negotiators move forwards.

How not to disagree

Negotiators begin with different solutions to the same problem and, hopefully, end with a common solution. Different solutions, like different opinions, are a cause of tension. When our interests are at stake, we do not like people disagreeing with our views as to what should happen. The beginning of a negotiation is usually more tense than the later stages (indeed, the close proximity of a solution often induces degrees of euphoria, which are dangerous in themselves). If the gap is large, we are tense. If the gap is narrow but the issues are highly contentious, we are also tense. If we feel threatened, or badly let down, we are tense. The other negotiator is both somebody who can help us to get what we want and somebody who can stop us from getting it, at least in a form that meets our expectations. Not surprisingly, we have an ambivalent attitude towards the other negotiator. On one hand, we are ready to be helpful, and on the other, we are ready to fight back if our darkest fears are realised.

With tension comes mistakes. We misjudge, or judge too quickly. Given that people tend to highlight their differences when they start discussing what to do about them, we react emotionally to what (we think) we hear, as if their first statements are the extent of their intentions towards a settlement. Not taking too seriously (in the sense of letting it determine our attitudes) what people say at the beginning of a negotiation – particularly where the issue is fraught – is good advice, though it is seldom taken. It is as if our worst fears are realised immediately – 'they will never accept the legitimacy of our position' – when in fact all they are doing is setting out their views, perhaps to give themselves negotiating room.

There is also the possibility that we have made a mistake in our assessment of the situation. We might believe, on the evidence that we have available, that we have a strong case for, say, compensation for some misdemeanour on the part of one of our suppliers, or that, say, a supplier is attempting to charge us excessively for a service. It would be difficult in these circumstances for us to remain casually indifferent in our emotional feelings towards the people against whom we believe that we have a grievance. Yet not to do so could undermine our negotiating abilities.

> *Brindley Airport uses a computer bureau to manage the payroll of its 2,000 employees. Everything worked smoothly for the first year of the contract, but one month the payroll failed to be supplied and, by using the previous month's records, employees eventually were paid manually by the airport management. The disruption surrounding this unfortunate incident was extensive. Many employees left their posts to besiege the personnel office – causing a failure in service to passengers and to the airlines – and it took considerable effort on the part of the management to prevent a total stoppage of work.*
>
> *Following numerous telephone calls between Brindley and Omega, the computer people, a letter was sent to Omega setting out a claim for compensation for the disruption (including the cost of paying cash to the employees) and asserting that Brindley regarded Omega as responsible for any liquidated damages claims the airport received from the airlines. Brindley's management were determined to punish Omega for their failure and to withdraw from further discussions on Omega computerising personnel records, traffic management and scheduling.*
>
> *Both parties met to discuss the claims for compensation and the decision not to proceed with negotiations on future business. The atmosphere was not pleasant. On Brindley's side, they were still smarting under the robust criticism they had received from their colleagues for the disruption and what they felt was a failure of Omega to act promptly when the crisis struck. On Omega's side, there was considerable anger at what they saw as an attempt to blame them for something that was not entirely their fault and that also caused them to suffer disruption in their services to their other clients. The situation was primed for a blazing row.*
>
> *Brindley's side led with a catalogue of complaints about the failure of the payroll to appear on time and a detailed analysis of the telephone calls they had made to Omega. They spoke about compensation claims from the airlines, without being specific about the amount (in truth, the only serious claim for a delayed departure amounted to £17,000 and this was felt to be a 'try-on' from an airline whose record of punctuality was notoriously bad anyway). They bluntly asserted that they had no intention of extending their dependence for computer services to a company as 'incompetent' as Omega.*
>
> *For their part, the Omega managers repudiated the charge of incompetence, countercharged Brindley with causing the problem in the first place (without detailing how), threatened to sue Brindley for defamation following the statements about Omega that the airport personnel manager made to local TV during the disruption, and counter-claimed for an unspecified amount that they had lost in servicing their other clients.*

It would, of course, have been better for one or both sides to have spent less time asserting its own case and more time finding out what the other side had to say about the problem, *and its solution*. A dose of professional calmness was needed but was absent. It is as if they had come for a fight and were going to be

Integrative bargaining, pt. 2: Debate

disappointed if they failed to have one. Each blamed the other. Moreover, their attitudes coloured their approach to the new information each had to offer.

Even in the opening session, there were warning signals that all was not as each had conceived it. If all is not as it is believed to be, it is essential to find out the extent of the deviation of reality from perception. The emotional and adamant approach of Brindley's people smothered their curiosity about the implication of Omega's statements that they too had a claim against Brindley for the failure of the payroll. They simply dismissed the whole notion that Brindley could, in any way, shape or form, be liable for Omega's manifest incompetence and took its mere assertion as further proof that Omega were not just bad, they were wicked too.

What else could they have done? Apart from any failings in their preparation – had they asked which was more important: punishment or solution? – they were badly in need of skill in handling a disagreement. Of course, this was partly caused by their self-assurance that they were completely in the right: it was Omega's contractual duty to provide the payroll; they had not done so, therefore, Omega was totally in the wrong. If Omega dissented from that evident truth, more's the pity for them. Not only would it cost them a compensation claim, but it would also cost them additional business.

The first thing to be aware of when faced with a disagreement about anything is the possibility (no matter how remote) that you, not they, are in the wrong. Being wrong is not serious, providing you have a means of correcting your error without a complete loss of credibility. But being wrong without such a means – even deliberately eschewing the need for one – is a serious mistake in negotiation. This applies particularly when we are *absolutely* convinced that we are in the right, as we could be when we are dealing with an area in which we are totally competent, or where the facts are so well established that we believe only the ignorant are unaware of them.

Let me illustrate the most effective way of dealing with disagreement over a self-evident truth by way of a parable from the world of competitive sport:

> *Suppose you are a keen follower of rugby, and this season your team, the Foxes, scored the most tries, won the most matches and earned the most points to become league and cup champions of the year. You are celebrating your team's success with your family and happen to open up Twitter to boast of your team's great year. Someone on your timeline posts up, just before you do: 'What a season! The Bears are undoubtedly the best team this year. Nobody else came close!! Celebrating with friends as we look forward to next year!'*
>
> *Now this is astonishing news to you because the Foxes, for the reasons rehearsed above, are the 'best team in the whole country' and your astonishment at the insult spills over into mild resentment that this 'idiot, fool and ignoramus' is deliberately provoking you by his wild assertions.*

> **Exercise 4D**
>
> *Consider what you would do in such a situation before reading on. (I exclude the obvious choice of minding your own business and leaving the ignorant to wallow in their illusions.)*

Suppose you have an opportunity to challenge this assertion – it's almost unthinkable that you would forgo the opportunity to comment on his tweet – how would you tackle the disagreement? Most people would simply tell the stranger that he did not know what he was talking about. And the more convinced they were of their facts, the more assertive they would be, perhaps even being sarcastic or mildly mocking of him:

> *'Come, have a drink and we'll tell you about a real team of real champions', is about the nearest to being conciliatory you are likely to be. However, the stranger holds his ground by replying:*
>
>> The Foxes are not the best team in the country by a long way, and, moreover, the Bears are so far ahead over the Foxes in 'bestness' that it is a great mistake for you to celebrate, rather than commiserate, over their many failures.

I am sure many of you have followed a Twitter spat like this and watched enthusiastically to see who comes out on top. Yet the fact is that you could be in the wrong in your assessments of the relative merits of the two teams. Your assurance that you were right factually is no protection against manifest error. You have made the elementary mistake of disagreeing with somebody without discovering the source of their assertion. The more sure you are, the more assertive you will be, and the more likely that your inability to accept that you could be wrong will drive you towards a breakdown in your relationship with the offending person. This is a common route to deadlock in negotiating situations.

Returning to Twitter, what could you do at the start of your discourse with the stranger that will protect you from both error and angry deadlock or humiliation? The main thing you must do is find out the basis of the other fellow's assertion of something that you know to be counter-factual:

> *'On what basis', you might ask,*
>
>> are you convinced that the Bears – worthy as they are to have reached half-way up the points table, to have scored an average number of goals and to have won about half of their matches – are the best team in the country?

By asking a question, you both inform and protect yourself. If he shows that your own factual beliefs are wrong, you will learn something that you ought to know. (Even though, in this case, he is unlikely, in your view, to produce any worthwhile evidence that contradicts the public record, it is still worthwhile in principle to check in case you have missed something.) Also, by asking for the basis of his views and not attacking his holding of them, you protect yourself – in the (admittedly improbable) circumstance that he is right about the Bears, and you are wrong about the Foxes – from having to make a humiliating climbdown. In a negotiating context, so serious is the prospect of a humiliating climbdown that negotiators have been known to cling to their beliefs, long after the evidence is available that they were wrong, for the simple reason that they have no ready means of abandoning them without impairing what they perceive to be their negotiating credibility. What they usually do is refocus their attention on the personalities or other behaviours of those by whom they perceive they have been humiliated (though, of course, it was their own misguided handling of a disagreement that caused them to be vulnerable to humiliation in the first place).

What might the stranger answer in response to your question?

> *'Well, Sir', he might have said,*
>
> I am celebrating the conclusion of my studies of the nation's rugby teams – I am Professor of Abnormal Psychology at Riccarton University – and my research shows that the Bears, as a team, have the best psychological profiles of all teams in the country. Do you know, Sir
>
> *he might continue,*
>
> that in the terms of psychopathic tendencies, neuroses, schizophrenia, manic depression, and catatonic relapses, the Bears have the best scores of anybody I have ever studied. Indeed, Sir, compared to a team like the Foxes– by far the worst team in the country on these measures – the Bears are positively brimming with good health.

Asking questions therefore is a brilliantly simple device that both informs and protects you from charging in at the first sign of a disagreement (they may not be wrong, you might just be uninformed). It also enables you to lay the groundwork for them to back off from a wrongheaded position without carrying with it the risk that to do so in some way humiliates them. People will hang on to strange notions long after objective evidence suggests that they are in error, if only because their personal (and perhaps public) investment in the notion is too large for them to disregard. By asking questions, we let the perpetrators of nonsense condemn themselves when they are patently incorrect, or we allow them to redefine their position in such a way as to qualify it into a new category (by 'best' the professor was not talking about the team that had the best scoring results; he was talking about their psychological health). By qualification we identify that we are in contention about different things and, therefore, we are not really in contention at all.

Suppose we also disagree with their qualification? Fine. We have identified where we disagree. We can move on in the debate phase to explore what prospects there are for both of us to mediate our differences in a deal acceptable to both of us. Negotiations begin in disagreement and, hopefully, end in agreement. The process of getting from one to the other is fraught with risk. Negotiations break down because the disagreement is too fundamental or because it is badly handled – the people get in the way of the deal. The negotiator is trying to find a solution even where there is fundamental disagreement and trying to avoid a situation where the people – including himself or herself – get in the way by snatching deadlock out of the jaws of compromise.

One way to make a fundamental disagreement worse is to require the other negotiators to acknowledge that they are in the wrong and that they must drop their views or perceptions as a precondition of reaching a settlement. Rhetoric and negotiation do not go well together. People sometimes have a need to cooperate in some measure despite their fundamental differences. If the negotiators concentrate on their fundamental differences only, there will be no negotiation.

It is unlikely that a person with strong views on religion would recant them merely to agree with an unbeliever on the price of a house. This is obvious when presented in this way. Yet negotiators in these circumstances have been frustrated in the past by the perceptions of the other side that some form of recantation is what is required or implied in the search for agreement. Public comments on the other negotiator's religion, politics, motivation and culture are seldom helpful, though in free societies they are unavoidable. As a negotiator, therefore, you can help the search for agreement by refraining from commenting in this vein or linking your solutions to their views of the world. Negotiate on the direct issues that affect your relationship and ignore the background noise that, if excited, will soon drown out everything else you say.

Similar advice to negotiators applies when dealing with the highly charged problem of a hostage negotiation. If the security forces insist on the impossible demand that the terrorists cease to hold the views they do about the efficacy or truth of their cause, or they insist that they recognise the criminality of their actions, you can expect little progress to be made in arranging for the release of the hostages. Instead, the negotiators are advised to concentrate on securing agreement with the terrorists on the trivial issues – and the more trivial the better – of food, comfort and communications. The security forces have no more need to 'negotiate' a change of heart, politics or religion of the terrorists than they have to concede a change in their own status as the instruments of the rule of law. The distinction between the terrorists and the police is one that can, and should, be maintained, for it legitimizes what ultimately will happen to the terrorists, namely their capture and commitment to judicial processes. Attempts to do otherwise put at risk the safety of the hostages without gaining anything from their captors.

We handle fundamental disagreements by separating the issues for negotiation from the trenchant beliefs of the negotiators. We try to prevent people getting in

Integrative bargaining, pt. 2: Debate 81

the way of the deal. We focus on what can be achieved – no matter how small initially – and seek to build agreement step by step.

If we start in disagreement, how do we move towards agreement without somebody giving in? Having ensured that we are clear on what we are disagreeing about – by questioning and not challenging the disagreement – and taking care not to widen the issues that might be negotiable to beliefs that patently are not, we need to explore the potential for bridging the disagreement in some way that does not compromise the negotiators' wider interests. This requires that we discover and understand the inhibitions that prevent agreement.

What is an **inhibition**? Inhibitions are whatever motivates the other negotiators to reject our suggested solution. They are often hidden and require to be dug out – perhaps the negotiators are not sure themselves as to why they oppose our solution and prefer their own; perhaps they do not know how to search for their interests; perhaps they are less than candid about their inhibitions because of some shame or embarrassment in holding to their views; perhaps they do not understand what we are proposing. For you, as a negotiator, this situation poses some awkward questions, as well as providing a useful device to progress towards agreement.

Exercise 4E

What would the negotiator have to do to clear the way for an agreement in each of the following cases? Consider your answers carefully before reading on.

Example 4.1

A potential partner in a venture was not keen to accept the amount of the minimum investment it was proposed he should make. He criticised the numbers, questioned how they had been calculated, wanted them checked over again. His inhibition, however, was his nagging suspicion of his potential partners – 'Were they going to cheat me?' was how he put it to his advisor – a view he could not articulate openly without risk of insulting them and one he could not ignore in case they were up to no good. He chose instead to attack the details of the project.

Example 4.2

A union objected to new shift schedules on the grounds that they put at risk the safety of air passengers due to maintenance engineers working up to 12 hours a day. The management argued that this was nonsense, as with overtime working, many engineers were clocking 12-hour shifts on a regular basis. The union's inhibition was the fact that the new schedules

> would substantially reduce overtime working, but they could not present it this way without compromising the union's official stance against overtime working, nor could they antagonise their members by agreeing to any scheduling system that denied them opportunities to earn higher incomes from overtime pay.

Example 4.3

A buyer objected to the price. His inhibition was that the purchase would coincide with other peak expenditures and he wanted to minimise the price of this item. The seller pressed for the full price. His inhibition was that an additional discount on this price to meet the buyer's inhibition would undermine his own profitability by creating a precedent.

Example 4.4

A buyer was wary of accepting the same quantity of radiators for the new season. He had two inhibitions: first, he had been left with surplus stock from last year's mild winter, and second, the models were about to change their styling, and surplus stock this season would have no resale value next season.

In each of these examples, the negotiator would first need to identify the inhibition preventing the other negotiator from agreeing, and second, he would need to propose a solution that addressed the inhibition. This could come about by finding a form of words that took account of the inhibition, or by directly offering something that compensated for the felt loss, or that removed the prospect of a loss.

Much of the debate phase of negotiation concerns the search for inhibitions, not all of them hidden as deep as those in Examples 4.1 and 4.2, and of clearly understanding their content and their extent. You have to know how far you might have to go to make an agreement possible, if only to judge whether going that far made the deal worthwhile. Knowing what inhibitions the other negotiator has is a first step towards removing them as obstacles to agreement, or to concluding that the obstacle is irremovable.

In Example 4.1, the proposer of the joint venture might want to address the cautious partner's inhibition with some assurance that the investment was safer than he perceived at present. Perhaps this could be done by association – 'We are backed by the following blue-chip businesses'; 'We are already working with household names in the business' – or perhaps by lowering the initial entry price – 'You can make your investment in three parts: the first on joining, the second on our completing the building and the third when we let it'. None of these completely removes the risk, of course, but they might be enough to reduce the impact of his inhibitions on the deal.

Once the management in Example 4.2 spots the hidden inhibition on overtime working, it has the choice of being candid – 'Yes, it does reduce overtime working, but that is its intention' – and facing the consequences. These might boil down to some form of compensation – the consolidation of earnings from overtime into the normal hourly rate – or of trade-off in some other area – 'These proposals will improve our chances of surviving commercially and of your members keeping their jobs'.

In Example 4.3, a proposal could emerge that allows the buyer to pay the full price in a period when his other expenditures are below normal, and in Example 4.4, some proposal along the lines of the supplier taking back unsold radiators would overcome the inhibition of the buyer.

In all these cases, merely stating the inhibition suggests various ways of removing it, hence the pay-off from identifying inhibitions in others and revealing your own at some point. *To state an inhibition is to imply that if some way can be found to remove it, then there is a possibility of a deal.* You should, therefore, be zealous in your hunt for inhibitions in negotiation.

Signalling

Beginning in disagreement and moving towards a settlement, the negotiators face a strategic difficulty only partly addressed so far: 'How do we move without giving in?'

> *Consider Brindley's negotiators in dispute over Omega's liability for damages. Given that people claiming damages for losses seldom understate their claims, it is likely that Brindley would make high demands and back them with firm to rock-hard rhetoric to demonstrate to Omega their seriousness and determination. They might feel that any sign of a willingness to alleviate their claim could be interpreted by Omega as a sign of weakness, which could encourage Omega to make no offer of compensation, backing up their stance with tough talking. Both sets of negotiators might be willing, in principle, to mitigate their opening positions, given that the alternative of costly and time-consuming litigation is unattractive and has little to do with managing airports or computer bureaux. Here, a sign of weakness could be fatal, yet a deal has to be struck if the negotiators are to settle it without litigation.*

How can or do they move? Fortunately, humankind long ago developed the means for signifying movement without a collapse in their stances on contentious or competitive issues. If you listen to Brindley's dialogues carefully, you might hear something like this:

a) We have stated explicitly to you the costs of £110,000 that we have incurred as a result of your failure to deliver the payroll, and I must stress that, unless we receive compensation for our losses, we have no intention of continuing our discussions with you on future business.

84 *Integrative bargaining, pt. 2: Debate*

b) We have stated explicitly to you the costs of £110,000 that we have incurred as a result of your failure to deliver the payroll, and I must stress that, unless we receive some compensation for our losses, we have no intention of continuing our discussions with you on future business.

Consider carefully the difference between these two statements before reading on.

The difference lies in a single word, yet this single word transforms the sentence dramatically from a negotiator's point of view. In statement (a), the speaker says he requires 'compensation' for his losses, while in statement (b), he says he requires 'some compensation' for his losses. In both cases he mentioned the sum of £110,000 as the amount of his losses, and the intention of the first sentence is to claim that full amount, while that of the second sentence is to claim *some* amount, clearly less than £110,000, but by how much less is not yet decided. We speak of the negotiator signalling a willingness to move, usually by a shift in language from firm absolute statements to vaguer relative statements. Everybody signals – they learn it from normal human discourse – but not everybody is conscious of what form their signals take or why they use these forms at all. They just do it. You signal too, and once you recognise what you are doing, you will choose more carefully when to signal, and you will identify signals in others and choose to react to suit the circumstances.

Exercise 4F

Write down the signal from each of the following statements:

1. *'It would be extremely difficult to meet that delivery date'.*
2. *'We do not normally extend our credit facilities'.*
3. *'It is highly unlikely that my boss will agree to a free upgrade'.*
4. *'Under these circumstances, we cannot agree to compensation'.*
5. *'As things stand, our prices must remain as listed'.*
6. *'I can't give you a better discount on your current volumes'.*

The signals used in Exercise 4F are discussed below.

1. 'It would be **extremely difficult** to meet that delivery date'.

It is no longer impossible to meet the delivery date, merely 'extremely difficult'. This provides an opening for proposals to overcome the difficulty. This signal usually emerges after some considerable discussion on why they cannot meet the deadline.

2. 'We do not **normally** extend our credit facilities'.

'Normally' is a signal commonly used to indicate that, in special cases or circumstances, the normal rule need not apply. Many rules and regulations use this signal in their clauses to indicate the degree of discretion available to the authorities. For example, in universities, examination rules often use this signal to give the examiner's discretion: 'A student normally shall be deemed to have failed if he attends fewer than three out of four of his laboratory tests'. Find a convincing reason for missing some laboratory tests and you might be excused a failure.

3. 'It is **highly unlikely** that my boss will agree to a free upgrade'.

The subordinate is signalling that he does not have the authority, but that you might want to try his boss. The signal, 'highly unlikely', covers the subordinate's resistance to the free upgrade while inviting you to try harder.

4. '**Under these circumstances,** we cannot agree to compensation'.

Change the circumstances and we might be able to agree to your claims. By linking a decision to specific circumstances, the signal invites imagination in changing the circumstances in some way, perhaps by redefining them, or enlarging them or disregarding them. A common litany among shop stewards when they face the application of a rule in respect of one of their members is: 'Broken noses alter faces; circumstances alter cases'. Often, the shop stewards' advocacy skill relies on finding exceptions to tightly drawn rules.

5. '**As things stand,** our prices must remain as listed'.

If things stood differently, then we could relax our prices. Again, the signal invites you to help the other negotiator by finding an exception to the rules that bind his decision. It might mean your moving some way off your own stated position – 'as things stand' – and he will reciprocate.

6. 'I can't give you a better discount on your **current** volumes'.

An invitation to move off a discussion on current volumes to other, higher, volumes. Many people not listening intently would only hear the words 'I can't give you a discount'. Naturally, such cultivated 'deafness' prolongs or disrupts the negotiation.

The signal indicates an invitation to explore other possibilities. It is the weakest, and therefore the safest, commitment to a move. There is absolutely no danger of giving in because it invites the other negotiator to move – by following the signal – without commitment on the part of the signaller. Consider again any of the signals in Exercise 4F: none of them put the signaller at risk.

For example, consider (1): 'It would be extremely difficult to meet that delivery date'. On its own, this is a statement that, if not responded to by the listener – who offers no suggestions on how it could be made less difficult – does not weaken the speaker. He is merely stating a fact about the extreme difficulty of meeting some requirement of the listener. If the listener ignores the signal, the speaker's invitation to consider a movement is also ignored and his negotiating stance is not compromised. Similar considerations apply in each of the other examples.

Signals are something like a 'safe-conduct pass' that protects the bearer from molestation he otherwise might experience. Without a signalling device in our discourse, we would be at the mercy of the interpretation the other negotiator puts on our evident willingness to move. The signal is, in effect, a bridge to a possible proposal, though the negotiator must be wary as to what the proposal might contain until he is sure that he is addressing the right problem. There is a close affinity between inhibitions and signalling – the one usually identifies the other. To state an inhibition explicitly is, in effect, to signal along the lines of: 'address this inhibition and I can consider coming to an agreement'. Hence, spotting an inhibition is a clue to a possible solution. To hear a signal usually identifies an inhibition. Both require the same response.

A signal is only an indicator of a potential solution, and an inhibition is an indicator of a potential problem. Before making a proposal to deal with either, we must clarify the signal/inhibition to ensure that we understand its scope and therefore its potential:

> 'When you say that you must receive some compensation for the delays at the airport, could you be more specific as to what compensation you are looking for?'

This tells the signaller that you have noted the distinction he is hinting at between £110,000 and 'some compensation' and, while asking him for more details, signals back that you are not averse totally to paying some compensation, presumably as long as it is a small amount. Now both sides can move from their opening stances of '£110,000 and not a penny less' versus 'absolutely nothing and not a penny more'.

> 'While acknowledging your difficulty about increasing the discount level for our current volumes, could you perhaps indicate what discounts are available for much larger volumes?'

Here, the negotiator is sending an assurance ('acknowledging your difficulty') with a positive response in favour of higher-volume discounts. Even the use of the word 'difficulty' subtly protects the negotiator from a formal acceptance that a discount for current volumes is precluded; after all, a difficulty is not an impossibility. He is suspending that line of argument to explore the relationship of discount to volume. The other negotiator can now indicate his schedule of volume discounts as a way out of the problem. It is no longer the case that the seller is offering no more discount with the buyer insisting on getting one because they have now moved to discuss not the principle of the discount, but its application to levels of volume.

Signals do not in themselves break deadlocks – the indicated area for potential compromise may not be attractive to the other negotiator; indeed, it may be totally off-limits, as far as he is concerned – but signals do indicate that compromise, in principle, is not excluded. They point the way out of the debate phase towards proposals.

Conclusion

In negotiation, we cannot negotiate a debate, nor can we negotiate principles, beliefs, prejudices, feelings, hopes, ideals and attitudes. We can only negotiate proposals. But before we can safely get to proposals, we must spend some time in debate. How long we spend cannot be determined unilaterally, nor can it be predicted. The interaction between the negotiators precludes detailed planning. Each responds to the other. It is more like a game of football than a symphony. In football, the players take off in pursuit of the ball and each other in all directions – whatever their managers had planned beforehand! There is no ordered scripting, no planned performance. That is the joy and the tears of the game for players and spectators alike. In a symphony, each member of the orchestra (and most of the audience) knows exactly what notes to play and when to play them, and woe betide any violinist or bassoon player who gets them wrong – conductors and fussy *cognoscenti* of music are unforgiving. The joy of orchestral music is its absolute and unvarying predictability.

In debate, we are setting out our views, creating our negotiating room and probing the prospects of a deal with each other. We do not know for sure what they will say, let alone what they will accept. To prolong debate longer than necessary is a major source of risk in negotiation. The sensitivities of people in debate are sufficient to provoke rounds of destructive and frustrating argument, and the longer we take to make constructive movement possible, the more we risk an outbreak of destructive argument. When people get in the way of a deal, it is almost always caused by the mismanagement of the debate phase.

What could Ben have done to set his negotiations with Jackie over the engineering failure problem onto a constructive plane? For a start, he should have listened to what Jackie had to say. He needs to know on what precise basis Jackie was looking for compensation. He will not find this out by giving Jackie the benefit of his own assumptions (invariably negative) of why he believes Jackie thinks she deserves compensation. Ben should listen more than he talks, not because he might be softened up by what Jackie says, but because the clues as to what Jackie might consider an acceptable settlement will be buried in what she says and how she says it. Also, the case for compensation might have merits that will prove irresistible in the business, and it might be in Admin Xpress's interests to make the best of a poor situation. Competitive changes restructure remuneration and the terms of business, and if Jackie is merely articulating the coming irreversible changes, Ben ought to be interested in knowing why and to what extent these changes are going to affect his business.

Jackie might, of course, be so out of touch with the competitive realities that her claim for compensation has no chance whatsoever of being considered. Again, Ben has an interest in getting Jackie to see this without unnecessarily antagonising a customer. Why? Because today's irate and insulted customer might influence tomorrow's business. I know of a management consultant who, when he was a junior sales representative on the road, was so antagonised by a hotel chain by their arrogant attitude to his complaints about their lack of attentive service, that 20 years later, when his office is booking hotel accommodation for several dozen seminars a year, he will instruct them to choose any other hotel chain but that one to place his business (even though it is now owned by another company). Brand sales rise and fall, and it does not take too many Jackies exercising their powers of discriminating purchases to cause modest but cumulatively damaging fall-offs in sales of a particular brand or company. Moreover, with rising costs and market uncertainty, Admin Xpress could very well find themselves at a disadvantage if their sales were marginal against their rivals. And what impact do you think there would be to expansion plans in the area if Jackie were to have an influence on the other businesses within the park?

In listening to Jackie, whose complaint was her loss of performance with the equipment failures, Ben might have detected a signal that Jackie did not mind how the money was restored — whether by compensation, credit or discount — which might suggest to Ben a possible joint solution to benefit both Admin Xpress and AppItAll (bearing in mind that the constant call-outs/repairs are having cost implications for Admin Xpress too). Suppose Ben could formulate a proposal that combined a guaranteed call-out time for Jackie with some training for Jackie's staff on use of the equipment, perhaps even teaching them some basic repairs to reduce minor call-outs. Instead of a bitterly angry Jackie (and let us not forget, an equally angry Ben) and a damaged relationship, they could have found a way out of the deadlock towards a better business deal for them both.

The power of effective debate is its direct route to effective (and winnable) proposals. True, not all differences are reconcilable. Negotiation is not a panacea for solving the unsolvable. But effective debate that discovers the irreconcilability of the aspirations of two negotiators is well worth its outcome. Better to discover the truth that our interests are irreconcilable *as things stand* than to err into believing them irreconcilable when in fact it is our debate behaviour that has made them so. Moreover, discovering the nature of the irreconcilability is also a gain because it indicates what has to change if the parties are to be reconciled. For instance, discovering that a deadlock over the future of the Falklands/Malvinas is based entirely on the unwillingness of the British to discuss sovereignty and the Argentines not to discuss it, at least eliminates the possible belief of either party that the other is bluffing. If they are clear that there is no bluff, at least neither side will take risks to call it, which is a degree better than going to war to prove there is no bluffing about our intentions.

Debate opens the way to proposals, but it does not follow that we debate in only one session, never to return to it throughout the negotiations. Any time we ask a question or make a statement, we are in debate, irrespective of what we are questioning – it could be the other negotiator's proposals – or what we are stating – perhaps our views on the other negotiator's bargain. You should see debate as an ongoing activity that takes up roughly 80 per cent of the time spent in the face-to-face interaction. It may be that there are prolonged periods of debate in the early stages of negotiation with shorter bursts of debate as we approach the conclusion. Of course, a negotiation that deadlocks could have 100 per cent of its time spent in debate (or, more likely, argument). How we allocate our time is all important. If we cannot negotiate a debate, it follows that we must move towards proposals (via signalling), and it is to this phase that we turn in the next chapter.

Checkpoint 4

4.1 In the debate phase, you should aim to:

   a) Complete it as quickly as possible to avoid argument.

   b) Discover the other negotiator's interests and inhibitions.

   c) Ensure that the other negotiator understands your positions.

   d) Inform the other negotiator of your interests and inhibitions.

4.2 Negotiators signal in order to indicate:

   a) A willingness to move.

   b) A desire for the listener to move.

   c) That a proposal is imminent.

   d) A preference for a compromise.

4.3 The most effective way to handle a disagreement is to:

   a) Point out where the other negotiator is factually wrong.

   b) Ask questions.

   c) Explain with great courtesy the grounds for your disagreement.

   d) Summarise the case against the other negotiator's views.

4.4 Are the following questions open or closed?

1. Do you have a safety policy?

2. Will it pass inspection?

3. How did you calculate those figures?

4. Is that important to you?

5. What aspects of my proposal are acceptable to you?

6. Is that agreed?

7. Have you changed your mind?

8. How do you expect me to accept that proposal?

9. Can you do better than that?

10. How can you improve on your offer?

4.5 Find the signal in the following statements:

a) I am unable to meet your current terms on delivery dates and penalties.

b) I can't accept an annual review.

c) Before we move forward, we need to discuss some discounting on bulk orders.

d) These timelines are very difficult to commit to.

5 Integrative bargaining, part 3
How to propose

Introduction

> *Amanda Levin (AL): Let me get this clear. You cannot accept our offer of a 5 per cent increase in price per photo as an incentive because this barely covers your additional costs?*
> *Tony Marks (TM): That's correct.*
> *AL: OK. How about if we made it 7 per cent?*
> *TM: Sorry. I'd love to be more reasonable, but we just can't afford anything under 10 per cent.*
> *AL: 10 per cent? Well, if I made it 10 per cent, would you accept a penalty clause?*
> *TM: We're not interested in penalty clauses.*
> *AL: It would make life easier for me if you were. Can I not tempt you to think about them?*
> *TM: Sure, I'll think about it, but I also think that at this meeting we should settle the incentive price first and leave the pros and cons of the complications of penalty clauses to another day. We'll accept your offer of 10 per cent and we suggest that it applies for every single-point improvement over the target of 25% error rate.*
> *AL: We were thinking of applying it to every five-point improvement . . .*
> *TM: Too high a barrier to jump in one go. It will take us a while to get momentum going, to fix all the little causes of error, before we see real improvements. If performance is measured in five-point blocks, we could be working hard for some time before we get paid, even though you would be benefiting from a reduced error rate almost immediately.*
> *AL: Well, if you are prepared to consider a penalty clause, I'll accept single-point improvements. What about sliding scales for increased incentive payments?*
> *TM: Sliding scales are very complicated. Why don't we keep it simple and do it on a straight-line basis?*
> *AL: I'll drop sliding scales if you can look again at the maximum target of 25 per cent.*
> *TM: Is that your final position?*
> *AL: Well, I . . . er. . . ..*

Exercise 5A

Identify and note from the text all the proposals made by Amanda before reading on. You should be able to find seven.

A proposal is any statement that makes a suggestion about how to proceed during the negotiation, or that indicates a possible solution to the issue under discussion. It can vary from the simple statement: 'Let us take the warranty issue first and then deal with the other matters', to the more complex offer of a solution: 'OK, I'll drop that demand if you'll reconsider the overtime rates'.

Proposals crop up all the time. They are different from any of the behaviours in the debate phase because they make a suggestion, albeit tentative, of how the two negotiators might agree on some issue that they are discussing. The problem for most negotiators is the tendency to use slack language in the proposal phase (a tendency that becomes even more damaging in the bargaining phase later) that directly, though not always obviously, undermines the impact of their proposal and contributes to the other negotiator perceiving that they have a weak commitment to it.

I can illustrate this assertion through a short diagnosis of the errors made by Amanda during her negotiation with Tony, the supplier of the photos causing error problems at Forth. I have cut out some of Amanda's supporting speech during this stage of the actual negotiation on errors and recorded only those sentences directly concerned with proposing.

Let us examine each of Amanda's attempts at making proposals to Tony.

1. **'How about if we made it 7 per cent?'**

Asked as a question, this is the weakest form of proposal. It leaves it to Tony to decide whether 7 per cent is good enough. When asked as a question, this proposal is far too easy to reject out of hand, or, as Tony is not required to do anything in return for accepting 7 per cent, his best bet – and the one he took – is to challenge the offer with a higher counter, to which Amanda gave in.

2. **'If I made it 10 per cent, would you accept a penalty clause?'**

Another weak approach. Amanda is improving on her offer of 7 per cent and also asking Tony to accept an onerous penalty clause. Why Amanda thinks that Tony should concede a penalty clause on the basis of a request after Amanda has moved to 10 per cent is a matter of conjecture. Experience suggests that negotiators are not overly generous in response to free gifts and certainly not when an onerous condition is presented as a question. Negotiators (rightly) react to these types of question-proposals, as in the example above.

Integrative bargaining, pt. 3: Proposing 93

3. **'Can I not tempt you to think about them?'**

Another example of a question-proposal. Why should the listener volunteer to think about something – a penalty clause – onerous to him? If you want someone to do something for what you are offering, make it a condition on your doing something for them.

4. **'We were thinking of applying it to every five-point improvement . . .'**

About as tentative as you can get! Amanda betrays here her lack of confidence in her proposal. From Tony's point of view, Amanda can think as long as she likes about the five-point threshold, but there is little likelihood that Tony will agree to something onerous to him as long as Amanda implies by her language that she is not too sure of his demands.

5. **'If you are prepared to consider a penalty clause, I'll accept single-point improvements'.**

Sounds far more impressive than it is. Amanda is only asking Tony to consider, not commit himself to, penalty clauses, as yet unspecified, in exchange for her acceptance of Tony's specific demand for single-point improvement schedules. Tony could say 'yes' to Amanda's proposal, and give purely nominal consideration to penalty clauses (rejecting them, of course), and thereby gain an important demand of single- – not five- – point thresholds for earning a performance bonus. For this exchange, Amanda gets nothing, which, to be fair, is all she asked for.

6. **'What about sliding scales for increased photo payments?'**

An almost pathetic plea from Amanda for something she wants. Tony is very unlikely to agree to anything presented to him so tentatively. He merely rehearses his arguments against sliding scales and leaves it to Amanda to pursue the matter, which she does by offering another weak proposal.

7. **'I'll drop sliding scales if you can look again at the maximum target of 25 per cent'.**

A classic example of Amanda offering something tangible – dropping her demand for sliding scales – for nothing. Tony is only required to 'look again' at the maximum target. Anybody can 'look again' at anything without changing his mind, and when he gets something in return for nothing, he is neither under pressure to trade, nor under serious threat that his intransigence will not be rewarded.

In this chapter, we examine effective and ineffective proposal language and what makes a proposal different from a bargain.

What is a proposal?

Movement in negotiation is essential if a solution is to be found. If we have no need to move, then we have no pressing reason to negotiate. Movement on one issue can be traded for no movement by ourselves on another, but the viability of this trade depends a great deal on how important it is for the other negotiator to secure movement on the issue upon which we are prepared to move. But movement there must be, if two negotiators with different solutions to the same problem are to secure a deal.

Where signalling is a tentative hint at the possibility of movement, proposing is a tentative suggestion of what form that movement could take. Signalling slides into proposing. It has also been described as the bridge to a proposal.

For example, the signal, 'It would be **extremely difficult** for me to accept an **unlimited** penalty clause', could become a proposal along the lines of, 'If you were willing to limit my exposure to penalty by some form of capping within the clause, I would be willing to consider adjusting to your performance standard'. Whether the proposal, and what form it takes, is presented after a signal or not would depend upon the other negotiator's reaction to the signal. It is not inconceivable that a proposal will be made after a signal has been ignored, though manifestly negotiating is more productive when the signal is followed by a signal question: 'Given that penalty clauses are part of our **standard** terms and conditions, how can I make it easier for you to accept them?' This invites the negotiator to make a proposal.

You should be able to see why negotiators who choose to argue against statements – in this case, the penalty clause – only muddy the waters because they force the other negotiator to defend the penalty (which, after all, protects his company from a failure in performance by the supplier). It is much more productive to signal and propose, or to question a signal and invite a proposal.

Why then does it matter what form the proposal takes? Surely a proposal, any proposal, is better than no proposal? This is true in much the same way as, when playing golf, scoring par is better than scoring ten over, but scoring ten under is even better. Poor negotiators sometimes stumble from an argument to a proposal, which is better than stumbling from an argument to a deadlock, but by presenting the proposal incorrectly, by not being aware of the importance of language and order in the proposal phase, they still do badly (in terms of meeting their own interests) when they could do better.

Proposal behaviour appears from the start of the negotiations. Merely suggesting that you meet at your office, not his, is a proposal. 'Let's sit over there' is a proposal; 'I think we should discuss the agenda' is a proposal. 'We should adjourn until Tuesday to consider what each has said' is a proposal, and so is the statement, 'We do not consider assignments valued at under £100,000 a year'. Each of these, and similar statements and suggestions, crop up all over the place during the debate phase of negotiation. You would be hard put not to propose anything in negotiation because the mechanics of meeting, interacting, pointing the way and stating your own position or aspirations involve loose proposal language, which for the most part is quite harmless to your interests – indeed, it might even enhance them in so far as it helps the debate phase move forward – but which, if carried on indiscriminately throughout the proposal phase, can severely handicap your position.

It is the ability to shift from loose informal proposal language to tight formal and assertive proposal language that improves your performance, but this is easier said than done. The very habit of loose language indulged in throughout the debate phase, where it does not present any threat to your interests, creates its own barrier to using formal language when it is needed. Many negotiators show no evidence of appreciating the distinction because it is not easy to shift gears from one situation to the other when the differences in the two situations are not easily identified.

Negotiators sometimes raise the objection that the shift from the looser language of proposing to more formal language is too risky because the change in language is noticeable and sounds almost aggressive. They do not want to appear to be aggressive (quite rightly) and they believe that any step down that road via assertive statements is to be avoided (quite wrongly). Lack of assertiveness leads directly to an unconvincing performance. If your proposal is meant to focus the attention of the other negotiator on a potential solution, it undermines your cause if the language of your proposal encourages the other negotiator to believe that you do not mean what you say, or that you have little confidence that your proposal will be accepted. Suspecting that you are ambivalent about what you want provokes the other negotiator to demand more from you – even when you are giving away the store because of your proposal language.

For example, negotiators often use very weak language to express their needs. They do this without thinking about it – we know because it often takes a video recording of their proposal language for them to realise that they actually are speaking in this way. Examples of non-assertive, and ultimately self-defeating, language take the form of:

> 'I wish . . .'
> 'I hope. . .'
> 'I would like. . .'
> 'It would be nice. . .'
> 'Could we. . .'
> 'Would this suit you. . .'

None of these forms would convince a negotiator that you were determined or committed to your views. There might be occasions and circumstances where you might find it useful to use such language (there are always exceptions to everything), but do not make the mistake of generalising from the exceptional to the particular. What might be appropriate in a minority of situations is not appropriate in most others. It would be far better that you adopt assertive language (said nicely and not arrogantly or aggressively). Examples include:

Integrative bargaining, pt. 3: Proposing

'I need . . .'
'I require . . .'
'We prefer . . .'
'We want . . .'
'It is necessary that . . .'
'We must insist . . .'
'If you do . . ., then we could consider . . .'
'We will . . .'

A proposal is a tentative suggestion that builds on a signal sent or one received. It is not a final solution (that is the role of a bargain). The earlier in the negotiation you are, the more tentative we expect proposals to be. We are exploring possible solutions, not putting forward final ones, and the less we know about the other negotiator's views, the less certain are we about which proposals are likely to be worth exploring. Hence, the extent to which we are tentative reflects the degree of our current prudence.

Tentativeness is its own protection. Saying, 'We could **make it** four visits a week', is far more specific (and on its own very dangerous if the number of visits was of crucial importance to them) than saying, 'We could **look at** the number of visits'. In the first case, the response could be, 'Fine. Now let's look at duration', leaving the proposer in trouble because he got absolutely nothing back for his specific movement and because, if he carries on like this, he will be picked off, item by item, by the other negotiator who is no doubt warming to the task at the thought of such easy pickings. In the second case, the response could be, 'Fine, but how many visits could you make a week?' To this, the negotiator can reply, 'That would depend on what we agree about duration, working hours and maintenance costs'.

Indeed, rather than wait (hope?) for the question, 'how many visits?', the negotiator could join his tentative suggestion or signal-proposal to his follow-on answers to the other negotiator's question by proposing, 'If we can agree about duration, working hours and maintenance costs, I could look at the number of visits'. This is a better approach because it does not rely on the other negotiator's alertness to pick up your signal-proposal ('We could look at the number of visits'). Not all negotiators listen very clearly, nor does everybody see all that quickly the implication of those signals you send. It is not unusual for the other negotiator, deliberately or otherwise, to move on to another topic, leaving your signal-proposal high and dry.

Exercise 5B

*Consider the construction of the proposal: 'If we can agree about duration, working hours and maintenance costs, we could look at the number of visits'. What do you immediately notice about it compared with the signal-proposal: 'We could **look at** the number of visits'?*

Yes, it is longer. The additional words preface the offer to look at the number of visits. These words also immediately place a protective cordon round his proposal and signal that the number of visits is negotiable (i.e. that they are tradable for things he wants in exchange). This is the essence of proposal language – it enables you to indicate movement without the risk of being ambushed or the risk of encouraging greater intransigence. You move from debating issues to tentative suggestions about how the issues might be handled, while making clear that the decision arrived at will be by trading and exchange and not by a one-way street of concession-making by you.

Effective proposals consist of two parts: the **condition** and the **offer**. Ineffective proposals only consist of offers.

> **Learning point:**
>
> *Effective proposals follow the simple format:*
> *Condition (first) + Offer (second)*

The language of a proposal is *always* tentative. Consider the proposal: 'If we can agree about duration, working hours and maintenance costs, we could look at the number of visits'. The condition requires the negotiators to 'agree' about some issues but does not specify what that agreement should consist of; the offer is for the negotiator to 'look at' something but does not specify what the results of his looking will or must be. There is a deliberate vagueness about both the vague condition and the vague offer in this proposal. The proposer cannot be ambushed with an 'OK' from the other negotiator because an 'OK' can only be a response that indicates a willingness to discuss the proposal and to explore the specific content of the vaguely presented condition and offer. If the other negotiator says 'no' to the whole proposal, then both negotiators go back to debate to see if there is some other way of solving the problem. By saying 'no', the other negotiator states his opposition to considering either or both the condition and the offer. A useful first question in debate, assuming that the other negotiator offers no reasons for his rejection, would be to find out what he does not like about the proposal.

Proposals decrease in tentativeness as we approach the bargaining phase. For example, you could propose that a specific condition is met: 'If you accept that the maximum duration of a maintenance visit is to be set at two hours, then we could re-examine the number of visits per week'. The condition is specific, but the offer is still vague (to 're-examine' something is a vague commitment). But whatever form the condition takes – specific or vague – the offer is *always vague*. This is summed up in Table 5.1.

Table 5.1 Components of a proposal

Condition	Offer
Vague/specific	Vague

How to make proposals

Negotiators often ask whether it is better to make the first proposal or whether it is better to respond to the other negotiator's proposals. I know some negotiators who boast of their principled opposition to proposing first, which if it works for them is probably a fine idea, but what happens when they meet somebody who holds the same principle of always proposing second? They could be in for a long session!

Some negotiations almost impose on the negotiator the task of making the first proposal. When a client asks you to send them a proposal for some new business, you are under pressure to put forward your solution – and often in writing. Another example is when two parties are working together, under a previously negotiated agreement, but one party wants to make changes or re-negotiate part way through.

> *Brian Denvor, a clothing manufacturer, was mid-way through a five-year contract to supply a national supermarket with part of their extensive clothing range. Everything had been fine with the work, and the income was certainly sufficient, until a few months ago. Changes in the local economy had put up all of his input costs: from electricity charges, materials and even transport costs, and now a minimum wage requirement was about to be brought in by his local authority, which would affect around one-third of his workforce. The contract would be worthless, unless he could re-negotiate.*

Negotiators wanting to change the status quo, by renegotiating a clause or even an entire agreement, do not have the luxury of moving second, and they risk irritating other negotiators if they persist in waiting for them to make the running.

It is in many ways an unhelpful approach to put too much into a single proposition about who should move, or avoid moving, first. If we perceive the process as one of debate and signals through which we move towards tentative solutions that do not commit the proposer, then who moves first becomes of less importance. We cannot endlessly go over the same ground with both stating their views but neither suggesting what might be possible. The purpose of proposals is to test the water – 'Is this line of thought productive? If it is, what are the likely costs in terms of the conditions that might be imposed?'

The conditionality of the tentative proposal protects the proposer. Presumably, the condition imposed as the entry price of benefiting from the offer is expected to be stiffer than the exit position of the proposer. By implication – it is, after all, a negotiation – your conditions are negotiable. And even if you price your offer too low in terms of your conditions, the vague nature of your offer leaves you some room for manoeuvre.

Perhaps a more important question than 'who proposes first?' is that of 'where should you open?' A fear of being caught short with an under-priced offer is counter-balanced by a fear of going too far over the top and alienating the other negotiator (as discussed in Chapter 2). Advice to open 'realistically' leaves open the question of, 'what is realistic?' The best **guide** to being realistic is to consider the credibility of your case for a particular entry position. Is there a credible reason (i.e. credible to the other negotiator and not necessarily to an appeal court of experienced judges) for adopting that opening proposal? Again, the vague content of your proposal helps you. The first and early proposals are likely to be vague in both the condition and offer. It is not difficult to be credible with a degree of vagueness covering the detailed content of what is on offer. For example, to require them to think about the distribution coverage (your condition) in return for your considering the proportion of in-house transport facilities (the offer) is hardly open to a charge of non-credibility, whereas a proposal requiring them to cut their drivers' hours by 20 per cent from midnight tonight (your condition) in return for your *considering* the proportion of in-house transport facilities over the next six months might well be. It all comes down to balance and circumstance, and this is helped by the vague content of your conditionality.

Negotiators can only make sensible proposals when all the issues are on the table. It makes little sense to make conditional proposals when you do not know enough about the other negotiator's attitude towards, or his perceptions of, the issues to judge the price you could get (i.e. your conditions) for whatever it is you perceive they want (i.e. your offer). Proposals should emerge from debate (via signals) and, by their nature – vagueness – cannot be settled without moving on to the bargaining phase.

> **Learning point:**
>
> *Vague proposals protect the negotiator from making mistakes in the value of the exchange. Mistakes in value can be hard to fix once the other party has accepted them.*

How can we make an effective proposal? One thing that is always going for proposals is the fact, from observation, that people give them their attention, or try to until they are put off by the surrounding verbiage. To announce to a meeting that you have a proposal usually creates an expectation and a higher degree of attention than you will get from announcing that you disagree with what somebody has just said and then proceed to tell them what it is you disagree with. How long the attention lasts and whether the expectation is fulfilled is partly down to the way you present your proposal. The most common mistake negotiators make when presenting a proposal is to drown it in irrelevant verbiage by confusing the proposal and debate phases. In short they propose and explain their reasons for the proposal at the same time.

Proposals, like humour, gain from brevity. If the signal is more of a hint than a banner-sized headline, the proposal is more of a tactful message than a sledgehammer. Language, I say again, is all. The tone is significant. It has a purpose. You are trying to entice them into an area where you can do business with them on the basis that you get some of what you want and they (might) get some of what they want. The tentative, even tempting, nature of the proposal is summarised in its vague content:

> 'I could consider . . .'
> 'We could perhaps look at that'.
> 'It might be possible to do something'.
> 'We might be able to adjust our terms in some way'.
> 'Perhaps we could go over that area again'.

The important message is carried in the vague but, nevertheless, conditional offer, and to drown it in verbiage not only detracts from the hinted deal but also can have the effect of, perhaps wrongly, implying to the other negotiator that you are less than comfortable with your own position. Let us look at some scenarios to illustrate this point.

---

1. 'How much do you want for the vehicle?'

Well, my Uncle George who knows about cars – he worked with the AA, or was it the RAC? – well, he thinks this car is a real goer. It can do at least 90 miles to the gallon – I have no idea what that is in litres – the European Union and its regulations, would you believe it? – well, taking all that into consideration, I would think it's worth at least £5,000, perhaps more, considering the work I've had done. Look at that inside trim, real leather. Had it done only a month ago. Perfect match. And the top-of-the-range sat-nav system. Had it put in by Balfords – what they don't know about sat-nav you can forget about. I'm telling you there's no better supplier in Europe. In fact, it even has maps of Europe, really useful on my last holiday to France. So what do you think?

I'd only offer £3,500, purely on the strength of his prevarication.

---

2. 'Omega's position is quite clear. We do not accept liability for third-party damages'.

Ah, yes, but we are not asking you to accept total liability. What we are proposing is that you accept about 50 per cent of the damages, should they arise. After all, it was your computer that went down – don't they all? – and we were left with the mess. Even the catering staff went off, which is something I thought they left to their dishes (ha, ha), and we had a terrible job getting the unloaders back to work – they had their meeting in the bar, and I blame that shop steward of theirs . . . Cassidy, I think – anyway, he's Irish, though he pretends to be from Liverpool, goodness only knows why – he insisted on a free round

> of drinks while we tried to calm the nerves of the outraged baggage handlers, more like a mob I would say – whipped up by that fellow Cassidy (we're checking to see if we can sack him on some technicality) – and it took ages for us to get the bar under control again – not that there was any threat to public safety, of course . . .

I'd press for absolute recognition that we were not in any way liable.

> **3. 'We need a much higher licence fee'.**
>
> Well, I suppose we could entertain some movement on the licence fee, but only to get this venture going. I'm not at all happy that we have to pay you $200,000 in advance for a project with a forecast income of $220,000 a year, assuming everything goes all right. And what happens if we don't make the target? Who bails us out? That's what my shareholders will want to know, especially Zenith Insurance, with their 14 per cent lurking in the background, and ever ready to put in their own people as soon as I falter. I don't know whether it's worth it at all.

I'd want to avoid doing any business with these people, except at the full $200,000 in advance.

These examples of the shambolic style of proposing are all too familiar across the negotiating table. The proposers waffle on, drowning their proposals in verbiage and disheartening the listeners, or worse, inspiring them to increase their demands on someone clearly unconvinced of the merits of his case. If only it were a rare occurrence. Unfortunately, it is all too common.

To make an effective proposal, three main 'rules' should be practised:

1. It should be conditional
2. It should be presented unadorned, without explanation
3. On completing the proposal, you should go silent (or, to be frank: shut up!)

A subsidiary rule is that it should be presented with the condition first, followed by the offer.

> **Exercise 5C**
>
> *Consider what is wrong with the following proposals, noting your thoughts before reading on.*

1. 'I'll accept your proposal for landing and pick-up rights for ten flights a week into Singapore if you support our claim for landing rights in Germany'.

2. 'If we provide you with more bed nights a week, will you accept two persons to a room?'
3. 'If we accept an 8 per cent differential on the shift allowance, will you look at the manning levels?'
4. 'How about if we made it £2 million? Would that meet your client's needs?'
5. 'OK. I'll make an offer. If you accept changes in your vendor's contract, I'll agree to you becoming our sole supplier on our three sites'.
6. 'If you agree to clauses 6 and 7 as they stand, then I will reconsider our policy on third-party maintenance'.

The errors made in the proposals in Exercise 5C are discussed in detail below:

1. Two errors: first, the offer is presented before the condition, which always weakens the impact on the listener (and, on the phone, could jeopardise the deal if the phone is cut off before you get to your conditions), and second, the offer is specific (ten flights a week) while the condition is vague, which is the wrong way round: conditions are specific or vague, but offers are always vague. What is meant by 'support' a claim for landing rights – a letter to the Airport Authority? a delegation to the respective governments? a £2 million donation for legal costs? or what?
2. Two errors: first, this is a question-proposal (it asks the other negotiator to judge the merits of the proposal), which does not put any pressure on the other negotiator to accept. Indeed, it could encourage him to be more demanding ('No way. We require single rooms'.). Second, the offer is placed before the condition.
3. Three errors: first, it is a question-proposal, which is always weaker than a statement-proposal; second, it puts the offer before the condition; third, it is specific in the offer but vague in the condition.
4. Four errors: first, it is a question-proposal; second, it is a specific offer; third, it is unconditional; fourth, it only requires the other negotiator to declare whether or not the offer meets his client's needs, which places a lot of faith in his ability to resist temptation and say, 'No, it doesn't', and then wait and see if the answer provokes a further concession from you. (What has the other negotiator got to lose?)
5. Single error: the offer is specific while the condition is vague. (What changes in their contract would justify making them the sole supplier?)
6. No errors, assuming that the proposed trade-off is considered to be acceptable.

Exercise 5D

Recast each of the proposals in Exercise 5C into effective proposal language. Then check your answers against my suggestions in the answers to Checkpoint 5 at the back of the book.

How to receive a proposal

Let's return to the example from the start of the chapter about Amanda and Tony.

> *AL: 'Our view is that we need some combination of a penalty clause and an . . .'.*
> *TM: 'Penalty clause? We're not interested in penalty clauses. There are enough penalties in this unprofitable contract as it is. No. You will have to find some other solution than that. What we want are incentives'.*

Interrupting a negotiator is always risky. It can lead to an increase in tension and ultimately towards deadlock. Interrupting a proposal is doubly risky. To the risk of deadlock there is added the risk of missing out on an opportunity to hear what the other negotiator is proposing in total and not just on the topic that we feel strongest about.

By interrupting the first part of Amanda's proposal – at the mention of penalty clauses – Tony misses finding out what proposals Amanda has (and even if she has them) on incentives. Indeed, there is a risk that Amanda's irritation at Tony's interruption on the issue that is important to her incites enough emotional reaction for Amanda to stiffen her resolve on the incentive side by making it a tougher scheme than she might otherwise have done. Not having heard what Amanda would have said if she hadn't been interrupted, Tony has no way of knowing whether the incentive scheme he eventually hears is better or worse than the one he might have heard.

Some negotiators argue that interruption can also intimidate the other negotiator into making deeper concessions. This often appears to be a plausible reason for interrupting, but it relies on the other negotiator succumbing to intimidation, which is a wholly unreliable assumption. And anyway, those intimidated today may not be tomorrow, and it is a short-sighted business plan that sets out to intimidate one's business partners. I can only offer my own observation that negotiators tend by a large margin to react negatively to the bruising, bustling and intimidatory approach. In my experience, it does not often pay off, and on the few occasions where it does, it achieves success over the other negotiator at the expense of their spending much resentful time working out how to get revenge. It is down that road that many an embattled relationship has led to a company's ruin, either with its own workforce or with its customers.

The nature of proposals as tentative suggestions, usually combining a condition, specific or vague, and an offer, always vague, suggests the appropriate way to respond. Listen to a proposal in full, including any extended elaboration of it (however unwise it is for you to elaborate on your proposals, you cannot expect to hear everything in the tidier order advocated here). Do not interrupt, and wait for the proposer to conclude. Even a tactical touch of silence at the conclusion can help you (yes: be silent for a few seconds) because experience shows that people making proposals sometimes add in extras, perhaps by way of clarification, when their proposal is met by a *little* silence. Silence also gives you an opportunity to think about, or appear to be thinking about, what you have heard.

> **Exercise 5E**
>
> *Consider and note your response, as a negotiator, to each of the following proposals before reading on:*
>
> 1. *'If you can improve your response times, we could look at training our staff in routine maintenance'.*
> 2. *'If you improve your offer of £7,060 for my trade-in, I might consider placing the loan with you'.*
> 3. *'Can we settle this purchase this afternoon? If we can, I could discuss with you bundling in some training for your operators'.*

Possible responses would be as follows:

1.
   a) 'By how much would we have to improve our response times?' or:
   b) 'How many staff would you make available for routine maintenance?'
2.
   a) 'By how much must I improve on the trade-in price for the car?' or:
   b) 'On what terms would you take the loan from me?'
3.
   a) 'What sort of training did you have in mind?' or:
   b) 'When you say, "bundling in", do you mean at no charge?' or:
   c) 'Does that mean we can also settle the training this afternoon?'

What is the common feature of these responses? They are all questions. They seek to clarify what the proposer means; they try to tempt him into being more specific, to give content to his vague offers; and they ensure that the listener understands what is being proposed.

You should not give an immediate negative response to a proposal, no matter how little the proposal interests you. It is much better that you fully understand what is on offer or in the minds of the proposers (their thinking betrays clues as to their priorities) than it is to leap right back into an argument. Questions are in the constructive part of the debate phase and not only provide you with, perhaps, vital information, but also demonstrate to the proposer that you are taking their constructive suggestions seriously, at least to the point of considering them on their merits. If they have no merits, your questions will soon confirm that.

Consider what some potential answers to your questions tell you and what you can do next:

1. a) 'By how much would we have to improve our response times?'

'We would be looking for a three-hour call-out'.

You now know their entry point on response times. Barring unusual circumstances, it is unlikely to get worse for you. Depending on your own circumstances (perhaps three hours is too short, or perhaps you can better it), you can be non-committal in your response: 'I see. Well, we would have to look at that in the context of the other details we must discuss with you'; or, you could link this issue to another one: 'To get anywhere near three hours, we would need to look closely at the incentive package to justify the high costs this would impose'.

1. b) 'How many staff would you make available for routine maintenance?'

'Probably one from each shift'.

Again you have learned his entry point, and again your business knowledge determines your response. If one person a shift is feasible for you (i.e. it is inside your settlement range), you can note this, but be non-committal (for why, see below), or you can link it to another issue: 'One per shift is not enough to stop expensive call-outs for trivial repairs. However, if you are prepared to pay for three persons per shift to be trained, we might be able to find a way of really denting the call-out charges'. (They might respond with a proposal to share the training costs, cut the number to two people or ask a question about your vague offer on 'really denting the call-out charges'.)

2. a) 'By how much must I improve on the trade-in price for the car?'

'I need at least £7,600'.

This is his entry price on the trade-in. If this is more than your exit price, you will want to see him come down to the settlement range (perhaps by trading something somewhere else); if it is less than your exit price, you know you have a potential settlement on the trade-in and you can move on to other issues. You can link a possibility of improving your entry offer on the trade-in with a condition that he places the whole loan with you at 4.25 points over base. In response, he might try to pull down that interest rate to at least 3 points over base.

2. b) 'On what terms would you take the loan from me?'

'2.75 points over base'.

This is below your exit point but, as it is his entry price, you know there should be a better (for you) exit price from him. You can respond to suit your judgement, either with a non-committal acknowledgement of his proposal or with a linked response of your own to another issue.

3. a) 'What sort of training did you have in mind?'

'Basic and introductory'.

If this meets your needs, you might consider pressing, now or later, for more advanced training to be bundled in, as generally an opening offer is his entry, not his exit, position. Clearly, if he can get a settlement that afternoon for his entry price on training, he is going to be quite happy, and if you were not expecting to get anything on training and you were able to settle that afternoon, then you too would be happy. Your question has elicited the useful information that a deal is possible.

3. b) 'When you say, "bundling in", do you mean at no charge?'

'Yes'; or

'No charge for the training, but you will have to pay for your own people's travel and accommodation'.

If the answer is 'yes', you have clarified his intentions. The second sort of response warns you of the below-the-line costs (travel and accommodation) associated with otherwise free training. You need this sort of information before responding with your own conditional proposal (he trains your people on site at his expense?).

3. c) 'Does that mean we can also settle the training this afternoon?'

'Yes'; or

'I think that might take a little longer, as we do not know who is available for this sort of training or when it can take place'.

Again, the 'yes' clarifies his intentions. The second response might send some red-light warning signals that require your attention in your own conditional proposals. Perhaps you could respond with: 'I would need to have details of your commitments to the training by this afternoon if I am to consider making a commitment to go ahead'.

Questioning to clarify, or to invite an extension of a proposal, is the most effective response you can make. All other reactions break up the momentum towards a settlement and can set back the debate phase – even into deadlock – for little gain. Proposals appear at every moment in a negotiation – some are purely administrative ('Let's have a break'), others are more contentious ('Let's deal with that later') – but as we can only negotiate proposals, it is essential to encourage negotiators to make them and for you to respond to them in a constructive way. Much of what you do in response to a proposal will signal to the other side how they should behave. If you say 'NO!', 'No way!', 'Do you think I am mad enough to accept that?' and such like, you cannot expect them to be less than decisive in their rejection, or interruption, of your carefully thought-out proposal.

Instant rejection is a less successful strategy than its prevalence in negotiating would suggest. He may only be testing the water by presenting a rather extreme (to you) solution, and you should be more relaxed about him exercising his right to do so. Some people do not like change, and proposals that require change are often rejected out of hand without explanation (usually from the fact that the listener has not thought about that sort of solution but does not want to admit to it), or he rejects it off the top of his head with a rapid-fire set of ten reasons why what is suggested would never work, won't work and can't be accepted, even if it did work. A proposal rejected out of hand usually changes the negotiation to argument. People do not like their suggestions dismissed instantly, and certainly not when it is done curtly, or worse. They like to think that their suggestions at least merit consideration, if only as a sign of respect for them as joint decision-makers in this negotiation.

What is the most effective way of responding to a proposal? First, clarify what is meant by the proposal by questioning its condition or its offer. If there is only a condition – a not uncommon experience in negotiating – you can ask the obvious question: 'If I were to consider what you have requested, how would I benefit from that/what would I get in return?'

Second, consider what the proposer is telling you about the scope for a deal on the issues he has raised. If there are other issues under discussion, be noncommittal (by verbal devices illustrated above) and seek proposals on these issues. Asking: 'What about these other issues?' is one effective way of shifting attention to the other issues. If the other negotiator wants a decision on the issue he has raised and not on the others until that is settled, you need not have a fight about this. The principle that 'nothing is finally agreed until everything is finally agreed' is one that you would always want to establish and maintain throughout any negotiation. You do this by reminding the other negotiator at appropriate moments – and this is a typical one – that while you are prepared to examine proposals on a single issue in isolation, and you are also prepared to indicate what you can agree to, no final agreement can be reached until you have examined everything under discussion. Hence, if he insists on settling a single issue, or a minority of the issues, you are negotiating before moving on, you simply state that your agreement – if one can be reached – is provisional, and its implementation is subject to final agreement on the other issues.

Tell the other negotiator what aspects of his proposal you like and don't like. You might want to make statements about them (you are in debate when you do this, so apply all the sensible points that are effective in debate: statements, assurances, questions, summaries and signals). It might be that the act of doing this alone encourages the other negotiator to respond with useful amendments to his proposal. That certainly moves things forward. He might also respond with comments on your comments (debate). You can handle these effectively using constructive debate.

Finally, you are ready to respond with your own alternative proposal. If you are in the proposal phase, you are in negotiation proper – you cannot negotiate a debate – and handling this phase as a prelude to the bargaining phase requires an ability to manage movement on several issues at the same time.

Summarising Issues

We trade because we value things differently, and the things we trade are **Issues** (see Chapter 3). In pre-negotiation, the preparation phase, we made estimates of the valuation that the other negotiator might have placed on the Issues by categorising them as of high, medium or low importance. In the debate phase, we discovered a lot about the other negotiator's thinking on all the Issues each of us has raised. From his proposals, and his comments on ours, we have gained an insight into his potential solutions and their match with ours. We work on the principle that what he values, he trades dearly for – and whatever he asks for, he values – and from this interaction we accept that some of the assumptions or valuations we made in preparation will need to be amended or modified. True, we might also have been misled by our interpretations of his remarks, and he might also be deliberately misleading us in respect of his wants. There is no way we can see into his head – nor he into ours – so we have to work on what we know (or think we know).

Most business negotiations cover a number of issues rather than merely one. Given that most negotiations are a rather untidy interaction – no pre-written scripts that each side could or would adhere to – the emergence of tentative proposals on each negotiable Issue is not synchronised either chronologically or even logically. They will emerge throughout the debate phase.

Some negotiations are slightly less anarchistic in that the negotiators are working on a single text, such as a contract or a list of items (for example, the typical trade union's 'shopping list') placed on the agenda by one or both sides. The negotiators might work their way through each item in order. This has the attraction of being orderly; it also has the risk of weakening the negotiator's ability to trade across the Issues. He is often reduced to negotiating within each Issue's settlement range, distinct and separate from other Issues (repeated forms of distributive bargaining, if you like). If their exit points overlap, they have the possibility of making an agreement, though not an ideal one if the Issue is less important to one negotiator than it is to another, and they are prompted to give way where, in other circumstances, they could trade movement for reciprocal advantage on something that they value more highly. You should be wary of pursuing tidiness in negotiating at the cost of narrowing your options. This orderly mind 'for its own sake' approach is often practised by solicitors and can lead to poorer deals, particularly where one side is pressed for time and the other is not (and meanwhile, no matter how long it takes, it costs both clients their solicitors' professional fees).

If, therefore, we choose to work in the more chaotic or disorderly atmosphere of the normal negotiation, we need a method of simultaneously handling several Issues together in the proposal and the bargaining phases. The device is interesting because, like signalling, it acts as a bridge from one phase to the other, in this case, from proposing to bargaining. Negotiators summarise each other's current proposals for the negotiable Issues and compare each other's conditional offers. Looking down, or listening to, the summarised list, you can see what is on offer (in regular negotiations over the same Issues, many negotiators can keep the details in their heads without recourse to a written list, though never be too proud to make notes – *as long as you watch where you leave or keep them*). The list is an indicator of how big the gaps are on the Issues, or whether there are overlaps with your exit point for any of the currently mentioned Issues (there may be other potential Issues you have not yet raised and for which, obviously, you have no information on exit or entry points).

It is amazingly simple to summarise as a means of keeping track of what is going on, yet negotiators constantly make life much more difficult for themselves by ignoring the simple things (and then make a bigger mess of the complex things). In debate, we summarise what people have said to each other; in proposing, we summarise what each has proposed. The summary introduces an element of order into our interactive chaos. It also sets up the bargaining phase. It creates the possibility of either negotiator moving from tentative conditional proposals (i.e. conditional vague offers) to the bargain (i.e. conditional specific offers).

Consider Maria and Bruce and their negotiation over the upgraded GRAPE 3000 IT system. Maria's summary might follow this pattern:

> I do not know whether I can accept that offer, or whether your problem with carrying too much stock is something I can do anything about. However, let me summarise what we have covered so far. You are prepared to reduce the price of the GRAPE 3000 and improve the trade-in allowance for my GRAPE 2010 . . .
>
> *'Only if we can agree on the loan you require and the borrowing rate'.*
>
> I was just coming to that. You have also offered to train one of my people in the upgraded systems and permit my staff to hot-line you for advice for a nominal charge. I have to accept your standard maintenance charge of 8 per cent of the current purchase value for three years, but you will provide me with some free software for my accounts processing and allow six months' warranty. The best you can do on delivery is within 30 days of placing the order.

Bruce has the opportunity to correct errors in Maria's summary and to elaborate on any item, perhaps hinting at further movement. Both negotiators will wait to see if the other moves. They could swing right back into debate (with its attendant risks), particularly if the gaps are too wide. This depends a great deal on whether they feel that the other has taken account of their inhibitions, as revealed in earlier debates, and which they signalled for attention. The negotiation is at a critical stage. Either it goes back to the debate phase (and, hopefully, to new signals and new proposals), or it goes forward to the bargaining phase. Timing the latter is important. An attempt to enter the bargaining phase too early is an attempt (almost pre-emptive) to close the deal. If the current proposals in no way address important matters of concern to the other negotiator, he is not going to respond positively to a closing bargain.

The summary of the current proposals either invites new proposals or a bargain. If central inhibitions have not yet been addressed, then new proposals are required. You are as well to summarise after each proposal and to include the previous proposals in each summary to manage the untidiness (and your proneness to error).

Conclusion

Negotiators thrive on handling proposals. Because we cannot negotiate debates or arguments, we are not making progress in the negotiations until we get to proposals. They are best encouraged rather than discouraged. An indicated willingness to listen to a proposal, even one that you disagree with, is positive negotiating behaviour. Like a poor argument, a poor proposal wilts sooner under open questioning than it does when under fire.

The most effective proposals consist of both a condition and an offer, and your response to them should always be to clarify and understand what the proposal means. In reality this will be less tidy than the model suggests. Some proposals will consist of an offer only – demand that you do something for nothing – and some will consist of a condition only – a unilateral concession. In the first case, you must question the condition (presumably the condition is onerous, or, if not, as it is an early proposal, is there some more leeway in it?) and question the missing offer: 'What do I get if I consider (NB: *not* agree to!) your proposal?' In the second case, you are faced with a unilateral offer and you may choose to accept it without fuss – free gifts do not have to be negotiated – or to note it as the boundary beyond which he might move at a later stage.

In the proposal phase, which emerges from various points in the debate phase, there will be a lot of untidy ends sticking up all over the place, reflecting the tentative nature of the proposals. Each one might represent a tentative proposal from each of you. Regular summarising of the proposals, whether they have been agreed to or not (you can present your alternatives within your summary), keeps the focus on what each thinks is a solution of the negotiation. Either this provokes new tentative proposals, or it sets you up for the final bargain, the explicit conditional offer that invites the closing agreement.

Checkpoint 5

Answer the following self-assessment questions on a separate sheet of paper before checking the solutions given in Checkpoint Answers at the end of the book.

5.1 Your terms and conditions include a protection against consequential loss, and the other negotiator has signalled his unwillingness to accept this. Do you:

   a) Ask him to explain his objections to consequential loss?

   b) Defend the necessity of your business having a consequential loss provision?

   c) Ask for a proposal on how he intends to cover your need for protection against a failure of performance?

   d) Tell him that a failure to sign a consequential loss provision means that no business can be concluded with him?

5.2 Any proposal is better than no proposal. True or false?

5.3 An unconditional proposal is better than no proposal. True or false?

5.4 A conditional proposal is better than an unconditional proposal. True or false?

5.5 An unconditional assertive proposal is better than a conditional unassertive proposal. True or false?

5.6 Which of the following is correct? Proposals should be:

   a) Short

   b) Unexplained

   c) Conditional

   d) Relevant

5.7 Which of the following is correct? A negotiator wishing to change the status quo should:

   a) Avoid proposing a change and wait for the other negotiator to propose a change.

   b) Propose a change and not wait for the other negotiator to propose.

   c) Avoid proposing a change until the other negotiator asks for a proposal.

   d) Propose a change only if the other negotiator signals a willingness to change.

5.8 The other negotiator makes a proposal with which you are in total disagreement. Do you:

   a) Say 'No'?

   b) Stop negotiating?

   c) Ask for an explanation?

   d) Counter-propose?

5.9 Which of the following is correct? When dealing with a number of issues in a negotiation, it is better to:

   a) Insist on them being linked together.

   b) Judge them as separate issues on their own merits.

   c) Decide upon nothing in finality until agreement is reached on all of them.

   d) Be tidy in your approach to difficult issues.

6 Integrative bargaining, part 4
How to bargain

Introduction

What do the following have in common?

- You are in a supermarket. You take a bottle of cooking oil to the check-out. The cashier scans the bar code and the price rings up on the till.
- You open your e-mails and one of them is a price quotation from a plumber for clearing and reconstructing the drains to your house.
- You are in your office. An IT salesperson has just handed you for signature a printed copy of his company's contract for supplying, installing and maintaining your company IT systems hardware and software for the next three years.
- You are in negotiation. The union official says: 'If you make it 3 per cent, I will call off the strike right now'.
- You are a diplomat. The intermediary says: I am authorised to say that if your government goes on record in condemnation of these hostile and unjustified attacks on human rights, then my government will arrange for the release of your two citizens, held in protective custody by our compatriots in the capital, by Monday of next week.
- You are a parent. Your son says to you: 'If you take me to the match this afternoon, I will clean your car'.

Answer: they are all bargains.

Now, to say they are bargains is not a comment on the merits of what is offered, though that is one common meaning of the word bargain – some kind of exceptional benefit, suggesting good value for the price. By bargain, negotiators mean something different. We mean that the statement contains *an explicit and conditional offer*.

The bargain offered by the supermarket takes the form of an explicit conditional offer: if you pay to the check-out person the price of the bottle of cooking oil, then you can take the bottle of cooking oil out of the store. Otherwise, it stays here. If you say 'Yes' to the bargain, the contract between you and the supermarket is concluded; if you say 'No', it is either because you disagree with the price (the condition), or you disagree with what you get for it (the offer).

The plumber's quotation takes the form of a bargain: if you meet his price and terms (percentage cash deposit with acceptance of the quotation and payment of the balance on completion of the work), then he will undertake the work detailed in the quotation, including the removal from the site of all rubbish, and the making good of the trenches he digs across your lawn. If you say 'Yes', the contract is made, you pay him the deposit and he starts the work (you hope!); if you say 'No', because you disagree with the price or the terms (the condition), you do without the work (the offer) or find another plumber.

The IT vendor's contract takes the form of a bargain: if you say 'Yes' and sign it, you and the IT firm are bound by its contents – the conditions, which you meet, and the offer, which they meet (though as it is their written contract, it is more likely to bind you more tightly than it is them – the proverbial small print); if you say 'No', you do without the computers and software, or find another IT company.

The union official is offering you a bargain: meet my terms of 3 per cent (the condition) and I will call off the strike (the offer); otherwise, by implication, the strike will continue. Whether you accept his bargain or not will depend on your assessment of the credibility of his implied threat (his ability to continue or stop the strike) and your assessment of the efficacy of meeting the 3 per cent claim.

The intermediary is offering you a bargain: accept his conditions (agreeing to lie about the human rights record of his government), and he will carry out his offer and the kidnappers of your citizens will release their hostages. This example shows that there is no implication in negotiation that a bargain is necessarily good value or not. It is a verbal device that offers a deal. Whether the deal is worth taking or not, and whether it is morally appropriate, is another matter.

Your son is illustrating the keen sense of bargaining that appears early on in children (and then, for various reasons, tends to be curtailed by the time they become adults). Meet his condition, attendance at the match, and he will clean your car (the offer). Has he pitched it high enough? Does attendance at a match with your son have less disutility for you than your staying home and washing your own car? Or were you planning to take him to the match anyway, and his bargain gives you something back, virtually for nothing?

These are examples of bargaining, and this chapter is about the role of bargaining, the form and content of bargaining language and how to make the most effective use of the bargaining phase.

From proposals to bargains

A proposal is not a bargain. A proposal is a tentative solution. A bargain is a specific conclusion. The distinction is more than pedantic. In negotiation, language is everything, and the language of proposing is critically different in one crucial respect from that of bargaining. In a proposal, the conditional offer is non-specific; in the bargain, the conditional offer is *always* specific. This is summarised in Figure 6.1.

A bargain is always a specific condition attached to a specific offer. There is no room for ambiguity. There is nothing tentative about a bargain. It states precisely

	Proposal	Bargain
Condition	Non-specific or specific	Always specific
Offer	Always non-specific	Always specific

Figure 6.1 Distinction between a proposal and a bargain.

what you get for what you give. The specific condition is the price tag of the specific offer. If you say 'Yes', you have a deal; if you say 'No', you don't; if you say 'Maybe', you are close but not quite there yet. You choose to stay in the bargaining phase and move to a close, or return to the debate phase, because the offered bargain does not suit you. Staying in the bargaining phase by offering an alternative or amended bargain might lead quickly to agreement; returning to the debate phase might put you further back – though it may be important for you to take that risk if the circumstances dictate it.

The two essential ingredients of effective bargaining are: all bargains are explicitly conditional, and all offers are explicit. In terms of preferred language, the format that is recommended is to use the keywords 'if' and 'then':

> *If* you do such and such, *then* I will do so and so.

When you hear any explicit formulation similar to 'if – then', you know that they have entered the bargaining phase; if you use the explicit format of 'if – then', you have entered the bargaining phase. Where the negotiations go from here is determined by circumstance.

> **Learning point:**
>
> *When bargaining, always use the conditional assertive language, 'If you . . ., then I . . . .'*
> *It is a clear and explicit statement of what you want in return for movement on something they want.*

In the supermarket, the bargain is made explicit by price scanning the products with a hand-scanner or the one at the check-out. You decide whether to buy or not at the instant that you see the product's price. If you agree with the bargain, you pay the price and take the product from the check-out; if you don't agree, you leave it in the store. You could ask here: 'What else am I supposed to do? Take it to the check-out and haggle?' You would be most unusual if you took several items to the check-out and tried to bargain with the assistants. They neither are trained nor have the authority to haggle with you ('If you take 10 per cent off, I will take two bottles of cooking oil instead of one'). The reason is almost obvious. Supermarkets have a pretty good idea of how many of any item in their product lists they can sell at their set prices in a shopping day. If they get it wildly wrong over the medium term, they go out of business, while almost minute by minute they can see at a glance along their shelves if their products are selling at their stated prices or not, and Electronic Point of Sale (EPOS) systems, loyalty programs and intelligent marketing enable them to make these judgements, or to have them made by computer algorithms, at the push of a button in the manager's office. Your offer to bargain would cut across their preferred way of conducting their business. If you do not want to accept their 'take-it-or-leave-it' bargain – the price tag on the product list – that is fine by them. Just leave the product on the shelf and leave the store. Out of the next wave of customers coming through the store, some – enough – will buy at the listed prices. Your offers to purchase in a busy day are not significant enough for them to go to the trouble and the expense of setting up arrangements to haggle with you. Your attempt to bargain would be of no interest to them.

The fact of annual – or more regular – 'sales' does not challenge this assertion. These are corrective devices under controlled conditions to maintain volume sales throughout the year. The annual – or quarterly – sale is at the stores' discretion. Some stores are in a permanent state of 'sales' (a friend of mine who has been engaged to her partner for over ten years was asked, 'When are you two finally going to get married?', to which she replied, 'When the DFS sale ends!'); for a minority of others, it is an unusual event. Even at the sale, the sale price is still on a tag with the same implied 'take-it-or-leave-it' conditions. Only in so-called fire sales, and closing-down sales, is the customer invited to make offers to bargain.

The supermarket, and most businesses in retail, know their margins and their markets sufficiently well to set take-it-or-leave-it bargains. Their decisions on price are confirmed every minute of every shopping day. Only when we move out to the high-value sale, or the industrial sale, does the element of uncertainty creep in and provide the basis for a negotiation. The price of a building that has been on the market only twice in 50 years is not as certain as the daily tested price of a bottle of cooking oil in a supermarket chain. The building's advertised price is a best estimate that may or may not be justified when real buyers meet real sellers in the market. The offered bargain may not be put together by the negotiator until several rounds of debate; the demanded bargain in the selling particulars forms the basis of a negotiation rather than an ultimatum (unless the buyers, for their own reasons, decide to 'give in' and take the offered bargain without further ado).

Moving from these fixed-price bargains to the previously undefined bargain of the normal negotiation, we can see the similarities and dissimilarities of the effective bargain arising out of the proposal phase. First, the language is analogous: if you agree to this explicit and specific condition, then I will agree to this explicit and specific offer. Second, so is the choice: a 'Yes' means agreement; a

'No' means continue the debate or deadlock. The difference is that neither negotiator is able, or likely, to fall back on a 'take-it-or-leave-it' stance. They are in negotiation, not on a shopping trip. Both have options (other plumbers, other computer suppliers, other customers), the existence of which gives them an incentive to negotiate a deal; and where they don't have options, they have an even more pressing incentive to negotiate a deal. For example, we do not normally change our children to suit our domestic arrangements, nor do we normally swap employees because they are on strike (though we might if the dispute is long and bitter enough).

Even when there doesn't seem to be an opening for negotiation, the bargain is negotiable. Services that we buy, like insurance, broadband and digital TV, all come with a 'take-it-or-leave-it' price tag, which usually goes up annually and automatically renews. If you don't want to pay, you cancel the contract. If you have ever tried to cancel the contract, you will know that this is not a 'one price' system. You are put through to the customer retentions department, where you can often get a much better deal, but only once you explain that you are definitely not remaining a customer. At this point, you will find a plethora of new payment and service options, all of which will leave you better off.

A negotiator cannot sensibly say 'Yes' to a tentative proposal and leave it at that because there is still some work to do in unravelling what is meant by, or implied by, or hinted at, in the non-specific attribute of the offer (and perhaps the condition) before an agreement can be made. The effective bargain stretches the proposal to a conclusion. It strips the proposal of its tentativeness. It makes it specific. It is a proposal that the other negotiator can say 'Yes' to and, by doing so, end the negotiation in agreement.

Consider the following scenario:

> *Mr Quinn, his wife Mary, and their two guests entered the Italian restaurant on time at 8 p.m. The owner welcomed them and apologised for the fact that their table was not yet ready, as the previous diners were running late, having just got through the main course. He estimated that it would take about 15 to 20 minutes for them to have their table ready. Mr Quinn, a project engineer, knew that an estimate of '15 to 20 minutes' always meant 20 minutes-plus, and that the 15 minutes mentioned was to make the delay sound shorter (did not his suppliers always promise 6 to 8 weeks when they meant 8 or 10?). He was less than pleased with this eventuality – it was his wife's birthday and he had been away for a month in the Gobi desert troubleshooting the building of a desalination plant that was three months behind schedule.*
>
> *Mr Quinn remonstrated with the owner and manager about the incompetence that had caused his party to be held up – 'What is the point of reserving a table if it is not reserved when you get here?' – and within a short while, he and the owner were having a public row. Unable to get what he wanted – access to his table immediately – he led his party out of the restaurant, vowing never to return.*

That Mr Quinn had a complaint, even a grievance, is beyond doubt. Whether he handled the situation effectively is open to question. By now you are well aware that arguing does not get you what you want – you cannot negotiate an argument – which is all that Mr Quinn had to offer. If, instead of offering an argument, he had offered a practical remedy for his and the owner's problem – demanding that they throw out the slow diners is neither practical nor a remedy – both he and the owner might have been able to find a way to remain on business-like terms.

I do not know why the owner did not propose a discount off the meal that Mr Quinn and his party would consume in due course: 'If you will have a little patience and wait for a while, I will knock something off the bill for the evening'. This would have been a practical remedy, and if it was what Mr Quinn would have settled for, he could only *hope* that the restaurant manager would have made the offer if he did not take the initiative and make the proposal himself. Even at this stage, such a proposal would still be just a tentative solution: how much would be taken off the bill? for how long must I wait? If Mr Quinn wanted to make sure that a discount was considered, and that it was for a specific amount, he could have proposed it himself: 'I am disappointed that we have to wait. However, if you were to agree to a 25 per cent discount for the meal this evening, I am prepared to wait'. This is a bargain. The owner may or may not respond positively – he might just do so for peace – but the focus of the debate between him and Mr Quinn would have shifted from placing blame, towards what should be done about the situation.

A bargain then is a specific remedy. It should be proposed as the final solution to whatever the negotiators perceive to be the issue. Where time or circumstances do not permit an informative debate and the exchange of tentative proposals that identify what might be the Issue, going straight to a bargain can be a stab in the dark. If the bargain is much too unrealistic for other negotiators to consider seriously, damage might be done that time and circumstance prohibit putting right. In this situation, a more modest self-denying bargain is more likely to be proposed. Instead of the ambitious target of a 25 per cent discount off the meal, Mr Quinn might have plumped for the lesser remedy of a free bottle of Prosecco, or perhaps a single round of drinks for himself and his guests at the restaurant bar while they waited to take their seats.

> **Learning point:**
>
> *Don't just complain, propose a remedy.*

Negotiation permits each to weigh up and assess what could be the content of the likely bargain that could finalise the deal. Hence, bargains tend to be offered near the close of a negotiation, unless the negotiation is about a formal offered bargain – a contract, for example – presented at the start of the meeting. This does not alter the role of the bargaining phase, which is to finalise the potential agreement on the basis of what has been said in debate and what proposals have been put forward. Many bargains may be offered by either negotiator, including the formal written one that started the meeting, but this does not mean that any of them are acceptable. The offering of a bargain is not the end of the matter – the offered bargains themselves are subject to the same process of consideration (i.e. debate, propose and bargain) – but the difference with other phases in negotiation lies in the fact that when we are negotiating bargains, we are generally closer to a conclusion than when we are making opening statements in the initial debate phase.

Linked trading

If we negotiate because we value things differently, it is in the bargaining phase that we focus on the differing valuations. Nothing, absolutely nothing, should be given away, no matter how little it is worth to you. The paradox of bargaining is that those things that are worth little, or less, to you in themselves, could be worth a great deal to you in the bargaining phase if they are worth more to the other negotiators. The form of the bargain is the conditional offer, and the Issues available to the negotiators are the potential content of the conditional offers.

A local council authority owns a ten-acre derelict site close to a main road and within driving distance of 300,000 potential consumers, whose combined spending power is in excess of £500 million per year. The council has zoned the site for light industrial use (until two years previously, it had been occupied by an engineering plant that went into liquidation, with 600 redundancies). A property development company approached the council in an attempt to persuade it to re-zone the site for retail units. The council has publicly stated that it is opposed to re-zoning because it still hopes to attract industrial employment into the district.

Several meetings were held between the council planning officials and the developer's agents, and while some progress has been made, there is still a reluctance to re-zone. The question of employment has featured constantly in the discussions. For the council, this is its major interest; for the developer, employment is strictly related to the commercial criteria of a successful development. The developer has pointed out that by letting the development go ahead, the council will gain a business rate income of £90,000 a year, plus a rental of £140,000 per year (based on £6 per square foot on 6.5 acres of buildings), where at present it is earning nothing from the empty site. As an alternative to a 25-year lease, with upward-only rent reviews, they offered to buy the site from the council for £2.5 million, but only if it were re-zoned.

The developer's approach to the final meeting was to consider whether to increase their rental or purchase offer, in the knowledge that they could probably achieve a rental of £9 per square foot from tenants in the first five years, followed by upward-only reviews every five years throughout the terms of the lease. In return for this increase, they wanted the council to grant them a 99-year lease instead of the original 25 years, enabling them to

> have the option to sell the unused portion of the lease at some point in the future. However, this still did not address the council's inhibition about jobs, particularly for those redundant engineers remaining unemployed after two years, and whose plight remained a sensitive issue in local politics and within the ruling party.
>
> At the meeting, the developer's agent made the following proposal:
>
> On rental income, we are willing to increase the amount from £6 to £7.50 a square foot on a FRI [Full Repair and Insurance] basis, provided you make it a 99-year lease for the site, with rent reviews every seven years.
>
> 'What about employment targets'?
>
> 'I think we should settle the financial aspects first and then go on to discuss the other issues'.

Developers, who think in terms of financial yields, are not always sensitive to the non-financial considerations of non-developers. Council officials, professional though they are normally shown to be, are under different organisational pressures that reflect, broadly, the values of the elected officials of the council. The developer, correctly, wanted something back for improving on the rent by 25 per cent; incorrectly, they tried to separate this Issue out from the whole deal, which for them centred on the high priority of having the land re-zoned (unless that happened, nothing else was possible). They also had neglected to address their bargain to the inhibitions of the other negotiators, thus making it more difficult for them to agree to what was proposed.

Issues widen the focus of a negotiation; the more Issues, the easier it is to avoid deadlock.

Exercise 6A

How many Issues were there in the developer's bargain?

1. Rental price per square foot
2. Full Repair and Insurance (FRI) lease
3. Length of the lease
4. Intervals between rent reviews
5. Open rather than upward-only reviews

The developer has some leeway to negotiate between these Issues. It can come down on the length of the lease or the intervals between the rent reviews and accept the 'upward-only formula' for reviews. It can also slightly increase the money. So in one sense, the developer is correctly using Issues to arrive at an agreement, though note that the only way they are likely to move is towards improving their offer from the council's point of view – thus worsening it from their own. By using the bargaining language of 'if–then', the developer could hope to mitigate movement on the Issues that merely worsened their position while finding out the limits to which the council would push on the financials. If the developer slipped into unconditional bargains ('OK, if we move on the rent reviews, will that satisfy you?'; 'How about if we made it £8.15 a square foot?'), they would stride, alone, along a one-way street towards giving in.

True, they could box and cox between the Issues they have – conditionally moving on the rent for a longer interval between reviews, or for the council's dropping any demand it might entertain in respect of the upward-only provision. It could be that the developer could hold the ground here but only if the council were less than serious about the employment Issue. In the actual case of this negotiation, this was not the situation. The local mayor was one of the redundant engineers still without a full-time job and he had little prospects of getting one. This personalised the employment Issue and made the negotiations more complex (and never underestimate how details like this can make a straightforward commercial deal more difficult). The developer's point that the site with retail units on it would bring hundreds of construction jobs to erect it and about 300 permanent jobs afterwards (half of them part-time) did not carry much weight with the elected councillors.

To break through the impasse and to avoid being milked on the financial details, the developer had to address the unemployment Issues head-on. It was no good throwing money at the problem, particularly when money was not the problem. A solution was found by extending the negotiable Issues. The retail units for the site took the form of a central six-acre shopping mall around which there was to be a car-park, plus a small petrol station and some office space. By taking the rear strip of the site and designing low-cost small business units for it, the developer was able to offer the council a feasible, though modest, contribution to the Issue of local light industrial employment. From the planning officials' view, this was a distinct planning gain, as the original plans had merely landscaped this strip, which was an eyesore of debris from the old factory, including a rusting rail-siding. The developer's bargain thus became in its (almost) final form:

> If the council re-zones the site for retail use, provides us with a 35-year FRI lease, clears and prepares the site for construction, and puts in the basic utility services, including the slip roads to the public highway, we will agree to an initial rental of £8 a square foot, with five-yearly rent reviews, and we will construct small workshops for light industrial tenants.

The developer did not completely 'rescue' itself from concessions on the financial details before they switched bargaining tactics to bring in the other unrelated Issues that met the higher of the council's priorities. It is impossible to know now, but I suspect that they might have done better on the financial details if they had deployed earlier the deadlock-breaking Issue of the small-business units at the rear of the site.

The principle enunciated here is that of **linking the Issues**. The principle of trading off one Issue against another allows for marginal movements in one Issue to be compensated by marginal, though more highly valuable, movements in another. The fewer Issues that are linked, the further you have to go to get agreement along whatever dimension that Issue is measured in. It will cost you more to get agreement with only one Issue than with several – on equity grounds alone, you would have to share at least 50 per cent of the negotiator's surplus if there were only one Issue and no other pressing reasons why you should get more (see Chapter 2). With only one Issue, the burden of meeting each other's wants falls entirely on that Issue. For example, if money is the only Issue, then the negotiators will fight exceedingly hard over that single Issue. This explains the ferocity with which people sometimes fight over single Issues like wages, prices, territory and such like. The result is often a lose–lose outcome for the negotiators. If one negotiator feels compelled by circumstance, time and perception to give ground to the other (for which, perforce, with only one Issue he cannot get anything in return), he is not only a loser, but feels one as well. Bitterly contested management–union negotiations can get into the single-Issue trap. Neither dares give way, and each goes to extremes of cost and consequence to avoid doing so.

An example of how the bargaining phase can suddenly turn in new directions is by the introduction of new 'Tradables' (see Chapter 3). Remember, Tradables are anything that you have discretion over, that you can use to gain movement in the deal. It can be seen in the following exchanges from the Forth negotiations:

> *Amanda Levin (AL): If you agree to a penalty of £500 a point below the target performance of 15 per cent error rate, averaged across all paperwork submitted, and calculated on a monthly basis, we will agree to pay an incentive bonus of £100 for every five points you achieve below 15 per cent error rate, calculated on a quarterly basis.*
>
> *Tony Marks (TM): There is an inequity in your proposal. In our view, rewards and penalties should mirror each other. Therefore, if you raise the incentive bonus to £500 a point and calculate it on a monthly basis, we would be prepared to accept a penalty rate of £200 a point, on the basis you have proposed.*
>
> *AL: In principle, I am prepared to accept the notion of equity. However, I cannot accept incentive rates of £500 a point for error rates below 15 per cent. What I will suggest is that we agree to a penalty rate of £200 a point above 12 per cent performance, calculated monthly, and that for every point below 12 per cent, calculated quarterly, we award an incentive bonus of £200 a point.*
>
> *TM: You have raised the performance target for a penalty to 12 per cent . . .*
>
> *(Debate on this issue ensues.)*
>
> *AL: To try to reach a final settlement, I am prepared to make the following offer. If you accept a penalty of £200 a point for every point any paperwork goes above 12 per cent error rate, and £500 a point for every point below 12 per cent error, calculated monthly from the beginning of the next quarter, and issue credit notes against our main*

> account for any penalties, and agree to adopt our IT and accounts system with a new team member, I will agree to a cash incentive bonus of £200 a point for every point that paperwork goes below the 12 per cent error rate, calculated monthly from the end of this month, and a bonus of £500 per point for all error rates below 8 per cent.
>
> TM: *I see. Well, I cannot accept a new team member to run the paperwork systems without some extra remuneration from your account. However, if you were to agree to the purchase of all IT hardware and software and provision of any training for our staff to help us integrate to your accounting systems, I could agree to hire a new part-time member of staff to solely deal with your account.*
>
> AL: *In that case, let me amend my offer. If you agree to pay for a new full-time staff member, to fully integrate to our accounting systems and give us regular admin updates, then we will give you a fully funded new IT system with staff training and an extension of one year on your contract.*
>
> TM: *I agree.*

The negotiation was see-sawing on the issues of penalty and incentive payments, with Amanda raising one or lowering the other in the search for a deal. She introduced the Tradable – adopting Forth's IT and accounting system – and used this both to drive Tony towards taking income in a performance-related scheme and to fund his proposals of additional bonus for lower error rates. For Amanda, the error rate was the high priority; for Tony, his high priority was to maximize earnings from this contract. But Tony also needs to be better at producing the back-end paperwork; a new IT system and staff member (paid for by hitting targets) will not only help with this client but with many others. For Amanda, this new Tradable – which would pay for itself in reducing the time taken by her staff if they can use integrated systems – also worked towards her own objective of lower error rates. By linking the new Tradables to the offer, they moved the bargain to an agreement.

Where do we get new Tradables from? Of course, circumstances do not produce neat rows of convenient Tradables for you to choose at your will. But you can help yourself to generate lists of Tradables by engaging in a simple exercise you can apply to whatever business you are in.

Exercise 6B

What are the negotiable Tradables in your business?

The list could prove to be surprisingly lengthy. In workshops for computer field sales personnel, I have seen small break-out groups develop as many as 64 Tradables available to them and to their customers, though not necessarily for use in all negotiations. Some of the main list headings of their Tradables included the following:

- Price
- Business allowance (another name for a discount)
- Trade-ins and disposal of old equipment (especially from rivals)
- Maintenance charges (on list price or actual paid price)
- Peripherals
- Software (dedicated or proprietary)
- Integrated with original manufacturer's equipment – supply parts (e.g. local lights supplied to Ford cars)
- Warranties
- Consultancy
- Training
- Reference sites (useful to sales negotiators)
- Facility visits
- Previews of coming developments in IT
- Installations
- Site preparation
- Delivery
- Have now – pay later/Pay now – have later
- Hot-line emergency help

An audit practice in one of the Big Eight accountancy firms developed a list of Tradables, available even to them in the increasingly competitive profession to which they belonged, that was so impressive that it was circulated to every partner and every senior manager for them to keep on their desks.

In every business, different Tradables are culturally specific. Part of the task of learning your business is to learn about what is and what is not (normally!) Tradable. For example, a firm of chartered surveyors conducted Exercise 6B in small groups of partners and discovered a market advantage that they were not using when they compared the outputs of each group. One group had listed 'minimum length of lease' as a Tradable and caused a minor rumpus by insisting that the traditional (at that time) convention of the minimum length of a lease being five years was unsuited to a fast rising market. Price inflation made some rents look decidedly weak after only two or three years (of interest to landlords), while five years was too long a horizon for a growing company to be locked into a lease in a property too small for it after two years (of interest to tenants). As professional surveyors work for both landlords and tenants (though not for both at the same time!) this new situation created a Tradable, or more correctly, raised the importance of a Tradable, previously only deployed in exceptional circumstances, above its normal inflexible value.

Creating lists of Tradables – properly a task of the preparation phase, but also a task when stuck in the bargaining phase, where its significance is more easily recognised – is only part of the creative work of the negotiator. The bargainer has to use them effectively and in a timely manner. The key to the effective use of Issues is always to link them, using movement on one as a condition of movement on another, or the introduction or acceptance of a new Tradable as a condition of accepting those Issues already on the table.

Bargaining to close the deal

The bargain in negotiation is the equivalent of what salespeople call a 'close', which is a verbal device they use (and spend endless hours practising) to persuade potential buyers to place the order. When a negotiator says 'Yes' to a bargain, the game is over. It only remains to write up what has been agreed. There is nothing more to discuss once a bargain has been accepted because the terms of the bargain are an explicit condition attached to an explicit offer. Clarification questions of a bargain usually precede its acceptance or rejection, though it is not unusual for the negotiators to clarify items while they are attempting to write up the agreement, and, sometimes, for negotiations to recommence when there is a misunderstanding on the details.

In the bargaining phase, there is a convergence of the negotiators' positions towards each other, but not necessarily by one or other making concessions across the gap that separates them on each issue. By linking their conditional offers across each Issue, they engage in what has been described as a 'negotiation dance'. The image is evocative for it captures well the bobbing and weaving of movements on some Issues in one direction with movements on others in another.

Technically, the problem of the bargain is *when* to propose it, rather than *what* it should contain. The timing is driven by the nature of your business, the content by your judgement, tempered by experience, and, of course, the enigma of opportunity. Bargains proposed too early – unless in the form of a written proposal and part of the normal structure of the negotiation – are vulnerable to antagonising the listener because they perceive you as too pushy and not properly responsive to their inhibitions, some of which they may not yet have had time to express, and are vulnerable also to a quick settlement before you have fully explored what it is that you are getting into. Bargains can also be too late, in that the negotiators spend all their time debating and proposing with nobody apparently willing to take the lead and go for a decision. Some deals just wither on the vine.

To offer a bargain is to call for a close to the negotiations. It is an explicit statement of an agreement that you are prepared to settle for without further elaboration. This itself makes the decision of when to close a lot easier – by offering a bargain, you are asserting your readiness to close, and it follows logically, if not always in practice, that if you are not ready, don't bargain! You can protect yourself to some extent by ensuring that there is no ambiguity in your view that nothing is agreed until everything is agreed and, therefore, that bargains offered during the course of negotiations on individual issues are not separable from other decisions on other issues. You are only making a provisional agreement on the individual issues, and the negotiation cannot close until you have completed bargains on all the issues that are linked.

You have already seen the 'new Tradable bargain' used by Amanda and Tony in the Forth negotiations, when Amanda introduced an integrated IT and accountancy system and Tony introduced the prospect of staff training for the system. Another example of that popped up in the shopping precinct negotiations with the council. While the offer of the rear strip for business units (a new Tradable) broke the deadlock, it was not yet sufficient to close the deal. The developer, however, did not have anywhere really to go, in terms of improving the offer on the other Issues, but they were acutely aware by now of the pressing significance of the council's inhibitions about employment. What they did was offer the following bargain:

> *Developer: We think we can make a suggestion that will help us to get an agreement. If the council agrees to our proposals to re-zone the site for retail use, provides us with a 35-year FRI lease, clears and prepares the site, puts in the basic utility services and slip roads and accepts our offered terms on the rental, we will construct up to ten small business units at the rear of the site, and we will undertake to press the contractors and tenants to give preference in their local recruitment to the families of former employees of the engineering works, providing that they are otherwise suitable for the 100 jobs likely to be on offer when the shopping precinct opens.*
>
> *Council: Are you prepared to make that a public commitment?*
>
> *Developer: Yes, though we would rather we did not release details of our financial arrangements just yet.*
>
> *Council: I think we have an agreement.*

The developer not only introduced a new Tradable, he used the **traded concession bargain**. This device helps a bargain over the last hurdle, when the negotiators are close but not yet closed. In the shopping precinct case, the worth of the actual traded concession, 'press the contractors and the tenants', is hardly a binding commitment, and a lot will depend on how genuine the developer was in his intent to carry out the promise. He can press with all the strength of a feather or take a virtual sledgehammer to this issue when selecting contractors, and can add it into the deal with the tenants. However, the outcome in this case is less important than the device used.

Traded concession bargains – the traded concession is the final movement for the deal – can take many forms. They could be an extra quantity of something (I have seen an extra peripheral for the MD's desk seal a large mainframe order), or a special colour strip added to a van fleet's livery, or something less tangible, such as a commitment by the union negotiators to positively recommend the deal to the workforce. They tend to be small and, because there is often not much left to trade on the main issues, they often are intangibles ('use best endeavours' is a common one).

Another device in the bargaining phase to secure the deal is the **summary bargain**. This replicates in form the summary proposal that leads to the bargain. You simply summarise everything that has been put forward as a bargain and ask for the deal:

> . . . If we can agree on that basis, let's write it up.
> . . . therefore, I think we have the basis of a deal.
> . . . I think when we both consider what I have summarised, we will conclude that we have made a lot of movement to accommodate each other's requirements, and therefore I recommend that we go ahead.
> . . . If that summarises your understanding of what we can agree upon, I suggest we shake hands and sign the agreement.

What happens if they raise an objection or an issue with which they are not quite happy? Fine. Decide whether the concession bargain will be relevant, and if it is, proceed as above; if it is not, repeat the summary:

> I can go no further, having made as much movement as is possible, and I must ask you whether this minor issue should stand in the way of a major deal we have worked so hard together to construct. I must ask for your decision on the proposal as it stands.

Circumstances will dictate which is the appropriate route forward. The repetition of a summary bargain, or the refusal to consider further small movements, leads you to the **or-else bargain** – probably the most risky of the bargains. It is close to the take-it-or-leave-it implications of a price tag in a shop, or the declaration that it is your 'final offer' (which, woe betide you if that is a bluff and they call it!). And what happens if the other negotiator decides to take the 'or else' (she thinks you are bluffing) and forces you into your threatened action, at a heavy cost to you and to them? It takes time to repair the damage of a bruising dispute, when, instead, if wiser counsels had prevailed, you could have presented your bargain in a less haughty or provocative manner. Presented properly, more in sorrow than anger, and with a solemnity that reflects the seriousness of the options, an or-else bargain can achieve its goal of impelling the meeting towards a decision if it is necessary to reach a decision there and then.

Somewhat less risky than an or-else bargain (though it has its own risks) is the **adjournment bargain**. In this case, you summarise the bargain as you see it, highlighting, of course, the contributions that they made to its final form, and say something like:

> If that summarises what we have before us, I suggest that we adjourn/sleep on it/take counsel from our own advisors/(and such like), and meet again (specifying a date, time and place) to present our views, and hopefully at that meeting we will be in a position to come to a final agreement.

The risks in the adjournment are that in your absence, they get a better offer from your rivals, that they take new inspiration from a change in their perceptions or information, that a distant player in their team intervenes and frustrates a perfectly good deal with awkward or obstructive objections, that you have timed it wrong and your deal elsewhere collapses, or that they use it as an excuse to get out from the deal. But bearing in mind that the adjournment bargain is a last resort and is an attempt to avoid the or-else bargain, it is probably inevitable that you should take those risks.

The agreement

The outcome of a negotiation is a decision, and that decision is either an agreement or a failure to agree. If nothing is agreed until everything is agreed, then the negotiators must agree on whatever it was that they agreed to. This somewhat circular presentation of the imperative to be clear that when you leave the table you know what you and they have decided is of the utmost significance. Countless errors and conflicts could be avoided if only negotiators would avoid a 'sign, grab it and run' approach. The euphoria of coming to the end of their negotiation – with the final bargain accepted verbally by both negotiators – tempts the participants to relax and leave the details to later. This is dangerous.

Exercise 6C

Without any reference to previous pages, write down on a separate sheet the final bargain offered by the developer's agent to the council in the shopping precinct negotiations.

Compare your answer with the text of the bargain earlier. Did you get everything exact in every detail? What did you miss? Most people will have missed something, or some detail or some nuance of what was said. For example, it could be that somebody would assert that the developer was committed to finding jobs for all the unemployed engineers when in fact he only offered to press the contractors and tenants to give preference to the families of the former employees, not the engineers themselves, in their local recruitment and only if they otherwise met the requirements of the job vacancies. Out of such confusion, a terrible myth of a broken promise could emerge.

During the negotiators' interaction, so much comment is made about the proposals and bargains that reach the table, and so many explanations, promises and clarifications are made, that negotiators have plenty of opportunity to confuse one set of proposals with another. Mostly, these confusions seem to work in favour of the person claiming them as fact – though, occasionally, we can be surprised because we had thought the offer was worse for us than it was in fact, and we are pleased to see that there was more for us in it than we supposed. Regular summarising should help clarify the contents and meaning of statements, proposals and bargains. Verbally restating what has been agreed or, preferably, writing it up there and then, to record that the negotiators agreed to what has been agreed, is another example of the usefulness of summarising in negotiation. It is the last (and best) chance, while the negotiators are still together, to be clear what they have decided, and I know of no better way than by jointly agreeing to a (written) summary.

If the negotiations are conducted on the telephone, then a verbal agreement must suffice, supported immediately by a written confirmation of the details (and do this on your own behalf, irrespective of arrangements made by the other negotiator to do the same).

Learning point:

Agree what has been agreed before you 'finish' the negotiation.

Mistakes made in implementing a decision can have a variety of causes. Where the mistakes are genuine – and obviously this is fairly common – they still have an unfortunate effect on the person affected. He or she can hardly be damned for the lingering suspicion that what is claimed to be a genuine mistake is in fact a case of one person taking advantage of another. In short, the genuine mistake is treated almost the same as the deliberate attempt to cheat on what was agreed. No force on Earth can convince someone that they have not been cheated when they firmly believe that they are the victims of a conniving cheater.

Ask yourself why it is that hotel accounts invariably show errors of overcharging, double charging and unbought items from the dining room charged to your account and always in favour of the hotel – exceptions the other way in your favour no doubt exist statistically, though they have not yet been given to me. Even stating this experience illustrates how easy it is for suspicion about somebody else's motives to become embedded in one's thinking. Yet it is avoidable: agree what has been agreed and avoid difficulties later.

Conclusion

The bargain is the crunch of the negotiation process. It is the statement of the intended output of the negotiators' labours. It is an implementable decision that, if agreed, closes the deal. After the bargain is agreed and recorded, there is no more work to do by the negotiators. They transform from negotiators into suppliers and customers, management and employees, colleagues and partners, or whatever. Their role as negotiators is over, for the time being at least. They get on with other aspects of their lives. Maria gets on with running her business, and Bruce gets on with finding buyers of his GRAPE systems; Amanda moves on to look for another process to improve her company's drive for quality, Tony to managing the supply of photographs to clients; the council officials step into their professional role as planners, and the developer's agents to servicing another client; most importantly, you watch the match with your son, and he washes the car.

By observation, the bargaining phase is proportionately a short phase, perhaps 3–5 per cent of the time taken by the face-to-face interaction (compared to 80 per cent-plus by the debate phase). It may be short proportionately, but it is no less critical for that. Loose or careless language in bargaining is extremely costly. What may be a weakness in proposing becomes a positive danger in bargaining. Weakness in proposing can shift the psychological balance against you by encouraging the other negotiator to be more demanding as he obtains concessions from you for little or nothing in return. Unconditional proposals undermine your negotiating room and encourage the habit of expecting something for nothing. But the proposal is protected by its tentative nature and the fact that nothing is agreed until it is finalised. The other negotiator cannot accept a proposal as a final and implementable offer. There is still some work to do.

The bargain is anything but tentative. It is a final statement that, if agreed to, is to be implemented as it stands. There is no protection for mistakes. An unconditional bargain is simply a 'giveaway'. It is an unpriced concession. It is like the supermarket labelling its bottles with the statement, 'you may take these home with you', and forgetting to add the price, 'for only 65p a bottle' (causing consternation – and accusations – at the check-outs as you march through without attempting to pay).

The only technique the negotiator can employ to prevent unpriced concessions slipping away is to make them conditional: *if* you accept these specific conditions, *then*, and only then, will I deliver this specific offer.

Not only is the form important, but so is the order. In bargaining, conditions are always stated first (that way they are not forgotten) and the offer follows second. It is a mistake to reverse the order because the slightest carelessness turns the bargain-statement into a bargain-question: 'If I deliver this specific offer, will you accept these specific conditions?', to which the answer is often 'No' (to test your resolve), or 'Not quite' (to demand an added concession). Once the habit of bargain-questions is caught, it is not long before the negotiator gets into the rut of offering first and then forgetting to add in his conditions, and he or she becomes a regular unconditional bargainer.

In the bargain-statement, the rule is: **conditions before offers**.

Checkpoint 6

6.1 What is the difference between a proposal and a bargain?

6.2 List 10 Tradables you could use in a pay negotiation.

6.3 Which of these is an effective bargain?

a) Let's do the deal at £16,950 for the car.

   b) If I give you a discount, then will you buy an extra 100 units?

   c) If you give me a shorter delivery date, then I will give you a bigger deposit.

   d) If you give me a 3-year warranty, then I will give you £8,995 for the machine and extend the delivery date to 8 weeks.

6.4 Rewrite the following as an assertive, conditional bargain:

   a) I would like £500 off the list price if we buy the full kitchen today.

   b) If I give you a discount, then will you buy an extra 100 units?

   c) If you give me a shorter delivery date, then I will give you a bigger deposit.

   d) OK, I can live with a 20 per cent Liquidated Damages cap.

7 The styles of negotiation

Introduction

> *Susie was an avid collector of rare pottery pieces. She had wanted the set of four porcelain 'Dogs in Poses' for years but had never managed to find a complete set to buy. By chance, after a late night browsing online, she came across a full set for sale. They were in 'mint' condition and very reasonably priced. In fact, they were a full £200 below normal market value. Susie had a brief chat with the seller and found out that Bob lived on the other side of the country and was keen to sell as they had been left to him by an aging aunt and he had no interest in them. Bob suggested that Susie go to her bank the next morning to send the full £1,000 to his bank account, and tomorrow he would also parcel up and post the pottery to her. Both the money and the parcel would take around three days to arrive with the other sender.*

What would you do in this situation if you were Susie? Assuming you were as keen on pottery as Susie, would you risk sending £1,000 to a stranger, with no guarantee on getting the pottery? If we take the risk of something going wrong out with the terms of the transaction (i.e. no pottery is broken or damaged, nothing gets lost in the post and the money is sent to the correct account), how risky is the actual transaction itself?

Let's answer that by considering the possible outcomes:

a)   Susie sends the money, *and* Bob sends the pottery.
b)   Susie sends the money, but Bob does not send the pottery.
c)   Susie does not send the money, but Bob sends the pottery.
d)   Neither Susie nor Bob send anything.

They were both clearly keen on the transaction, but both were nervous about sending and not receiving anything in return. By both agreeing to send at the same time, they would be sharing the risk equally. However, they are acting independently and have no real knowledge of the other or how the other is reacting. They are unable to maintain contact and do not know how each other will behave in any given situation – they are strangers, after all. Each will have to decide what to do based on the anticipated action of a stranger they have no control over. They can, however, make an estimate of what they think most people, on average, would do in this or a similar situation. And that is the purpose of the exercise: to get you to consider what you think other people are up to when you cannot communicate with them and when you are dependent on what they do for an outcome that you regard as important in your business, or even personal, life.

Suppose Susie knew for sure that Bob would post the pottery to her; would she still go the bank and send the £1,000, or would she cheat? Setting aside the ethical issues of cheating and not completing the deal, let's consider the outcome of behaving in this reprehensible way. Susie would have the pottery collection and Bob would be £1,000 out of pocket. As the transaction was brokered online, perhaps there is no real way of knowing who or where either of them truly live, leaving a trail very difficult should Bob ever manage to convince the local police to investigate this 'theft'. Effectively, Susie would be beyond retribution (especially since she had the parcel sent to a post office box, not her home).

Suppose now that Bob knew for certain that Susie wasn't intending to send him any money in exchange for the pottery collection. Would he go ahead with his side of the bargain? Extremely unlikely, I am sure you would agree. Neither of them in these circumstances would be worse off if they both cheated (neither would have to make the trip to the bank or post office), and one of them, perhaps, could be better off if she or he alone cheated, though, by cheating, they forego the benefits of joint cooperation in which each would gain something from the transaction. Susie gains the pottery collection she has always wanted, and Bob gains cash to spend on something he wants.

The problem is that neither Susie nor Bob knows what the other intends to do. They must rely on their judgement. Their choice is between defection from their decision to cooperate, and cooperation to their mutual advantage: the former either prevents them from being cheated by the other, or it enables them to cheat the other; the latter enables them both to gain. Why, then, do they fail to cooperate? Because the outcome is dependent upon their own and their partner's *simultaneous* choice between cooperation and defection.

Faced with the choice between defection and cooperation, we can set out in a simple diagram what each of them gets – their pay-off – for any combination of possible choices they both make simultaneously. First, we name the choices facing Susie and Bob 'Cooperate' (C) when they choose to fulfil their part of the bargain and 'Defect' (D) when they choose *not* to fulfil their part. Then, we enter the outcomes in a diagram (see Table 7.1) for all possible combinations of choices they can make.

To read the diagram, taking Susie's pay-offs, we read horizontally along either the row marked Cooperate or the row marked Defect and check the outcome for the corresponding choices Bob makes, shown by reading down the columns marked Cooperate or Defect. The first number in each square is Susie's pay-off for that combination and the second one is Bob's.

Table 7.1 Payoff diagram for Susie and Bob

		Bob	
		Cooperate	*Defect*
Susie	*Cooperate*	Pottery, £1,000	-£1,000, £1,000
	Defect	Pottery, 0	0, 0

For example, look at the top, left-hand square and note that this combines a Cooperate choice by Susie with a Cooperate choice by Bob (i.e. they are both cooperating by sending the appropriate goods or money). Susie gets the pottery, and Bob gets £1,000. They are both better off, and this is the preferred outcome. Now look at the bottom, right-hand square. What combination of choices does this represent? Yes, they are both defecting (i.e. a Defect choice by Susie is simultaneously met with a Defect choice by Bob). What is Susie's pay-off? She gets nothing because Bob did not send the pottery. What is Bob's pay-off? He too gets nothing because Susie did not send £1,000 to his bank. Both either tried to cheat the other, or believed that they would be cheated by the other, and hence protected themselves from a con trick.

The top, right-hand square and the bottom, left-hand square are interesting combinations in that the participants' choices did not coincide. In the top, right-hand square, Susie chose Cooperate and sent her money, but Bob chose Defect and did not send the pottery; therefore, Susie lost her £1,000 and Bob gained Susie's £1,000. In the bottom, left-hand square, Susie chose Defect and did not send £1,000 to the bank, while Bob chose Cooperate and sent the pottery in the post. Susie gained Bob's pottery, and Bob lost his £1,000. In either of these two squares, one of them gains and the other loses. Whatever motivated one of them to defect, the loser is likely to perceive the defector's motivation as an intention to cheat. They feel conned.

This takes us back to the original question. What would be the likely outcome of this exchange?

Exercise 7A

Suppose you were Susie. What would you do? Cooperate and make a possible gain but risk losing £1,000 to a conman, or defect and earn a reputation for cheating (if he cooperates) but risk nothing (if he defects)?

You face a real dilemma. There is no resolution to a dilemma in an abstract sense. Given only two choices, you resolve the dilemma in the practical sense by choosing one of them. The game highlights the nature of a dilemma by highlighting the tension between what is, on one level, the rational best choice – both cooperate – and, on another, the rational defensive choice – both defect.

In negotiation, and business generally, we face similar dilemmas, though we may not think about them very often.

- How should we behave when we are uncertain of the intentions of the other negotiators?
- Are they going to be cooperative or will they defect?
- To what extent will they be open and trustworthy, in which case we can safely reciprocate in kind, or will they be devious and untrustworthy, in which case we must protect ourselves?
- How do they see our intentions?

If we misread them – they cooperate when we defect to protect ourselves, or vice versa – we could unintentionally damage the relationship because we have not influenced their perceptions appropriately; or, perhaps, we did influence them correctly – we convinced them that we were open and trustworthy and they responded in kind, but at the last moment we lost our nerve and protected ourselves by a defection. You can see that the options are recursive:

> If we knew that they knew that we knew that they knew . . . we would both know what to do, but we don't; therefore, what is he thinking about what I am thinking he is going to do?

The existence of these and similar dilemmas influences our negotiating behaviour whether we are conscious of it or not. Our approach to other negotiators and our perceptions of their intentions determine our style of negotiation.

Trust in time

> *Rodney was not a keen collector of rare pottery pieces. However, after a night out with some friends he was looking online for a gift for his new girlfriend, Susie. He came across an advert to sell a rare collection of four 'Cats in Poses', and knew that it was something Susie would love. He contacted the seller, Bob, and discovered he lived on the other side of the country. Bob was selling the 'Cats' for £1,000 and suggested Rodney send the £1,000 by bank transfer, and at the same time Bob would go to the local post office and send the pottery.*
>
> *Rodney, though, had a problem with this. He needed to space the transactions out over a longer time so that he could afford it with his weekly wages. Bob agreed that, on Monday of each week, they would go to the bank and post office, respectively, where Rodney would send £250 and Bob would post one 'Cats in Poses' per week.*

136 *The styles of negotiation*

Table 7.2 Payoff diagram for Rodney and Bob

		Bob	
		Cooperate	Defect
Rodney	Cooperate	1/4 Pottery, £250	-£250, £250
	Defect	1/4 Pottery, 0	0, 0

Table 7.3 Sequence of choices for four rounds of the pottery game

	Rodney	Bob
Week 1	C	C
Week 2	C	C
Week 3	C	C
Week 4	C/D	C/D

What do you think of Rodney's cunning plan? Was he smarter than Susie in devising a system by which he minimised his risk? Let us examine the possibilities.

Each week, Rodney and Bob face the same choice of whether to cooperate or defect, and they receive a pay-off dependent both on what they do and what the other negotiator does simultaneously. These are set out in Table 7.2.

There is an additional complication, however. After the first week, Rodney and Bob know what happened on the previous week and this influences how they will behave that Monday. Hence, if on the first week either of them defects, it is unlikely that the other would risk the transaction as arranged the second week or any week thereafter. The game would cease and it would be extremely unlikely that it would start up again. Therefore, there is a good chance that both would cooperate. But what about on the last week when the exchange takes place? On the one hand, a degree of trust would have built up over the successful transactions they completed on the three previous weeks and this might create enough momentum for them to cooperate on the final week; on the other hand, it is the last day of the game and the pressures of the single-shot game between Susie and Bob could reassert themselves, causing either or both of them to defect.

Exercise 7B

The possible choices of Rodney and Bob from Week 1 to Week 3 are set out in Table 7.3. Complete your assessment of what is likely to happen on Week 4 and state your reasoning.

If you decided that they would *both* choose to cooperate (Week 4 = C, C), you are assuming that the trust they have built up over the exchanging of the £750 for three 'Cats' is sufficient to carry them through to the exchange of the last £250 for the last 'Cat'. Rodney might consider it worthwhile to risk cooperating with his last £250; he has a lovely collection already and it seemed worth the money (he was sure if it all went wrong he could still sell the set of three cats for more than he had paid). Bob might reason similarly with his last 'Cat'; the money was way more than he was expecting (and frankly, what would he do with just one?). They both might have been influenced by their successful transactions over the previous three weeks and this has compelled them to cooperate without concern for the risk in doing so. If they were overly concerned about the risk, then they would play differently.

If you decided that one of them would cooperate and the other defect (Week 4 = C, D or D, C), you have to explain why one of them is compelled to defect by the situation and the other is compelled to cooperate. Rodney could consider that he already has a good gift for Susie (they've only been dating a few months, so maybe what he has is already more than enough). Bob might reason similarly with his last 'Cat' (perhaps he could sell it at a higher price for someone to complete their set? These pottery items certainly seem ridiculously popular!). If they react differently to each other, then one of them was strongly influenced by the success of the previous three weeks, and the other was strongly influenced by the possible failure of the last week. Why should one be more concerned than the other? Because he became concerned about his vulnerability on the last week, perhaps, and saw a defection as the least risky choice.

If they both choose to defect, you are assuming that the fear of a loss compelled them both to protect their interests by defecting. Their concern at losing £250 and one 'Cat', respectively, because of their perceptions of the likely behaviour of the other, led them to defect.

However, this last circumstance raises interesting thoughts. If Rodney perceived that Bob would be likely to defect on Week 4 and he therefore defected in self-defence, where does that leave them both on Week 3? If we suspect that the motives of the other person are based on an intention to cheat on Week 4, how can we be sure that he would not cheat on Week 3? It would make sense, Rodney could reason, for him to assume that I would realise my vulnerability on Week 4 and defect also, but that I might not be so vigilant on Week 3; therefore, he is likely to defect on Week 3 to catch me unawares, so I had better defect in self-protection too! In this frame of mind, Rodney might reason that Bob might defect on Week 2, in which case it makes sense for Rodney to defect too! Hence, once Rodney reasons in this way, under the suspicion that he is vulnerable to Bob's defection, he has no reason not to defect on Week 1. In short, the whole transaction aborts because neither trusts the other.

Despite this somewhat pessimistic conclusion that Rodney's idea to ensure the probity of his partner's behaviour contains the same destructive seeds within it as Susie's one-off deal, we do at least have the prospect that a repetitive deal could contain within it prospects of a trusting relationship building up. It is really a knife-edge situation: trust begets trust and cheating begets cheating, and the risk of cheating begets actions to protect ourselves that make us out to be cheats! Which way the game will be played is uncertain, and it is this uncertainty that creates the dilemma we are trying to resolve.

Interestingly, the introduction of a time dimension, with repeated plays of the game, does highlight the point that there is a better chance of a trusting relationship building up the longer the negotiators know that they are going to depend upon each other through repeated plays of their dependency; put another way, if negotiators do not know the finite length of time of their relationship, they are less likely to react to their pending and foreseen vulnerability in the final round of the relationship. For example, if Rodney makes an arrangement with Bob that they will go through their transaction each week for an indeterminate number of weeks (perhaps Bob has even more pottery to sell and Rodney has more than one woman in his life to keep happy), and consequently it is unknown to either of them how long it could possibly continue, their vulnerability to the other cheating on the final week, Week 4, is removed. The unknown duration of their relationship removes the motivation to cheat arising from their 'final-week' vulnerability, though other influences could motivate them to cheat. Presumably a motivation to cheat by Bob would arise from a calculation that the profit from a surprise defection – Rodney's £250 – exceeds the profit from selling any further pottery (the rest are damaged and would not be worth as much anyway). For Rodney, in this particular case, cheating on his last week – which week presumably he would know about before Bob – nets him a set of three 'Cats', but not a complete set. A more sensible suggestion would be for Rodney, on his last week, to announce the end of their profitable relationship, and instead of groping through the transaction, he could message Bob, perhaps mentioning that, in view of their successful business, he will recommend him to Steven, whose wife is always looking for rare pottery items.

In contrast, some transactions are known to be of finite number to the parties before they negotiate. The deals offered by a used-car salesperson, for instance, by their nature are one-off deals – you do not buy a used car (unless you are in the trade) every day. This affects the view that people have of a used-car seller – they are hardly perceived by most people to be a model of business rectitude. One-off deals excite suspicions. Many businesses, anxious to hold on to their customers, go to great lengths to promote the sense of trust that their customers can place in them. They want a long-term relationship with their customers and, with 'no-quibble' guarantees and instant refunds in full, they market their trustworthiness to persuade their customers to trust them. Brand (company) loyalty is very valuable, and some organisations go a long way to encourage repeat business, making the one-off transaction less likely, and building trust with customers.

Negotiator's dilemma

This is all very well, but this leaves the problem of how we arrange coordination to make two parties better off in any transaction. This is the negotiator's dilemma.

Merely deciding to be cooperative is fraught with dangers. The choice may be unilateral, but the outcome is dependent on the other negotiator's independent choice. Surely, you might interject, in negotiation we are not barred from

Table 7.4 Red or Blue?

		Negotiator B	
		Blue	Red
Negotiator A	Blue	+3,+3	-5, +5
	Red	+5, -5	-3, -3

communication, and with communication we can overcome the main barrier to coordination of choices. True, but the mere existence of an ability to communicate does not eliminate the imperatives of a dilemma; indeed, communication can make coordination as difficult as if we were playing a dilemma game.

Let me illustrate this assertion with a game we have played with thousands of negotiators in our workshops. The version presented here only sharpens the dilemma by adjusting the pay-offs. In its simplest form, the game can be played by any two negotiators, each of whom has two poker chips, one of which is Red and the other is Blue. The players independently choose which chip to reveal to the other (covered such as to be unreadable before the simultaneous revelation) and they score points dependent on the combinations of colours that are played in each round. They are told, without elaboration or interpretation, only that their task is 'to maximise their positive score'. The pay-offs are as shown in Table 7.4.

By now you should be familiar with how the game is played and you could usefully persuade a friend to play ten rounds with you to ensure that its lessons are fully understood. For the first four rounds we permit no communication between the negotiators. Each hands over a poker chip and receives a coloured chip simultaneously. On observing the chip colours, the negotiators note the combined plays and score them according to the pay-offs in Table 7.4. Thus, if they both have played Blue, each scores 3 points; if they both play Red, each scores −3 points; if negotiator A plays Blue and negotiator B plays Red, then A scores −5 points and B scores +5 points; if negotiator A plays Red and negotiator B plays Blue, then A scores +5 points and B scores −5 points.

After noting the scores for each round, the negotiators hand back the chip they received and then choose which of their colours to play in the next round, repeating the same performance for each round and scoring as above. At the end of four rounds, they may communicate with each other and choose to coordinate their play over the next four rounds. For example, they may choose to play Blue together. If they do so, and if they keep to their agreement (it is a non-enforceable contract!), they will score 4 × 3 = 12 points each. If either of them breaches the agreement, they will score differently, though how differently will depend on when they choose to defect.

At the end of the eighth round, they may again communicate and again they may seek to coordinate their choices for rounds 9 and 10. However, to make things interesting and to tempt defection, the scores for rounds 9 and 10 are doubled, both positive and negative: two Blues score +6; two Reds score −6; a Blue played

140 *The styles of negotiation*

to a Red scores −10 (or +10); and a Red played to a Blue scores +10 (or −10). At the conclusion of the ten rounds, each player totals his score.

The Red and Blue game permits two brief scheduled negotiations between the players after rounds 4 and 8. They can agree to coordinate their scores, but agreement and implementation are vulnerable to defection still. People do not automatically find the cooperative outcome merely because they can communicate. It all depends upon the communication and what has happened between them in the earlier rounds before they communicate.

Consider some results from our workshops. In round 1, the majority of negotiators (51%) play Red, not Blue; that is, they open with a hostile play. When asked why they do this, the most common answer is that this minimises their risk of a loss (i.e. the most they can lose is −3 and they have a possible gain of +5). This, remember, is the rational play. They do not appear to consider the impact on the other player of their opening with a Red, nor do they consider the fact that the game is played over ten rounds and, whatever gains they might make in round 1, they are going to be vulnerable to Red play for nine more rounds.

What of the negotiators – the minority – who open with a Blue? Their reasoning is that they want to signal a desire for cooperation which, though laudable, is risky. They risk losing −5 for a prospective gain in round 1 of +3. But though risky, this play is sensible if cooperation is to be assured. Evidence of a willingness to cooperate by playing Blue at the start of the game carries more weight with the negotiators after round 4 than evidence of distrust (or worse, a desire to trump with a Red) by playing Red in round 1. The Blue negotiator is definitely looking for cooperation, while the Red negotiator may or may not be, depending on how we perceive his motivations for playing Red (there are no prizes for guessing how most people perceive such play).

What about round 2? Should the negotiator who played Blue and received a Red continue to play Blue? Evidence suggests that the Blue player who has received a Red switches to Red in round 2. Sometimes the player who played Red in round 1 appears to regret his decision when he received a Blue and plays Blue in round 2. This is done to signal his regret and to show a willingness to cooperate from then on. Unfortunately, this is often too late to obviate a Red from the previous Blue player who has switched to Red in retaliation. However, if they can get to round 4 with at least a Blue play from each of them, it is highly likely that they will be able to negotiate a cooperative agreement from then on as their actions support their claimed wish to cooperate.

For some players, the communication after round 4 definitely helps and they are able to find a basis for cooperation for the rest of the game. This appears to be most common when there is an aggrieved negotiator who has played Blue at least once and received only Reds in return. Here the nature of a trusting act is revealed. Usually, the aggrieved negotiator who is at least − 5 points down on the first four rounds compared to the Red negotiator – they both have negative scores – proposes that they both play Blue over rounds 5 to 8, but because this calls upon him to show his trust in the face of four rounds of Red play from the other negotiator, it is only fair that he be allowed to play Red in round 5 to a

Blue. By agreeing to this move, the Red player demonstrates his willingness to cooperate and allows the Blue player to 'catch up' his score. If he delivers under this agreement, all is well and they both end up with positive scores; if he defects again, the Blue player reverts to Red and they both end up with negative scores.

Few pairs of negotiators end up with maximum positive scores of 36 points from 10 rounds of Blue play (and as few end up with negative scores of −36 each). Most have scores of less than 36, indicating that there has been some mixed Blue and Red play. A minority of negotiators fail to get a positive score and end up with negative scores in the range −6 to −24. The imbalance between those getting positive scores of less than 36 and those getting negative scores up to −24 suggests that communication does assist them to coordinate their play and recover from early Red play. Sometimes they apparently recover from early Red play and work together with mutual Blue play for most of the rest of the game, but the past Red play can still rankle enough for there to be a defection in rounds 9 or 10, which sets back their scores if they both anticipate a defection by the other and hence defect to protect themselves.

The negotiator's dilemma can be summed up as follows:

> If I act to protect myself from my vulnerability to the other negotiator's predatory behaviour, I will be assured of a smaller loss than if I actively trust the other negotiator's good intentions and discover afterwards that I was mistaken in trusting him. I know that my act of self-protection is likely to be reciprocated by the other negotiator and we will both be worse off than we might be if we could trust each other. I would like to be different, but can I take the risk? I wonder what he is thinking? *Therefore, I defect, not because I want to, but because I must.*

Negotiators face this dilemma every time they negotiate. They may not consciously think of themselves in a dilemma at all. They develop an approach to negotiation, however, that indicates how they have decided to resolve the dilemma. For some, their approach is blended with their personality; for others, it is adjusted to the circumstances. But resolve the dilemma they do, for otherwise they would be paralysed into indecision and no negotiations would take place at all.

Red, Blue and Purple styles of negotiation

The Red–Blue game is not identical to a negotiation because it operates under strict rules and communication is highly restricted, whereas in negotiation there are no set rules and communication is unrestricted. The Red–Blue dilemma has its lessons for negotiators and is ever present. We can also make use of the concepts red and blue for analysing aspects of negotiation behaviour. First, however, we need to shift the meanings of 'red' and 'blue' slightly and introduce another colour, 'purple'.

There are two main styles of negotiation behaviour. I shall describe them as Red or Blue. **Red** can be thought of as a sign of anger, of war rather than peace, and it describes somewhat crudely the negotiating style that is based on 'more for me means less for you'. In its more extreme form, it summarises the intentions of the negotiator in the distributive bargain: 'Whatever else happens, I intend to get the largest slice of the negotiator's surplus'. Red is *results* oriented. Blue is the opposite style to Red. **Blue** is a sign of submission, of a preference for peace not war, of a desire for tranquillity. It is based on the ethos that if giving more to the other player creates the conditions for a happier *relationship*, then it is better to save the relationship than risk it in competition for the 'largest slice'. In its extreme form, a Blue style can become so unselfish as to be positively self-destructive: 'Whatever else happens, I wish you to have as much as you want, even if there is little left for me because whatever makes you happy makes me happy'.

It is possible to conceive of these contrasting styles by the more emotionally loaded terms, competitive (Red) and collaborative (Blue). But emotionally loaded terms are not helpful when no moral judgement is implied, nor prescriptive preference intended. Neither Red nor Blue style is optimal – one *takes* at the expense of the other, and the other *gives* to the singular benefit of the other; therefore, neither is a preferred style.

From observation, negotiators in the main adopt combinations of Red and Blue styles according to their perceptions of how to do business. Some of this they learn for themselves, some from their mentors, but mostly they have not thought about their choices and, if pushed, they call it 'experience'.

Those who play Red in round 1 of the Red–Blue game do so because of their perceptions of how best to cope with risk – even in a game where the risk is obscure and the points have no intrinsic value. They seek to minimise their exposure to the behaviour of an unknown partner. Faced with the risk that the other player will play Red, they play Red to *protect* themselves ('I play Red not because I want to, but because I must'). Some of those who play Red in round 1 do so because it is in their nature to *exploit* others ('I play red not because I must, but because I want to'). These perceptions incline such people towards Red play in the game and Red style in negotiations. Those who play Blue in round 1 either minimise the risk of the other player playing Red, or they assume that the benefits of playing Blue will become obvious over ten rounds (mostly they are disappointed).

Business experience influences perceptions and behaviour. Small businesses are highly vulnerable to Red play by debtors. The construction industry, for example, is overflowing with firms that went bust because the main contractor failed to pay them on time for the work they did, and not always for legitimate reasons. Ruthless Red-style managers place sub-contracts with small firms at rock-bottom prices without the slightest intention of paying them on time, or at all. They get the work done cheap, save on their cash flow and leave it to corporate lawyers to sort out afterwards. Red-style small firm owners take on sub-contracts, skimp on everything they do (especially work 'below ground' or anything not easily inspected), pass fraudulent work dockets and move on once paid before the main contractor discovers what they were up to (hence, even honest main contractors tend to delay payments!). One Red experience leads to another. To avoid being ripped off by ruthless sub-contractors, the main contractors inspect everything in case sub-contractors 'cut corners', build in latent defects and charge for work that requires re-doing. This can drive small firms into bankruptcy unless, that is, they can successfully skimp, etc.! In this business sector, firms are notorious for opening 'claims files' immediately after they are awarded a contract, in anticipation of a battle over payments. The additional cost of the Red–Red styles to business can be eye watering.

Some companies celebrate their ability to avoid Red-style behaviour. They approach their customers with what they consider to be the opposite of a Red style ('the customer is always right'), advocate long-term relationships and stress the importance of the customers' goodwill over short-term profits. Unfortunately, these claims are obtained more in the breach than in the practice. If you talk to their customers – and their staff – you get a different picture. Their selective style does not extend much beyond a few favoured large customers and certainly excludes their suppliers, and often is absent from their treatment of their employees. Consider the big supermarkets, all of whom advertise about how great they are for their customers, all the while squeezing costs down from suppliers to almost a breaking point by using their buying power, not to mention their somewhat poor record for shop floor staff pay and conditions. There may be little visible evidence of Red style in the marketing and sales departments, but it is in abundant supply in purchasing.

Red style does not imply an absolute imperative to be overbearing and aggressive (though it does accommodate to such behaviour). The Red-style negotiator is dominated by the motivation to 'win' at your expense, but how that determination is expressed depends on many factors and can incorporate a wide range of behaviours. The Red player can be charmingly immovable on something as well as angrily dismissive of your right to a fair share. Therefore, do not judge a Red style solely on the basis of the tone of the negotiators; instead, rely always on your judgement of the content of their proposals.

Openly Red stylists normally approach negotiation with manipulative intent, using ploys, bluffs and counter-bluffs. You will recognise Red styles in other negotiators by the extent to which they are aggressive, domineering, immovable, devious and, in debate terms, bad mannered. Some Red stylists are typified by a bombastic and patronising manner that often hides a general weakness of intent or commitment. For some of these people, their Redness is a sham, easily pulled apart by a firmness of purpose by an assertive conditional bargainer. One problem for the unthinking Red stylist is their proclivity to say, or rather shout, 'No' to everything before they have thought about it, and this catches them out because their outrageous unreasonableness costs them their credibility and, if their bluff is called, their apparent strength is revealed to be a sham.

In some cases, the Red stylists are unaware of the negative impact their behaviour has on the other negotiator. This can be caused by inexperience or ignorance of the feelings of other people. But you can push people too far. The most difficult industrial disputes to settle are those between an aggrieved workforce that has had no experience of negotiations – they do not know how to compromise once they are worked up to the point of defiance – and domineering managements that have never chosen to compromise. It is also well attested by observation that a suppressed people let loose against their former oppressors can engage in violent acts that ignore any sense of proportionality.

But not all Red stylists are overt in their behaviour. Some are quietly resolute in furthering their own interests at your expense – and charming with it. They conceal the more obvious Red moves or behaviours and work away at your resolve with few signs of movement on their part – you move or remain in deadlock – and they rely on time or other pressures to produce the results they want. It is wise always to remember that Red style is not solely a set of behaviours. It is an intention to benefit at your expense, and while Red behaviour may be hidden by plausible distractions, the content of a proposal is always subject to your analysis.

The extreme Blue stylist is a pitiful sight. So low is their self-esteem that they need desperately to be liked, even loved, by the other negotiator, and in pursuit of this goal they concede everything, even cringing in their self-effacement. Far from achieving the love or respect they crave, they often provoke contemptible feelings in the persons upon whom they shower their concessions.

The Blue stylist is as difficult to deal with as a Red stylist. For Red stylists generally exploit moderately behaved Blue stylists (there is a continuum of behaviours within both Red and Blue styles; see Figure 7.1), and the best that can be done for this condition is to train them to be different.

Exercise 7C

What is your negotiating style? Given the information that you have on the differences between the styles and using the continuum shown in Figure 7.1, assess, frankly, your belief about your own style:

a) *in your work or business relationships*
b) *in your domestic relationships*

Observation of negotiations – and responses from negotiators at workshops – suggests that people have preferred styles for different situations. People switch styles between Red and Blue. Many people are fairly Red at work (unless they are in sales and promotion where a Blue style is trained into them – have you never

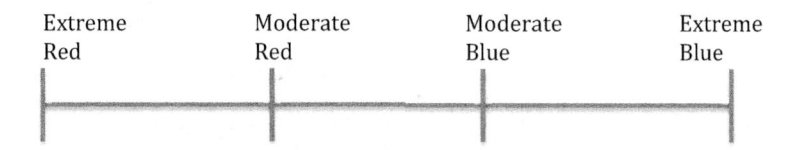

```
Extreme          Moderate          Moderate          Extreme
Red              Red               Blue              Blue
|————————————————|————————————————|————————————————|
```

Figure 7.1 The Red–Blue continuum.

heard of or recoiled from the 'smarmy salesperson'). They are more Red with subordinates and same-level colleagues than they are with the upper reaches of their hierarchy (some people acquire a reputation for 'crawling' before, or, as the Americans put it, 'brown-nosing', their bosses, which is an extreme Blue style). Domestically, people tend to be blue but that depends on the state of their relationship, as the divorce courts show.

Styles can also vary dependent on job culture or the types of negotiation that are required in your job. A survey of nursing staff within the NHS suggests a very aggressive Red approach to negotiation, but only because when they do negotiate it, is for extremely scarce resources, and they are fighting for their share for their patients.

Which style, Red or Blue, should you adopt? It is not much of a choice, is it? Fortunately, there is an alternative that excludes the two on offer. Because neither Red nor Blue is optimal, you need choose neither. Choose to be **Purple** instead!

This choice can best be illustrated by considering how the principle of **conditionality** derives from Red and Blue behaviours. A proposal or a bargain consists of two elements, the condition and the offer. The **condition** states what I want and is in the form: 'Give me the following'. It tells you what you have to do – what 'price' you have to 'pay' – for whatever you might want from me. It is my demand on you.

Let me ask you: 'how am I behaving if I merely *demand* something from you without offering anything in return?' By now you should recognise Red behaviour when you hear it because that is what it is – outright Red demanding behaviour. The *condition*, in other words, is my **Red** side.

The other element in a proposal or bargain is the **offer**, which tells you what I propose to give you in return for meeting my condition, and is in the form, '. . . then I will give you the following'. It is my offer to you.

Now answer the question: 'how am I behaving if I am willing to give you something without demanding something in return?' By now you will recognise Blue behaviour immediately – outright Blue submissive behaviour. The *offer* is my **Blue** side.

Now, this perspective on the conditional proposal or bargain is much like consumption of sodium and chlorine. By themselves, neither of these elements is good for you yet your body cannot function for long without them. Nature's harmless solution is to combine them in the form of salt. Likewise, the conditional proposal or bargain combines Red demands with Blue offers because, by themselves, neither of these behaviours (demanding without giving, or giving without demanding) is good for your negotiating effectiveness, yet together they are an assertive traded solution. In the form of the principle of conditionality, they are the alternative to the sub-optimal behaviours of Red on its own or Blue on its own: 'If you meet my (Red) demands, then I will make a (Blue) offer'. This is illustrated in Table 7.5.

This format specifies the exact nature of Purple negotiating behaviour: combine your Red side with your Blue side in assertive conditional proposals and bargains and do not let them be separated – ever!

Table 7.5 Red and Blue conditionality

Condition	+	**Offer**
Your RED side	+	Your BLUE side
If you . . .	+	Then I . . .

Table 7.6 Choice of styles

		Negotiator B	
		Blue	Red
Negotiator A	Blue	Joint gain	Exploited, Gain
	Red	Gain, Exploited	Lose, Lose

The difficult negotiator

By difficult I mean when a Blue-style negotiator meets with a Red-style negotiator and faces the problem of shifting the negotiations from competitive confrontation to collaborative joint problem-solving. To carry it out looks easier in theory than it is in practice. Yet it is one of the most common occurrences in negotiation, if only because we are always primed to believe that it is we who are being reasonable and they who are being difficult. I have never yet known a negotiator describe his behaviour as other than 'reasonable in the circumstances', which, of course, hides a great deal in the allusion to 'the circumstances'.

Let us first look at the potential outcomes when we select Red or Blue styles – see Table 7.6.

Two negotiators who adopt Blue styles for their negotiation will make joint gains ('more means more'), but the quandary is that neither negotiator knows how the other intends to play it, and if they play Blue to the other's Red style, they will be exploited. You will be exploited to the extent that you accept as true what the Red negotiator tells you (he bluffs, etc.) and if you do not accept it as true, you will be playing Red, perhaps to his Blue (he was not bluffing!). Thus, we return to the negotiator's dilemma: 'I play Red not because I want to, but because I must'. With both negotiators playing Red, they end up with a Lose–Lose outcome, defined as anything less than the potential joint gain they could have achieved by playing Blue–Blue.

Having established that neither Red nor Blue play is optimal, what can we do when faced with a difficult (Red) negotiator?

Iain Thompson, a convenor of shop stewards at a large transport company, had a reputation for his aggressive, almost over-the-top, style of doing business with departmental managers. He was verbally abusive, physically dominant and given to bullying any sign of weakness he perceived in a manager, especially anyone who preferred a 'quiet life'. Relations got so bad that Andrew Tyler, the General Manager, called a meeting of his departmental heads for a Saturday morning in a local hotel (he did not want to use company premises in case the meeting and its purpose leaked out). The one item on the agenda was how to deal with Mr Thompson.

The first hour and a half of the meeting was taken up by departmental war stories of the atrocities of Iain Thompson. These varied from fairly trivial incidents of exceedingly bad manners on his part to more serious disputes involving stoppages of work and intimidation of supervisors. After this session, Andrew Tyler called for suggestions of what should be done. These were equally varied (and imaginative). They ranged from finding an excuse, or creating one, to sack him through to offering him a large bribe and an excellent reference to transfer to another division of the company (which, it transpired, was how he arrived in this division, complete with a glowing reference). Other (not serious!) suggestions about having him run over by one of the company's trucks lightened the session (things were bad but not that bad!).

At this point, Tyler called on a consultant, who had sat through the meeting listening to what had been said, to make some observations. His first activity was to get every one of the managers present to play the Red or Blue game. The ranges of scores achieved by the 12 pairs of managers were slightly worse than normal, in that the majority had low negative scores and nobody had a positive score greater than 24, indicating a fairly Red culture.

The next thing he did was to draw up a table, an extract of which is set out in Table 7.7 This focused on some key behaviours and the managers' responses to them as detailed in the first session of the meeting.

The first two columns in Table 7.7 show what was happening in the main at present. When Thompson spoke, he did so loudly, and managers responded by speaking even more loudly until they were both shouting at each other. They spoke fast to pre-empt interruptions but ended up interrupting their own interruptions. Thompson had a gifted tongue for swearing – he could get swear words inserted within another swear word – and this brought out the worst in the managers. Frustration led to threats and counter-threats and many needless disputes as each side felt obliged to show how tough it could be.

In column three, the consultant listed the reactions that the managers should use in the future for a trial period of three months. He suggested that the managers should always aim

Table 7.7 How Thompson is currently handled and how he should be handled in the future

How Thompson acts	Manager currently reacts	Recommended future reactions
Speaks louder	Shouts	Speak softer
Speaks fast	Speaks faster	Slow down
Interrupts	Interrupts interruptions	Give way
Swears	Swears back	Never swear
Threatens	Counter-threatens	Ignore

to speak a little, but preferably a lot, quieter than Thompson at all times and to speak more slowly. This would leave them vulnerable to interruptions from Thompson but they should always give way when interrupted, listen out what he said, and then recommence (and give way if necessary if he interrupted again). Swearing should be avoided – 'we only swear at our friends' said the consultant – and Thompson should be treated with respect in every way and on every occasion. All threats should be ignored and no comment should ever be made on the consequences of his carrying out one of his threats, no matter how outrageous it was in terms of agreed procedure. To support the managers, an exercise in active listening was undertaken, for it was essential, claimed the consultant, that they listened to what Thompson said and got a clear picture of what made him tick.

Three months later, a similar meeting was held – this time on company premises – and the managers reported back what they had done. The picture was a bit messy. Of the 24 managers, only 11 had managed to carry out the assignment consistently over the three months, and another six claimed to have used the methods occasionally. The remaining seven managers said it was hopeless and Thompson would have to go one way or another.

Interestingly, of the seven who had given up from the beginning, four of them had high positive scores greater than their opponents in the Red–Blue dilemma game (the consultant had kept the score sheets for analysis), and two had scores that were greater than 36. This suggests that these managers were predominantly disposed to Red styles of play, including outright defection. Of those who had continued with the assignment, nine had negative scores in the Red–Blue dilemma game, and one of them had scored the highest negative score (−64) of the group, indicating that they were 'victims' of Red-style defections.

For the minority, it was business as usual with Thompson. But for the others, they had some interesting things to report. Relations had distinctly improved and, while Thompson was never going to become a tame pussycat (never an objective of this sort of exercise), he was easier to handle. As one manager put it, to much laughter in view of his unintended pun: 'When you listen to what Thompson has to say, he comes out with some rather Blue remarks'. This was generally agreed.

Thompson demanded things from the ridiculous to the justifiable (though mainly the former). But by addressing the demands that were justified, managers reported that the stress of previous meetings was avoided and the employees whom Thompson represented – 'my long-suffering members' was his catchphrase – were less prone to harass their supervisors, who in turn were less likely to complain to the managers. When, for example, Thompson angrily demanded that the toilets in one of the garages should be cleaned up immediately because of their dreadful condition, the manager immediately inspected them and agreed with Thompson about their condition and ordered that they be cleaned and replumbed forthwith. Thompson, on this occasion, was believed to have uttered the very first 'thank you' anybody could remember, though, typically he half-spoiled it by adding 'about bloody time too'!

The management were on their way to changing a stress-dominated relationship with a Red stylist towards a more Purple relationship – responding when the Red stylist played Blue with a Blue and remaining Red when he played a Red. Over time, it was hoped that Purple play – with a Blue tinge! – would predominate in their relationship.

First, you must separate people who are difficult only with you from those who cause problems for everyone. In the former case, it might be you that is the cause of the difficulty and not them. What are you contributing to the difficulty of the relationship? What have you done, or been perceived to have done? Whatever it is, you had better put it right.

Some people, however, are deliberately difficult because they have found that their behaviour usually produces what they want. For them there is a direct connection between their behaviour and the outcomes they seek. Their behaviour intimidates their 'victims' into submission, and where it does not have this effect, we get the kind of problem represented by the Thompson situation – bitter contests of will, much stress and tension and a totally Red–Red manner from both him and the managers. Dealing with these types of difficult negotiators sometimes prompts a debate on whether to match or contrast their behaviour. By matching I mean responding in kind – the way managers reacted to Thompson – by going Red on Red with him. By contrasting I mean responding in a different way – by going Blue on his Red.

The debate between matching and contrasting is inconclusive. The problem with matching Red to Red is that this often provokes an escalation in tempers that can get out of hand. After a couple of rounds it is impossible to settle on who started the Red-style contest. Once into a Red-style cycle, what do you do next? Matching also suffers from an inherent defect in that, from the Red style's point of view, Blue responses to his behaviour signify that his Red style is working and that you are about to submit. What happens if you don't?

The choices of matching or contrasting look like another dilemma because neither response answers the key question of what you are supposed to do next. The clue to the answer lies in what outcome the difficult negotiator is seeking from his behaviour – he intends that you will submit. Hence, your tactical aim is to deprive him of that purpose *by disconnecting his behaviour from the outcome*.

The response to all forms of difficult behaviour can be summed up in the statement that 'your behaviour will not affect the outcome'. Whether you express this statement directly to the difficult negotiator must depend upon the circumstances, but you certainly must articulate its meaning to yourself in all circumstances. Let it become your mantra!

> **Learning Point:**
>
> *Separate the effect of any bad behaviour from the possible outcome*

By disconnecting his behaviour from the outcome, you will also cease to make his behaviour an issue – how he chooses to behave is his business, not yours. Hence, all temptations to advise him on how to behave must be resisted. Statements like, there will be no negotiations until 'he changes his manners' or until the 'union is back into procedure' and so on, are a waste of time and re-connect the behaviour with the outcome. Realising that his behaviour is not going to influence the outcome – you are not going to submit to it – does more to change his behaviour

150 The styles of negotiation

than confronting the behaviour directly. Hence, in the Thompson case, the recommendations for future reactions did not in any way allude to him changing how he behaved – they only determined how the negotiators across the table from Thompson were to behave.

In the UK, we constantly watch government spokespeople and employers fall into the trap of reinforcing the behaviour of difficult negotiators, though, no doubt, they feel they are undermining it. A strike takes place, for example, and government spokespeople queue up to tell the media just how 'damaging' the strike is to the country and to the strikers. They appear to think that the strikers – behaving in just about as difficult a way as they can – will heed these warnings and return to normal working. They have the opposite effect. The strikers interpret the warnings of the 'damage' they are doing as confirmation that their behaviour is having some effect: 'If our strike is causing these important people to notice what we are doing and to inform us of the damaging effects of our actions, then we must be doing the right things to get our grievances addressed'. This usually prompts the pseudo game of passing the blame and responsibility for the alleged damage of the strike to the other side: 'Increase our wages and we will stop striking, and if you don't do this, then you are to blame for the damages caused by the strike'.

However, if the spokespeople were to shut up about the strike itself and were to concentrate instead on the disputed issues, they would weaken the commitment of the strikers to persisting with their actions. Keeping workers on strike is a difficult task for the union, and it must continually reinforce the employees' solidarity with assurances that their actions are having an effect, in order to stop erosion of support for strike action among the employees. Strikes can crumble quickly when their actions have no perceived effects.

Employers who agreed with their employees that they had a right to go on strike but that their strike would not affect the outcome would fare better in these disputes than employers who attack workers' rights to strike and also tell them how effective their strike is by the 'damage' it is doing.

Likewise, with difficult negotiators. Letting them know how effective their behaviour is by showing how much it upsets you only reinforces their behaviour: 'If my manner hurts you, the remedy is in your hands; give me what I want and I will stop bullying you'.

This still leaves us with answering the question about what to do next. Providing the first part of the strategy is in place and working – disconnect their behaviour from the outcome – the second part can be deployed. This requires you to assert – at all and every opportunity, if need be – that the only way in which the outcome will be determined is either by the merits of the case they have or by the principle of trading (and, of course, some combination of them both).

This is where a toughness of resolve is necessary. For the typical difficult negotiator, toughness is an attribute of their aggressive and bullying Red style behaviour. For the Purple negotiator, toughness is one of inner strength and determination that they won't be bullied into submission, nor will they accede to any determination of the outcome other than the twin principles of the merits of the case or of trading ('you will get absolutely nothing from me, unless and until I get something from you in exchange'). Toughness comes from resolve not abuse. In the Thompson case of the soiled toilets, the issue was decided by the merits of the case (the toilets were soiled) and not Thompson's rude and ignorant manners, which the manager ignored.

In another Thompson case reported at the follow-up workshop, we heard of an example of applying the principle of trading. Thompson had barged into a manager's office with a demand that the depot be closed on Saturday so that his 'long-suffering members' could attend a cup tie featuring the local football team. They would come in on Sunday at 'double time' and clear all deliveries. The manager said 'no' on the grounds that he saw no merits in Thompson's case – it was unlikely that the majority of the 120 drivers would want to go to the cup tie because many other teams were supported in the depot, plus a large minority did not follow the game, and working on Sunday would not be feasible because many customers were closed on Sunday and could not receive the deliveries they expected on Saturday. He suggested, however, that he was prepared to pay the men for a full Saturday shift if they completed all the day's deliveries by 12 noon, which allowed those who wanted to go to the cup tie to do so and everybody else to do whatever they wanted, but nobody was going to work on Sunday. Thompson went off muttering about this 'miserable' offer and called a meeting of the drivers. They listened to Thompson's report of the manager's offer and his recommendation of a walk-out and promptly voted to accept the manager's offer, much to the consternation of Thompson.

Making progress with a Purple style in a Red negotiation

The Purple stylist places an emphasis on what he wants to do rather than justifying what he feels he must do. Faced with a negotiator's dilemma, he manages it by dividing the difficulties of choice into smaller manageable risks. Instead of a single choice, as in the original dilemma faced by Susie and Bob, of cooperate or defect, which decides the final outcome, the Purple stylist breaks up the process into numerous little dilemma games. The single-play game becomes an iterative game played over a sequence. Think back to the contrasting games played by Susie and Rodney. For Susie it was all or nothing, as her £1,000 went on the block once and for all. Rodney turned the game into £250 a time. The purple stylist is closer to Rodney than to Susie. He takes measured risks that help judge the Red or Blue intentions or proclivities of other negotiators and that also train them to play Purple because each exchange demonstrates the benefits of conditional exchanges.

The debate phase plays a significant role in determining the other negotiators' games. If they are arguing, a Red game is under way and caution is advised. To open with a joint problem-solving approach – such as by revealing one's vulnerabilities to the pressures of deadlines or cash-flow shortages – could be dangerous. The determined Red negotiator always exploits the too-open Blue negotiator. The Red player's response to openness is to exploit what is seen to be a weakness. A deadline revealed is one that is run up to; the statement, 'We'll have to wait until our accountants report', leads to cash-flow shortages being exploited: 'I am sorry, but cash advances are out of the question'. The intention is to increase the pressure to force submission to onerous Red terms.

Given that the debate phase is a series of exchanges across a wide range of topics, there are plenty of opportunities to test the nature of the game played by the other side and to take measured risks that do not expose you to sudden-death exploitation. On each topic the negotiator must listen to what is being said and must ask questions that probe for information both about the issue and about the intentions of the other negotiator. How the negotiator answers – if at all! – tells you something about the game being played. A refusal to disclose information can send warning signals to you immediately, and the tragedy is that the signals may be clear but the cause of them may not be justified.

Nabwood Software were subcontracted to debug a pilot simulator for the BOE Airforce. They were given the job at extremely short notice by the manufacturer of the simulator to meet a deadline caused by the earlier-than-planned visit of the BOE authorities to the plant to have the simulator demonstrated. Faced with the client's deadline and the purchase order stamped in Red over it 'Priority One' (the highest level of urgency in the business), Nabwood withdrew staff from other projects, set up a 24-hour shift system, hired two specialist programmers, and reserved large time-shares on their mainframes to the exclusion of other work. When they completed the debugging on time and submitted their account, they were astonished to find that the invoice was challenged on the grounds, it was claimed by the manufacturer, that the invoice exceeded their budget for the debugging by 300 per cent.

Nabwood and the manufacturer's purchasing department met to discuss the problem. Things went from bad to worse. The Nabwood people were adamant that they had behaved impeccably in meeting the customer's deadline and successfully debugging the simulator (the BOE visit was a great success too). They resented strongly the implication that they were cheating by padding their account. They referred vaguely to the additional charges they had incurred and to the reassignment of personnel to the work. They did not go into details about the internal charges they had incurred in the substantial use of the mainframe computer, the consultants they had hired and the royalties they had to pay for using somebody else's unique software.

And that was the nub of the problem. They added to an already Red situation – caused by one side believing they had been ripped off and the other that their integrity was impugned by the implication that they cheated their customers – by being vague about their excellent case for full payment. Nabwood's failure to be open with the details of their costings – they felt that the mere reference to them ought to be sufficient – only excited the fears of the manufacturer's people that they were being taken for a ride by a supplier. Their evident scepticism further fuelled Nabwood's sense of indignation. Within short measure, both were muttering about litigation.

Red behaviour can arise from a misunderstanding as well as from the situation. When the negotiator is sending Red signals inadvertently, he can correct this mistake by taking a measured risk:

'Are you saying that it is the lack of information that is causing you to consider cancelling the contract?'

'Yes'.

Can I take it that, if I supply you with the information that you require and that if this information establishes to your satisfaction that we have made a legitimate claim for our services, that you will accept this information on a commercial-in-confidence basis and will pass our account, or that proportion of it that you agree is justified, for payment?

Dependent upon the answer, the negotiator will know what game they are playing. If they say 'No', and assuming they have understood the contents of the question (which is perhaps worth testing), you know that their Red stance has some other motivation (which is perhaps worth questioning too); if they say 'Yes', you know that your disclosure of information is a potential means of solving the dispute. Whether it does would depend largely on whether your figures will stand examination. If they do not, then your own Red stance is explained by your customer catching you out in a padded fiddle.

All the activities summarised by 'SLAQSS' (Statements, Listening, Assurance, Questions, Summaries and Signals – see Chapter 4) are measured-risk Blue behaviours. None of them are sudden-death risks. If you make a signal and get it shot down ('Ah, so we have been wasting time listening to your protesting that you cannot meet this deadline and now you suggest that it might be possible!'), you do not lose everything or even anything. The Red rejection of the signal tells you that it is not safe for the moment to make an overt advance along the lines you suggested. You could return to making a statement explaining your motives in trying to move towards a solution, perhaps summarising where you have both got to in your respective statements of positions or attitudes, and await a response from them. They might respond along the lines of: 'Oh, I see, OK, well go on. I'll listen to what you have to say', in which case you can make a tentative – very tentative – proposal; or 'That's a maybe, but if you think we are shifting from our deadlines to suit your convenience, you must think we are daft', in which case you do not propose anything and you will have to endure some unpleasant Red-style argument until an opening occurs through which you might try another signal, or, if you are listening carefully to what they are saying – listening is always Blue behaviour – you could respond positively to a signal from them (remember Thompson?).

Negotiations tend to concentrate on Issues and the positions people hold on the Issues. A wage rate is an **Issue**; £20 an hour is a **Position**. People also have Interests. An adequate standard of living is an **Interest**. These can be set out as follows:

Interests – overriding motivator – why somebody wants something
Issues – agenda item – what they want
Positions – focus of stance on the issue

The bitterest of disputes often concentrate on Positions, but the stances people take are driven by their Interests. A union announces the minimum wage it intends to get and publicly commits itself and its prestige to attaining that figure. Given that its prestige is an Interest, it finds itself unable to shift from its Position, and it digs in for a long and mutually damaging dispute.

Many Red behaviours actually make it difficult to reach a settlement because they offend the Interests of the other party. A Red ploy of 'take-it-or-leave-it' on a Position or an Issue, for example, can provoke resistance, even where the negotiator is willing to consider accepting the offer, because the way the offer was presented compromises the sense of dignity in the negotiator.

Purple negotiators seek to identify the Interests of the other side – and to be candid about their own – if only to assist them in addressing Issues and in shifting Positions. They have to be careful here because identifying somebody else's Interest and then making it public has the pitfall of announcing (or more usually denouncing) the alleged motives of somebody else. It is important, however, to attempt to identify Interests, if only for personal consideration. They are the drivers of negotiators to, or off, Positions. They may work on the surface or off it, and they may be understood and acknowledged by the other negotiator, or remain subconscious.

Dependent upon the circumstances, a Purple negotiator could choose to avoid publicly identifying the Interests of other negotiators, though this does not preclude, and must not preclude, identifying their Interests in order to understand their commitments to Positions and Issues. Take a negotiation between two parties who have a record of tensions with others, or worse, between them. It may not pay dividends to reveal Interests or to address them. Allowing for the expression of ideological differences can be fraught with danger (for the prospects of a negotiated settlement) if brought out into the open.

The broad principle for the Purple negotiator is to concentrate on reconciling Issues and Positions when the Interests of each party are effectively incompatible (as when ideological, religious or racial standards of conduct or governmental differences are too wide), and to concentrate on reconciling Interests when the Issues and Positions are effectively incompatible (as with fixed amounts of territory, money and resources that cannot be split satisfactorily). Neither approach necessarily permanently precludes the other because, in due course, by following one route, the prospect opens up of moving onto the other routes. By sorting out trading details between two irreconcilable political systems, for example, we create the long-term contact that can lead to a peaceful ideological shift.

A divide between secular and religious citizens is an example of how, by concentrating on the interests of the rival lifestyles, they end in a deadlock. You cannot reconcile the two lifestyles by expecting one or other to give up its preferences for its rival's. Instead, negotiations should concentrate on the substantive Issues and Positions – how to 'live and let live' – for be sure that attempts for one side to triumph over the other will lead to much unpleasantness for both sides and, perhaps, a total collapse of life as they presently know it. The fateful events in Bosnia stand as a stark warning to denying this advice in pursuit of 'victory' for one over the other.

Purple negotiators are aware of the linkage between agendas dominated by any, or all, Interests, Issues and Positions. They choose to switch between them to

The styles of negotiation   155

suit the circumstances in pursuit of an agreement. They have to be aware of the dangers of concentrating on one to the exclusion of another. When absolutely stuck in a positional confrontation, they can choose to move to look at broader Issues (a trade-off, perhaps?) or to examine the Interests that lie behind the other negotiator's (and their own) dogged persistence with their current Positions.

But there are dangers for negotiators, which if not controlled, can lead them into serious mistakes. They can be fixated by the high-sounding rhetoric of the general interest and forget the implications for the lower-level implementation of the details that flow from the rhetoric. This is a tactic that works whenever the negotiators take their eyes off the ball and get bamboozled with high-sounding rhetoric and then find themselves in no position to defeat detailed proposals that are slipped under the rhetoric.

Purple negotiators may also protect their negotiating stances by adopting measures that *test* the other negotiator's intentions. Ostensibly, testing the integrity of another negotiator is a Red act and this might seem odd behaviour for a Purple stylist, but it is not part of a negotiator's skills to confine himself exclusively and wholly to the Purple end (middle?) of the spectrum. The purpose of the Purple negotiator using a Red test is to allow the other negotiator to reveal whether he is playing Red or Blue. It is not to exploit him, which would be the intention and outcome if a Red player adopted these tactics, but to clear him of suspicion of trying to exploit the Blue player. If he passes the test, the Purple player can adopt a Purple response by doing what he wants (i.e. make a deal) and not what he must (i.e. play Red); if he does not pass the test, the Purple player avoids being exploited.

Consider the case of two consultancies negotiating over a joint venture that would bring their expertise together for a special event.

> *Snales Ltd, civil engineers, had entered discussions with Archways on the prospects of their jointly presenting a one-day seminar on the vexed question of securing payment for work done by subcontractors in the construction industry. The commercial prospects of the seminar looked good, though there is always a risk in such ventures that the market will not take up the places and that the marketing and other set-up costs will be lost. The principals at Snales Ltd were impressed with the public reputation of Archways and considered that their involvement would greatly assist them in making the seminar a financial success.*
>
> *When it came down to details, Archways was asked how much they would charge to present a half-day of the seminar. They did their calculations and decided that they would set a fixed fee of £800, plus £25 per person who attended, which they did not consider particularly onerous a charge. This gave them a baseline income no matter how few attended and an extra income if the seminar was so successful that it was a sell-out. On an expected turnout of 100 people at £100 a person, this left a great deal to Snales Ltd.*
>
> *Archways were informed by letter that their proposal was unacceptable as it left too little net revenue to Snales Ltd after they had met their marketing, administration and other costs. For Archways the question boiled down to whether this was a test of their resolve in a distributive bargain over the negotiator's surplus or whether it was an attempt to get*

> *Archways's unique services in this field on the cheap. Were Snales Ltd playing Blue (they had a genuine problem with their net fee), or were they playing Red (bluffing to force down Archways's share of the net proceeds)?*
>
> *Dropping the fee was no answer to the problem (and what then could Archways teach hard-bitten construction claims officers if they dropped a fee on the sole basis that they were asked to do so?). They decided instead to test the colour of Snales Ltd by writing back to them and offering them the following deal:*
>
> *Archways will undertake the marketing of the seminar, will bear all the administration and other costs and will confine its fee to the net returns after Snales Ltd are paid an £800 fixed fee plus £25 per participant.*
>
> *In short, Archways offered to Snales Ltd the very same deal that they had asked for. This obviously caused some consternation because it took two weeks for a reply to arrive. The reply consisted of a terse rejection of the offered deal and a withdrawal from further consideration of a joint venture.*

Exercise 7D

What did Snales Ltd reveal about their game by rejecting the offer from Archways? Consider your own response to this question before reading on.

They were clearly playing a Red game. If Archways's first fee was too high and left Snales Ltd with too little, then being offered the reverse deal (i.e. Archways's first fee, and avoiding all the costs of the seminar) must leave them better off – unless, that is, Snales Ltd's stance on Archways's fee was a ploy. By testing their erstwhile partners, Archways discovered what they were up to, which was to force down Archways's fee to gain more of the net income for Snales Ltd.

Similar tests can be applied by Purple negotiators to what they suspect are Red-style bluffs (or worse). Take the case of the person selling a business with a profit forecast that suggests that it is worth in excess of £10 million (based on a formula of the price being eight times audited net profit). How do we test the accuracy of the forecast? By suggesting a contingency element in the price package. If the business reaches its forecasted profit over the next three years, then the price will be £X; if it does not, it will be £X–n million. How the seller reacts to the proposal could reveal what game he is playing. If the seller rejects the principle of a contingency price out of hand, you might want to reconsider doing business with him; if he negotiates over the value of n, then it might be safe to assume that he is fairly sure of his forecasts but that they need revising downwards; if he agrees to a contingency without a quibble, he must be pretty certain of his forecasts. Similar tests are common with delivery dates and for performance standards (with penalties for failing to meet them).

Conclusion

The dilemma of trust in negotiation is ubiquitous. If you are too trusting, you risk exploitation (C, D; D, C); if you are not trusting enough, you risk a second-best outcome (D, D is always worse than C, C). Coping with distrust and building it into trust is a strategic aim of the Purple negotiator.

The prevalence of Red-style negotiation reflects the way most people cope with distrust. For the effective negotiator, however, rising above distrust –even with a hard-line Red stylist – is an essential skill, learned through a combination of insight and practice. The Purple stylist understands what the Red player is up to (a Red ploy recognised is a ploy disarmed) and can indulge in some controlled 'Red' behaviour to send a signal or to test the intentions of the other negotiator. Hence, I favour the colour Purple as the best description of the style of the effective negotiator.

A printed contract is the written expression of the distrust each partner has of the other. In some contexts it is a highly Red instrument (what else is the injunction to 'read the small print' but the cry of a Blue player at what he had discovered he had agreed to?). Those contracts with wide-ranging exclusion clauses that protect one party to the prejudice of the other are examples of Red instruments. In Japan, the presentation of a highly detailed contract at the start of negotiations to establish a joint venture arouses alarming levels of suspicion in the Japanese negotiators and their superiors. The overly detailed contract says that you do not trust them. They believe in establishing the nature of their relationship with you before they set about discussing a contract, and even then they regard it as a guide rather than a bible.

In other contexts, a contract is a useful test of somebody's intentions. If they are willing to sign the contract, then they are willing to be bound by the written obligations and promises they made in the negotiation. If they are unwilling to sign a contract, then they are not to be trusted at all. However, if you insist on a contract, you might cause offence by making them think that you do not trust them!

How you handle these paradoxes and dilemmas is a matter of personal experience and proclivity to a behavioural style. For some people, you would not take a small order unless it was accompanied by an official purchase order signed by a senior manager; for others, you would willingly undertake substantial expenditure without a written contract and solely on the word of the person you have dealt with for many years. How to tell the sharks from the dolphins is not made any easier by acting upon what they tell you about their natures. Trust is based on what people do and have done, not what they say they will do.

While considerable evidence can be assembled to show that Red-style negotiating behaviour has paid off handsomely for some highly skilled practitioners of the style, being Red for most people is a short-term advantage. The longer term pay-off is pretty poor from a monolithic application of Red styles to negotiations.

People, when they can, exact revenge for previous Red play against them. They also blacken your name to many more people if they feel aggrieved at their treatment. Deals that are based on fraud, or heavy manipulation of the negotiators, soon fall apart at the first loophole they can find in the contract. Remember how the people at Xander Enterprises were discussing how to get out of a poorly drafted contract they had with Phoenix in Chapter 1? Similar meetings are a daily occurrence somewhere in business.

The Purple negotiator, who constantly strives to move the negotiations over towards the exchange of conditional proposals, is strategically sound over the long run. He is handling distrust by building small pockets of trust through taking measured risks on myriads of smaller topics in the debate phase (every minute of debate provides opportunities to build small elements of trust). As he instils in the negotiations the tone of seeking a settlement; of not bowing to Red pressure tactics; of being creative in addressing the inhibitions and concerns of the other negotiator and assertively seeking similar attention to his own inhibitions; of being willing to switch from positions and issues to interests, and vice versa; and of being positive rather than negative in all aspects of the obstacles to a deal, he is laying a solid foundation for an endurable settlement that both sides can be happy with and be willing to implement.

Checkpoint 7

7.1 Read the following statements and write down whether they indicate a Red or a Blue style.

1. The man with money meets the man with experience. The man with experience ends up with the money, and the man with money ends up with the experience.

2. If you can't stand the heat, get out of the kitchen.

3. My word is my bond.

4. It's tough at the top.

5. If they want a price war, I'll show them what a low price means and we shall see who has the deepest pockets.

6. We are not in this venture for a quick buck.

7. Give me some of what I want, and I will give you some of what you want.

8 Rational bargaining

Introduction

With practical negotiation so messy and humans so unreliable, a preference for rationality in negotiation is understandable. By assuming that people are rational, it is possible to develop models of negotiation that produce normative principles for rational behaviour. You can contrast these rational behaviours with the kind found in everyday negotiations and you can use insights from the rational models to signpost ways to improve behaviours in the (irrational) negotiations we all take part in.

Economics, for example, uses assumptions of rationality to produce elegant mathematical models of concession–convergence negotiation, more appropriately labelled haggling. These models are largely of limited practical value. There is also a growing academic literature in philosophy that uses rational bargaining models and dilemma games to explore justifications for morals and ethics. Again, these models have limited practical value for practising negotiators.

The main problem with assuming rationality is that it is at variance with how people behave. While the derivation of rational behaviour from the assumptions produces insights into what would happen if people behaved according to the assumptions, it is more than a trifle academic to rely on rationality if people do not behave that way. And practitioners are at risk of compounding their errors if they follow plausible right-sounding but deductive prescriptions derived from preferences for rationality in circumstances that are contrary to the assumptions.

That negotiation research has travelled down the rational road is evident from published work since the 1950s. People do not instinctively behave rationally, and only a small minority opt for joint maximisation. The latter proportion can be increased by prompting and training, but it is still difficult to achieve – even approach – the much-lauded 'win–win' outcome without considerable investment in long-term relationship building. Companies that have tried to change to win–win relationships have found it difficult and many have been disappointed. In my classes, barely 8 per cent of delegates manage the 'win–win' in dilemma games, despite nearer 90 per cent saying that is the type of negotiator they are. It only proves that the coveted win–win outcome is much harder to achieve when you have to consider other people's reactions to the situation. Maybe negotiators ought to behave rationally but they do not, and while analysis of the defects of non-rational negotiating is insightful (and makes for good copy) it is not yet apparent that these insights influence practice.

Starting from observing how negotiators behave, you can improve your performance. To do this effectively, you must go from description to prescription and not from assumption to prediction, though this does not disallow considerations of both approaches. The very fact that people attend training courses to improve their negotiating behaviour is clear evidence that they do not naturally act as a rational bargainer, nor do they find such behaviour commonly exhibited by those with whom they negotiate. If it was natural to behave rationally, why would people need training?

The case for rationality in negotiating behaviour stems largely from observation of the common errors of non-rational negotiators. On the grounds that recognition of these common errors prompts a desire for alternative behaviour, you can identify the cognitive sources of these errors and learn how to avoid them. This alone causes negotiators to behave more rationally without having to take on board the formalistic models and analyses of pure rational behaviour.

In this chapter, we look at several Rational Bargaining models that have valuable lessons for everyday negotiators. They have their flaws as they rely on rationality and prescribed behaviours, but they have some good observations that can help us adapt to be a more effective negotiator.

John Nash and Utility Theory

Bill and Jack

Two young brothers, Bill and Jack, want to exchange some of their possessions and they want to do this without the kind of argument they had last time, when it ended in tears with Jack telling his mother that his elder brother had bullied him into giving away much more than he got in return. As before, they had no money through which to conduct the exchange. They asked their elder sister, Louise, for advice, after Bill had objected to Jack's suggestion that they ask Mother to supervise the swap (Bill suspected that she would be biased in favour of his younger brother). Louise was keen to give her advice, if only to stop the usual arguments that would otherwise interrupt her MBA studies that afternoon.

Louise told Bill and Jack to bring those possessions that they were considering swapping to her room. They returned with nine items, five of which belonged to Bill and four belonged to Jack. Bill's possessions consisted of a book, a whip, a ball, a bat and a box; Jack's consisted of a pen, a toy, a knife and a hat. Louise gave each of them a piece of paper and a pencil and asked them to rank all nine of the items in their order of importance. She suggested that they could think of the items as being of high importance, medium importance or low importance. With some obvious indecision, requests to remind them of what high, medium and low meant, and a few scorings out, Bill and Jack undertook this task reasonably quietly.

Table 8.1 Louise's flip chart

Bill's possessions	Value to Bill	Value to Jack
box	medium	low
book	low	medium
whip	low	low
ball	low	low
bat	low	low

Jack's possessions	Value to Bill	Value to Jack
pen	high	low
toy	medium	low
knife	medium	low
hat	low	low

Louise took the lists from each of them and copied them out onto a flip chart beside her table. Her combined lists looked like this (Table 8.1).

Bill and Jack, though somewhat puzzled by Louise's list, waited expectantly. It was not yet obvious how they would swap their possessions. Intuitively, they both knew which of the other's possessions they wanted, and they both wanted to be better off as a result of the swap, but they had no idea what to do next.

After some thought, Louise announced she knew what possessions her brothers should swap and, as she spoke, she picked up some possessions from Bill's set and moved them to Jack's, and moved some of Jack's possessions over to Bill's set. When she had finished transferring items between the two sets, Bill had 'swapped' his book, whip, ball and bat for Jack's pen, toy and knife. The boys appeared to be satisfied with the exchange and went off to their own rooms with their new sets of possessions, leaving Louise to get on with her MBA elective on negotiating.

> **Exercise 8A**
>
> a) *Did you recognise the planning tool that Louise used?*
> b) *What negotiating principle was she applying to the transaction?*
> c) *From the limited information given to Louise, can you explain her selection of items to be swapped?*

a) Did you recognise the planning tool that Louise used?

A simplified version of a Negotek® PREP Planner (see Chapter 2) showing Bill's and Jack's priorities of the items for exchange.

b) What negotiating principle was she applying to the transaction?

Items of low priority or value are exchanged for items of higher priority or value. For example, the pen is of low value to Jack and of high value to Bill, while the book is of medium value to Jack but of low value to Bill. On the basis of their relative value, an exchange is possible in which Bill gets the pen in exchange for Jack getting the book.

> c) From the limited information given to Louise, can you explain her selection of the items to be swapped?

Bill gives up four low-value items – the book, whip, ball and bat – and received the pen (high), toy (medium) and knife (medium); Jack gave up three low-value items and received the book (medium), whip (low), ball (low) and bat (low). As long as the items Jack gave up are of lower value to him than the items he received, he will willingly complete the exchange.

Nash and the bargaining problem

Economists, for more than a century, fully understood how markets set prices, but how bargainers set their prices remained for many years an irritatingly grey area. This was known as the bargaining problem. John Nash responded to the challenge in 1950 and his work initiated an avalanche of research contributions to the mathematics of bargaining theory. (He was awarded the Nobel Prize for economics in 1983.)

Nash asserted that the economic situations of monopoly versus monopsony, of trading between two nations and of negotiation between employers and labour unions are bargaining, not market-pricing, problems. He then made certain idealising assumptions to determine the amount of satisfaction each individual bargainer could expect to get from a bargained exchange.

Nash's solution to the bargaining problem is not about defining negotiation as a process or explaining why and how people negotiate. It is about what makes one particular solution better than all of the other potential solutions. The bargaining problem is not as easy to solve as at first it looks, so let me assure you that this topic is vitally important to anybody interested in negotiation.

You negotiate because it makes you, in some sense, better off. Given that you volunteer to accept or not accept the final deal, it follows that if you accept the deal you believe that you are in some way better off than if you reject it. What is true for you must be true for the other negotiator, so it is fair to conclude that you both negotiate because you both expect to gain something over what you have before your bargain. Briefly put, the Nash bargaining problem is not about how you arrive at a solution – it is solely about the content of the solution. This leaves the problem of *how* to arrive at a solution unaddressed and, therefore, unsolved by Nash.

For those not exposed to economic theory, Nash's assumptions seem naïve compared with the circumstances commonly found in real-world bargaining processes. Nash, for instance, assumes:

Rational bargaining 163

- highly rational bargainers who can accurately compare each other's desires for various things;
- bargainers who have equal 'bargaining skills';
- bargainers who have full knowledge of the tastes and preferences of the other; and
- bargainers who desire to maximise their gains in bargaining.

His model of bargaining uses numerical utility theory, which is an economist's way of 'measuring' the satisfaction, however defined, that an individual receives from possessing this or that set of goods. Nash, fortunately, provided an arithmetical example to demonstrate his solution. He refers to Bill and Jack, though they are not brothers, nor do they have a convenient adjudicator (their elder sister, Louise). That was my device to introduce you to the Nash solution.

Before trading, Bill and Jack enjoy various numerical utilities from their possessions (see Table 8.2). It is the differences in their priorities or valuations that enable Bill and Jack to solve their exchange problem. Because each of them wants something from the other, they can find mutually acceptable terms for the trade. The main difference between being in a negotiating process and defining a Nash solution is that the former have to work through a process to arrive at a solution, while Nash bargainers find the optimal solution without enduring the uncertainties of working through a process.

What I suggest we do is combine what we know about the negotiating process with what Nash solved almost 50 years ago. First, recall that in trading you exchange things that you value less (lower priorities) for things that you value more (higher priorities). Now ponder the arithmetical example used by Nash to illustrate his solution. By putting his example into a Negotek® PREP format, you can see directly how Bill and Jack accomplished their transactions. Prioritising into high, medium and low categories is a crude, though analogous, indicator of the relative valuation by Bill and Jack of the possessions available for trade. You simply stretch

Table 8.2 Utilities before trading

Bill's possessions	Utility for Bill	Utility for Jack if acquired
box	4	1
book	2	4
whip	2	2
ball	2	2
bat	2	2
	12	

Jack's possessions	Utility for Jack	Utility for Bill if acquired
pen	1	10
toy	1	4
knife	2	6
hat	2	2
	6	

164 *Rational bargaining*

Table 8.3 The Nash solution in a Negotek® PREP format

Bill's utilities		Jack's utilities		Priority
pen	10			high
	9			
	8			
	7			
knife	6			medium
	5			
box, toy	4	4	book	
	3			low
ball, whip, hat, book, bat	2	2	whip, ball, bat, knife	
	1	1	pen, box, toy	

the meaning of prioritising to indicate, in some way, the relative utilities of the goods to Bill and Jack.

First a brief note on 'utilities'. The book for Bill, for example, in Table 8.2 has a 'utility' of 2, and for Jack a 'utility' of 4. This does *not* mean that Jack values the book twice as much as Bill. Each individual compares the utilities of the possessions for themselves and not with each other. Crudely, take the utility of 4 to mean that, for Jack, Bill's book would have a greater amount of satisfaction (however Jack defines his satisfaction) than, say, Bill's ball (2), should he acquire these possessions. Meanwhile, for Bill, take the 2 to mean that his book has much less satisfaction (however Bill defines his satisfaction) than, say, Jack's pen (10), should he acquire it. By placing the utility rankings of 1 to 10 on the vertical axis, they align roughly with the three levels of priority: high utilities of 7–10, medium utilities of 4–6, and low utilities of 1–3, as shown in Table 8.3.

The slopes of the lines link the valuations of the possessions as they would appear if we contrasted their differing priorities for Bill and Jack. Items of low valuation to Jack, for example the pen (1), are higher on Bill's utility scale (i.e. 10). If both of them trade items of differing priorities, this confirms the particular exchange of items identified in the Nash bargain. Thus Bill, who values the pen highly (10), would be keen to exchange his book (say) for it, which is valued more highly by Jack (4) than his pen (1).

Given the utilities of their possessions, what exchange of the goods, asked Nash, would maximise their satisfaction after accounting for the loss of the utilities that they give up in the exchange? Nash postulated that the solution in this and every other case would be where the 'product of the utility gains is maximised'. The bargainers would agree to exchange the goods in whatever way that maximised their joint *gains* in utility.

For Bill and Jack, Nash asserted that they would trade as follows:

Bill gives Jack: book, whip, ball and bat
Jack gives Bill: pen, toy, and knife

Rational bargaining 165

This leaves Bill with his box and Jack with his hat. You should note that Bill would be unwilling to exchange his box for the hat because this would mean giving up a higher valued item for a lower valued item (i.e. Bill values his box at 4 and Jack's hat at 2). Jack is likewise unwilling to trade his hat for Bill's box, because he would be giving up his hat, which he values at 2, for Bill's box which he values at 1.

Exercise 8B

Can you explain how each trades the other items, using a similar argument? The summary details of the transaction are shown in Table 8.4.

Bill would be keen to exchange his ball and bat, say, for Jack's knife because he values the knife at 6 and his own ball and bat at 2 each, while Jack values the knife at 2 and he gets back a ball and bat worth 2 each, or 4 in total.

Nash (safely) assumes that the players will trade those goods that they value less for those that they value more (an important principle of bargaining). And as Bill and Jack have perfect information about each other's preferences, and, therefore, each knows the true value the other places on each possession, neither can bluff the other into 'paying' more for what they want.

Compared to their original utility positions (12 for Bill and 6 for Jack in Table 8.2) and given the utilities of the possessions they traded, they have both increased their utilities (to 24 for Bill and 12 for Jack). The product of their net gains in utility is $12 \times 6 = 72$. Nash affirmed that no other combination of traded possessions could produce a gain in utility that was greater than 72. The product of their net gains in utility was what it was worth to bargain.

That negotiators don't reach the Nash solution in practice is not a definitive refutation of Nash. Although his assumption on the behaviour of negotiators is unrealistic, his use of comparative priorities is something that all negotiators (consciously or subconsciously) do when considering exchanges. Natural biases and

Table 8.4 Net utility positions for Bill and Jack after trading across their varying priorities

Bill			Jack		
Goods received in trade	Utility		Goods received in trade	Utility	
	Gains	Loses		Gains	Loses
knife	6	2	book	4	2
pen	10	2	whip	2	1
toy	4	2	ball	2	1
		2	bat	2	
Total	20	−8	Total	10	−4
Net gains	12		Net gains	6	

errant behaviours can play a part in negotiators making less than optimal trades, but the basis of the Nash solution gives negotiators a clear guide on how exchanging goods we value less for goods we value more is where we should all be aiming as effective negotiators.

> **Learning point:**
>
> *We trade things we value less for things we value more.*

Looking at the Nash solution from the point of view of the dilemma games introduced in Chapter 7, we can see the idea of Nash attempting to move us all towards the win–win, non-zero-sum outcome. However, maximising joint gains as a bargaining objective is a minority choice of the thousands of negotiators playing the dilemma games that I have observed. Depressingly for the Nash solution, most bargainers behave as if they reject maximising joint gain as their objective in an, often futile, attempt to maximise their individual gains. The overwhelming majority of bargainers end up with sub-optimal, non-Nash, outcomes.

The benefits of bargaining

Negotiators have at least one common interest because the consequence of non-agreement means they must put up with the status quo instead of changing it in some way. As the benefits (however defined) of the status quo are available to both of them, without expending time and effort to negotiate a change, it follows that if they negotiate, it must be because they believe that they could be better off individually if they succeed in changing the status quo and, if they do succeed, then they are jointly better off too.

Apart from cooperating by negotiating, parties have common interests in a negotiated outcome. If they freely negotiate an outcome, then the benefits of their agreement will address some of the interests of each party. In so far as these interests benefit each party, they have a common interest in reaching and in implementing that agreement.

> *Two siblings, Morag and Andy, inherit their parents' farm and meet to decide how to divide it. They could agree to sell it and divide the proceeds. Now, suppose Morag is a farmer and wants to keep the family home as a working farm. Suppose Andy does not; he prefers his share of the money from selling the farm.*
>
> *It could be a stalemate, unless Morag can agree with her brother, say, that she keeps the farm and pays Andy a rental (how much?) for his half share. He agrees on condition that Morag takes sole responsibility for looking after Grandma and he gets their mother's Jaguar car.*

> Andy needs Morag's consent to pay him a regular income, to forego the Jaguar, and to take responsibility for Grandma; Morag, perhaps, wants the farm more than she wants the Jaguar. Alternatively, selling the farm at this time could mean a low price to be shared between them, with, perhaps, most of the money they raised having to go to fund Grandma's retirement in a home, rather than her continuing to live in the house that she has lived in for 80 years. In these circumstances, Andy and Morag (and Grandma) are better off if they can cut a deal.

Like other social skills, you negotiate with varying degrees of success. Your behaviour can also degenerate when you switch from voluntary trading to coercive relationships, or seek to manipulate perceptions by various forms of posturing. These defects are neither inevitable nor endemic in a negotiation process. Idealisation would suggest that two parties freely enter into a search for the terms upon which they can exchange what they value less for what they value more. If they find such terms, they agree; if they do not, the negotiation aborts, freeing both parties to attempt to contract with others. It also leaves them without the gains they could have made if they had found acceptable terms.

The real bargaining problem

The real bargaining problem lies in the dichotomy of **zero-sum** and **non-zero-sum**, or **non-cooperative** and **cooperative**, behaviours in negotiation. Achieving a maximisation of the net benefits in a Nash solution depends upon the behaviours of the bargainers, which in turn depend upon the coincidence, or otherwise, of their attitudes to bargaining.

Experience suggests that, in most cases, bargainers behave in ways that fail to maximise their potential gains. If you choose to be a **distributive** bargainer, you can only benefit at the other negotiator's expense. Only if you choose to be, *and meet with*, an **integrative** bargainer, can you both make joint gains at neither party's expense. This is a choice between being non-cooperative in behaviour or being cooperative, though, strictly, this is only a quasi-choice, because the gains you seek from your individual choice of behaviour are dependent on the other negotiator's choice of how she sees the appropriate behaviour to obtain her gains. This is the real bargaining problem – it's not just how people choose to behave that counts; it's how both independently choose to behave and then how their choices interact when they negotiate together.

Exchange can produce jointly created benefits, both tangible and intangible. That both benefit from agreement does not mean that it is, necessarily, a shared benefit. What benefits one may not have any corresponding benefits for the other. Benefits express themselves differently, use different currencies and may be invisible except to the party that receives them. Hence, there are two distinct methods of negotiation producing different solutions to the bargaining problem depending on the congruence, or otherwise, of the behaviours independently adopted by each of the negotiators. Not understanding this fact of life leads to many of the real problems you experience when negotiating. Idealising negotiation into a joint-gaining game, and acting as if your idealisation is always true, leads only to disappointment.

Lax and Sebenius (1986, *The Negotiator as Manager: Bargaining for Cooperation and Competitive Gain*, Free Press/Macmillan) make a revealing distinction between claimers and creators in negotiating. **Claimers** see negotiation as the distribution of a fixed amount between them and you. The bigger their share, the smaller is yours. It is a zero-sum transaction; what they gain, you lose. Where claiming predominates, manipulative ploys, tricks and power perceptions are the tactical imperatives of your behaviour, reaching their 'highest' level of competence in 'streetwise' negotiating.

Creators are different. There are three ways to create a joint gain.

First, an agreement that you both voluntarily enter into is likely to be better than no agreement at all, on the safe assumption that, as both of you have the right to veto any deal with which you are uncomfortable, it is the value created by the deals you agree to that makes you say 'yes' rather than 'no'. In saying 'no' to any deal, you prefer to forego what you would 'gain' from saying 'yes'.

Second, by accepting another deal, replacing the one that is unacceptable to one or both of you, it must create additional value to you both in some way. If it does not because, for instance, it made one of you worse off than no deal, the loser would veto it.

Third, negotiators, by iterating towards an agreeable deal that makes both of you better off, or no worse off, could create a previously unthought-of solution, which creates additional value.

That joint gains are possible from creating value, rather than merely distributing it, is unchallengeable. The real bargaining problem is that it is not easy in practice to do so and many (most?) negotiators behave in ways that make it unlikely that they will search jointly for opportunities for creative cooperative action. Thus, in practice, many potential gains are unrealised, and inferior 'solutions' are agreed.

This constitutes the essence of the real bargaining problem: if joint gains are preferable, how do bargainers achieve them, and why, we must ask, do so few negotiators seek them?

Learning point:

Recognising the tendency of players to behave as if a zero-sum gain is their objective alerts negotiators to the need to develop behaviours (through training, for example) that can successfully produce joint gains.

It is not all doom and gloom by a long way. The constant struggle between claiming and creating behaviours is the single most important feature of negotiation with which you will have to come to terms. There are no other routes open to practical negotiators. Acting as if Nash assumed behaviours are the behaviours of actual bargainers is naïve. Negotiators have a choice in the way they behave, and understanding the severe limitation of that choice – you are totally dependent on the other negotiator's choices – is the first step to proactively changing behaviour in the negotiation process towards the Nash solution.

Fisher and Ury on principled negotiation

Fisher and Ury's seminal work, *Getting to Yes: Negotiating Agreement Without Giving In* (1982, Century Hutchinson), has significantly influenced the theory and practice of joint problem-solving. Its prescriptive model is widely accepted among many practitioners in dispute resolution and mediation, though less so by practitioners of commercial negotiation.

Principled negotiation has a prescriptive sequence that is for a rational *individual* and not a negotiating *pair*. What works for the rational individual may be inadequate for the negotiating pair, if only because the pair are subject to conflicting prejudices and reactions to their interactions, whereas the individual can mediate between herself and her differing views on the options in private, and she can override certain of her private views (including rational views) by finding subjective reasons to justify whatever she decides to choose. In negotiation, most of this rationalising is necessarily in the semi-public domain. For instance, your justification for one option is subject to critical examination by the other negotiator.

The method of principled negotiation, write Fisher and Ury:

> is to decide issues on their merits rather than through a haggling process focused on what each side says it will and won't do. It suggests that you look for mutual gains wherever possible, and that where your interests conflict, you should insist that the result be based on some fair standards independent of the will of either side. The method of principled negotiation is hard on the merits and soft on the people. It employs no tricks and no posturing. Principled negotiation shows you how to obtain what you are entitled to and still be decent. It enables you to be fair while protecting you against those who would take advantage of your fairness.
>
> (p. xii)

Principled negotiation, or negotiation on the merits, asserts the debatable premise that traditional negotiation inevitably means positional bargaining, which, in turn, because of its alleged in-built defects, inevitably opens stressful fault lines between negotiators. Principled negotiation as a method, it is claimed, is the only alternative to the errors of positional bargaining. From Fisher and Ury's examples of these errors, however, they appear to confuse positional bargaining with positional posturing (where bargaining is certainly not manifest). Nevertheless, they enjoin practitioners to abandon traditional negotiation.

One example illustrates that positional posturing is not the same as positional bargaining. Fisher and Ury write:

> Each side tries through sheer willpower to force the other to change its position. 'I'm not going to give in. If you want to go to the movies with me, it's *The Maltese Falcon* or nothing'.
>
> (p. 7)

This is not evidence of positional *bargaining* at all. It is the antithesis of bargaining and perfectly describes posturing in the form of an ultimatum. If the listener gives in to the contest of wills, the outcome has none of the characteristics of a voluntary bargain nor is it the outcome of a process of negotiation. Contests of will are what happen when the parties fail to negotiate, not what happen because they do.

Fisher and Ury set up two extremes, 'hard' and 'soft' positional bargainers, to show that neither extreme can be 'efficient', or 'wise' or good for relationships ('bitter feelings generated by one such encounter can last a lifetime'). They also exclude the possibility of 'a strategy somewhere in between' the extremes, and they conclude that negotiators must change the 'game' of negotiation to the principled negotiation method (p. 13).

While practitioners can learn much from the method of principled negotiation, there is no need to throw the baby out with the bath water. You can reject the errors of positional posturing without rejecting the methods of traditional negotiation. By setting up two extremes and denying a third possibility, readers are driven to a forced conclusion, just as if our options as negotiators were governed by an algorithm.

As negotiators, we could decide to change the game from traditional to principled negotiation but only if it is to our benefit to do so. For the moment, I advise practitioners that they would be less than wise to abandon traditional negotiation just because of the avoidable (and objectionable) practices of positional posturing.

Fisher and Ury's prescriptions

Principled negotiation is a prescriptive method of negotiation to be 'used under almost any circumstance'. The four prescriptions are set out in Table 8.5. Its popularity is founded on these sensible strictures – they appeal to the good sense of people who want to resolve problems rationally and in good faith.

In examining the prescriptions of principled negotiation, I make some supportive as well as critical comments.

Table 8.5 The four prescriptions of principled negotiation

1	Separate the people from the problem.
2	Focus on interests, not positions.
3	Generate a variety of possibilities before deciding what to do.
4	Insist that the result be based on some objective standard.

Separate the people from the problem

There can be little to quibble about with what Fisher and Ury have to say on the people problem in negotiation, nor with their remedies, all of which are consistent with our advice on how to handle difficult negotiators and how to prevent others from becoming difficult, by adopting various assertive Blue-style behaviours to lead the other negotiator towards a joint problem-solving approach based on trading without giving in. At once, the appeal of principled negotiation is fully explained. This goes to the heart of the challenge to confrontational or adversarial approaches. People are often part of the problem (sometimes they are the problem!).

Everything people say is conditioned by who they are and the state of their relationship with you. They bring large emotional baggage with them too. When they throw this around during an interaction of any kind, it is more difficult for you to find a joint solution. Emotional baggage distorts perspective. Layers of abusive hostility make for poor problem-solving, and any advice to shift attention from the people to the problem is good advice, though like much good advice, it is difficult to apply if at least one of the parties is determined to keep it personal.

Emotional hurt from the collapse of relationships filters out good sense. In the heat of a conflict, you lose perspective. Normally decent people lose their self-control and behave beyond accepted frontiers of personal conduct. If you follow competitive sports at all, you will know how common it is for fired-up players to descend into unacceptable, even appalling, behaviour.

This is the bottom line, of course. Removing the people from the problem is a fine goal – and a necessary one to attempt, no doubt – but it is not so simple to enforce. The best you can do is make sure that on your side of the table you try to rise above personalities, whatever the other side decides to do.

If the prescription to separate the people from the problem requires that the parties cooperate in making it effective, this suggests that people problems are not standing in the way of solutions! The prescription is only required when people are in the way of creating the conditions to agree to a deal.

Focus on Interests not Positions

Much of what Fisher and Ury write on Red-style negotiating is absolutely on target. The adoption of inflexible Positions is clearly a barrier to negotiation, but in the Interests, Issues and Positions format, Positions are not a barrier in themselves, except when they are taken in isolation from the Issues that make up the agenda and that serve the overall Interests of the negotiators. Fisher and Ury prefer the parties to focus on Interests, not Positions, but Interests alone are not enough.

One Blue test of the commitment of the parties to keep to their promises is to be precise in the details, which means establishing the range of entry and exit Positions that would make the agreement acceptable to each side. This does not mean that, if the parties disagree, the negotiation collapses solely because of the difference in their Positions.

Positions are *what* we want, Interests are *why* we want them. The two are inseparable. Fisher and Ury appear to emphasise that the Interests of the negotiators are the only way to resolve disputes and to explore the acceptability of terms because attempting to resolve positional stances alone is likely to be unproductive. They are wrong, however, if they assume that considering the Interests of the parties removes the need to decide on Positions. As we shall see, Interests and Positions are not mutually exclusive; they are intertwined. It cannot be the case that Interests are good and that Positions are bad. That would be a profoundly silly error.

Issues are the agenda of the negotiation, expressed (normally) in Positions. It is not possible to negotiate without reference to Issues and Positions, except at the most general level of 'yes' or 'no'; but even that 'yes' or 'no' must come down to a reference to some Position, otherwise, to what are you saying 'yes' or 'no'?

Let us take the vexed question of a proposal to build a new runway at an airport, which is an event usually accompanied by intense controversy from those residents who are most immediately affected by the proposal. Some residents may decide against a proposed runway by how the new flight path affects their Interests in the quiet enjoyment of their property. It is their Interest that drives them not to want the runway, and the more their Interest in quiet enjoyment is affected – the closer, that is, their property is to the noise envelope of incoming and outgoing aircraft – the more likely that they will be against the proposal. Uncovering a party's Interests helps you to understand what they are about; identifying your own Interests likewise helps you to decide on your Positions on the negotiable Issues.

Not all people decide their Positions from their Interests. They could take a Position for or against the runway without considering their Interests first or at all. Some could deny that they had any personal Interests because they oppose the expansion of air travel facilities on grounds of political, or some other, principle.

The Issues are commonly addressed by some form of stance (build/not build; yes/no, etc.), and if the stances on the Issues, and the consequent alternative Positions that are possible on any one Issue, are in conflict, this creates the need for a process of dispute resolution.

If nobody took a stance on an Issue, there would be no dispute to resolve. What is non-controversial is not negotiated. Peace is the acceptance by all of the status quo. Disputes (from differences of view through to violence) arise when at least one person wants to change the status quo and at least one other person does not.

Negotiation is about the management of movement from conflicting positions towards an agreement, which often means getting beyond the positional posturing of some of the people with whom we must negotiate. To be sure, it helps in resolving disputes to focus on the Interests of the parties concerned, but it is not essential that we abandon traditional negotiation or positional bargaining to achieve a workable agreement.

Following the identification of Interests, Fisher and Ury recommend that you move from 'your interest to concrete options'. Now, what are 'concrete options' but just another name for Positions? Traditional negotiations accommodate such a progression from Interests to Positions, as shown in the Negotek® PREP planner. They also advise you to think in terms of 'illustrative specificity'. Again, what does 'illustrative specificity' mean if it is not yet another word for a Position? They assert that: 'Much of what positional bargainers hope to achieve with an opening position can be accomplished equally well with an illustrative suggestion that generously takes care of your interest' (p. 55). This is excellent advice, even though it uses words like 'concrete options' and 'illustrative specificity' to avoid admitting that the principled negotiator, sooner or later, must move from considering Interests to that of considering Positions.

They also insist that the principled negotiator must 'be concrete but flexible'; that is, in the terminology of traditional bargaining, it means to be specific in your opening Position but flexible enough to move along a range of Positions in search of agreement. Principled negotiation, on these admissions, is only a special case of positional bargaining, complete with negotiation ranges and entry and exit points. I have long found it remarkable that the negotiating literature has ignored Fisher and Ury's affinities with what they criticise.

Learning point:

Whether you focus on Interests or Issues in particular negotiations is a tactical question and not a principle.

Long-running disputes between two separate communities living in close proximity are examples of where it might be better to switch from considering the overall Interests of each side to negotiating on specific and immediate Issues. How do you reconcile differences that affect every aspect of the culture and lifestyles of their respective communities? We cannot hold our breath until a longer term accommodation is found when the two adjacent communities are so riven with conflicts of interest that they are in danger of slipping into violent confrontations, necessitating the intervention of the police to protect law and order. In these circumstances, negotiation on Issues is about here and now; negotiation on Interests might take a while longer.

You cannot avoid the immediate Issues and Positions in these conflicts because the disputed Issues are driven by the Interests behind them. As neither side will forego its principles or amend them, your attention must switch to what can be done about the disputed Issues.

You might be able to negotiate, for instance, an arrangement that determines for how many minutes a public road is free of cars on school mornings and afternoons so that parents and children from the other community can walk to and from school safely and unmolested. Residents can absent themselves from the roads for a short while without it becoming an issue of civil liberty. If some people feel strongly about it, they can seek redress through the courts, hopefully, in full knowledge of the consequences for the losers, civil liberties. Such disputes, obviously, can develop into severe civil unrest. What starts with verbal abuse leads to stone throwing, road blocking and eventually to petrol bombs. Demanding that one side or the other abandons their interests and beliefs is a ruinous route to civil disorder.

You cannot negotiate principles (if we could, they would not be principles!), but we can negotiate their application. To do this successfully you must be prepared to negotiate details, which implies negotiating ranges on your positions on the Issues. For the immediate negotiation, appealing to Interests may be less productive than concentrating on the details of a compromise.

This has long been a part of British diplomatic practice. In circumstances where it is near impossible to discuss the substantive differences between two hostile parties because of their bitterly opposed beliefs and histories, it can help to move things forward by focusing on the 'heads of a potential agenda' for the discussions. If the 'bigger' picture is fraught with pain, let us try looking at the 'smaller' picture to ease the pain while making progress on the details.

The reverse applies if you are stuck on an Issue: can you make progress by turning to the 'bigger picture' and to the Interests of the parties? Traditional negotiators are not frozen into either Interests or Issues. A dose of pragmatism is the antidote to restrictive negotiating practice. The negotiator should adapt her negotiating method to suit the circumstances and not try to suit the circumstances to her preferred negotiating method.

Invent options for future gain

Like the previous prescriptions, this one is widely accepted by practitioners, though less widely applied, largely because of the constraints imposed by higher policy-makers who often direct the negotiation activities and overtly restrict their negotiator's scope for movement. The extreme rational theorist argues in favour of surveying all of the options in any management decision process; the practitioner would likely retort that this is just not practical most of the time. But, to be fair, this is not what Fisher and Ury are prescribing. They are advising negotiators to do more than just accept what appear to be the only two competing solutions on the table, particularly as these may be narrowly framed and also, as they stand, mutually exclusive.

The principle of inventing options for mutual gain is a worthwhile activity and one that has been put to good use in quality improvement programmes, where a 'no-blame' diagnosis of a quality problem, involving everybody concerned, irrespective of rank, enables a frank attack on the cause of the problem with remedies to which everybody is committed. The tentative and uncommitted proposal phase of negotiation (following signals) can encompass Fisher and Ury's advice in this respect (brainstorming, joint brainstorming and the circle chart) to good effect, providing that the parties can shift from a Red stance towards a Blue stance.

Once the Interests of the parties are illuminated, other possibilities for solving the problem are highlighted. There is usually more than one possible solution, other than the first ones generated by the parties, particularly as their first reaction to a problem is usually to enter the negotiation with their least accommodating positions (it's called giving themselves generous negotiating room!). Recasting the problem by reference to Interests enables other options for a solution at least to be considered. Behaviourally, this requires a suspension of judgement while the possible options are identified and listed.

Brainstorming sessions are recommended for you to identify the options. Initially, you can conduct this with your own colleagues but, if confidence levels are high, a joint brainstorming session with the other negotiator is suggested. The rules are the same for a single or a joint session: no idea is too silly, nor rejected because of who suggested it, and all judgement is suspended until the well of ideas dries up. This atmosphere is reckoned to create the right conditions for looking at problems from new perspectives. Deadlocks can be broken by relatively risk-free consideration of other people's ideas.

How rich the well of ideas and options that emerge from brainstorming sessions depends on the size of the problem, the extent to which 'big-picture' macro-level solutions dominate over 'little-picture' micro-level solutions. Switching from the 'yes versus no' decisions based on conflicting principles, to the conditions under which a 'yes' or 'no' decision could operate, opens up lots of flexible possibilities, some of which could induce the parties to some mutual accommodation between their mutually exclusive initial principled positions.

Consider the dispute over whether the new airport runway can be built and the impossibility of reconciling a blanket 'yes' with a blanket 'no' at the local level. Higher level policy-makers – the government, for instance – may legislate over the heads of the local community in the 'national interest', and if they get away with this politically (not assured in a democracy), that could end the dispute.

On the way to the government securing the necessary legislative authority to implement their decision, the local residents can impose a price upon the nation for their acquiescence in an outcome conceived by them as contrary to their interests. In the extreme, as in the 2019 Hong Kong demonstrations, violent protests can heighten the tensions and shift from a focus on the extradition bill interests at stake to a test of the final authority of the State.

A brainstorming session on the micro problems raised by the local residents could produce various options palatable to them and the authorities. For instance, if the Interests of the residents have been identified – remember, Interests are the reasons, motives, concerns or fears that motivate the residents in this case to say 'no' – micro policy responses can be addressed if the parties are willing to try them. This can be done by the authorities (if they have any sensitivity or political acumen) or by the residents (if positions have not hardened to the point where to contemplate searching for other options is treated as a treachery by one's neighbours). In either case, it is a way forward, which is what motivates the principled negotiator.

Those in favour of the runway should consider meeting as many as possible of the objections of those whose Interests lead them to oppose the runway proposal as it presently stands. Among these objections will be the following (Table 8.6).

176 *Rational bargaining*

Table 8.6 Airport runway

The residents living within the noise footprint of the aircraft	They can be generously compensated with double or triple glazing and other sound-proofing measures, or their properties bought at fair market value.
The impact of airborne pollution	This can be treated by specifying and enforcing non-spillage standards for re-fuelling and tighter lean engine burn.
The effect on sleeping patterns	This can be addressed by restricting flying hours and engine noise levels.
The effect of increased airport-related traffic	This can be ameliorated by road re-design and landscape investments.

None of these options alone may be sufficient to break a mass consensus against an airport proposal, but together, with the micro details fully aired, they might be sufficient to reduce hostility to the proposals to manageable levels, even reducing opposition to the futile condemnations of a small, isolated minority. It is seldom possible to please everybody, but then you don't need to.

Again, the method of principled negotiation finds its best expression in assisting in the sorting out of public disputes. Just how far it is applicable to the myriad of small one-on-one negotiations that dominate private decision-making is debatable.

Insist on objective criteria

In my view, the fatal flaws of principled negotiation hide in this prescription. And these flaws cause the same frustrations that lead to positional posturing.

The prescription to agree to objective criteria is comfortable for those with a judicial mindset. Justice depends on objective criteria for consistently applying appropriate remedies when the facts have been established to the satisfaction of a jury. In some countries, the law is codified into specific criteria about what constitutes a criminal act, and, by default, what does not. In other countries, the law depends upon the precedents set by earlier courts judging the remedies that are applicable to the same or similar facts.

When we consider the principle of an insistence on objective criteria, however, we reach a potentially serious problem. The idea and intention is excellent; its universal application is doubtful. Why? Because the parties are likely to be partisan to different criteria, the selection of which would influence the outcome for or against them. Much of Fisher's training in the principles of law is apparent here. Legal issues are decided, in theory, by the test of whether the alleged events constitute a crime against a set of legal criteria (statute or precedent). The best brains in the legal profession make the best of their client's case. A crime is defined from proving, 'beyond reasonable doubt', etc., intent and action: the accused's guilt rides on whether his attorney can sow reasonable doubt that his client had no such defined intent or that he did not commit the alleged act, and on whether the prosecution can demonstrate the contrary. If it is difficult in practice to show this one way or another in a court of law – subject as it is to rigorous procedures and standards of debate – how much more difficult is it for negotiators operating in places and on cases where neither of these conditions is present?

When the authors of principled negotiation include the necessity for deciding disputed issues on objective criteria, they are introducing judicial methods into negotiation. What could be surer of rational support than insisting that decisions made by negotiation should conform to a basic principle of natural justice, namely, that the criteria for a decision should be objective for those who are to submit to its governance and not be the result of pressure or the whims of powerful individuals?

But what might work for the justice system may not work for the process of negotiation as it operates around the world, including in those societies where the rule of law is more of a lottery than a reality. Agreeing on objective criteria to settle a dispute has great rational appeal but does it have practical substance in a negotiation?

Principled negotiation sets a high and admirable standard by its insistence on objective criteria, but it cannot set a norm. Criteria are often controversial, as are 'facts', and we must accept that negotiators have to handle the practical problems as they arise in unscripted, private interactions where there is no body of precedent, no bench of independent judges and precious few people willing to forego the protection of their interests to some third party's objective facilitators.

It does not require an Einstein to make the connection between agreeing to use objective criteria and the predetermination of an outcome based on that criteria. Indeed, Bob, who cannot spell his name backwards, would have no trouble realising the implication of accepting a prior commitment to using 'objective' criteria. He would either resist the notion altogether, or he would endeavour to import whatever selective criteria best suited the solution he wanted, with, no doubt, his opposite number doing exactly the same in support of his contrary case.

Fisher and Ury's prescription 'solves' the persistent problem that negotiators tend to select criteria that support their own preferred outcomes, and thereby they produce a clash of solution criteria every bit as intractable as a clash over positions, by inventing a plausible, but impractical, device of the 'convenient third party', who just happens to be available to uncover objective criteria for resolving the disputes they cite in their text. Some examples will suffice:

- In the case of two partners designing their future home, there is a helpful architect who takes away their ideas – some of which are mutually conflicting – and re-designs the house to meet their expressed criteria.
- In a union–management dispute they cite there is a 'facilitator'.
- In a playground dispute over a ball, the teacher is on hand to help decide whose turn it is.

A principled negotiation apparently is no longer one between the two parties alone because an additional third party appears who gets them to an agreement based on the objective criteria he or she introduces. I find their examples unconvincing as a guide to the solution of the daily negotiations entered into by the rest of us for whom there is no convenient facilitator to hand.

Most private negotiating parties do not allow for third-party interventions because neither time nor resources permit a role for them. Left to the parties, predictable differences in objective criteria take them back to positional bargaining and they will only agree to objective criteria that predetermine the outcome in their favour, unless they are tricked into agreeing otherwise.

Negotiations I have participated in provide much evidence that each side, not surprisingly, selects criteria for settlement that are heavily loaded to support their own interests. Competing objective criteria often are immovable and can lead to the fallacious rhetoric of positional posturing. Battles over criteria need not improve the rationality of negotiators at all. They are just another facet of the bargaining process problem.

Principled negotiators who insist on joint agreement on the objective criteria by which an outcome is to be determined simply ignore the fact that much of the debate phases of negotiation are precisely a contest between the competing criteria selected by each party. To expect them to search for objective criteria to resolve the dispute is unrealistic because differences in positions usually reflect differences in the criteria they adopt to justify their positions. An individual making a rational decision probably can develop objective criteria because they only have to satisfy themselves. But negotiation is about joint decisions between more than one party which raises the complexity of the task by several magnitudes. The way through the dilemma is for the negotiators to trade themselves out of the impasse.

All that the search for agreed objective criteria achieves is to shift the focus of the negotiators' debate from their positions on the issues to their positions on their criteria for settlement. In an ideal world that may be a step forward, but in reality it achieves little for practical negotiators, particularly when the solution criteria are as controversial as their positions.

A dispute over which criteria to select could be just as unrewarding as a dispute over which position to adopt. Principled negotiation once again slides into a special case of positional bargaining.

BATNA

One of principled negotiation's main contributions to negotiating practice has been the idea of a negotiator's BATNA: Best Alternative to No Agreement. Basically, BATNA asks the negotiator to consider the very best that could happen if he fails to make a deal, and to compare the deal on offer with that alternative. This is a deceptively simple but very neat idea for it provides negotiators with a means of deciding the basis on which they would agree or walk away from a bargain. Understanding your BATNA should be part of the preparation phase of the negotiation (see Chapter 3).

The negotiator as mediator

In the absence of a third-party mediator, which for the overwhelming bulk of negotiations we must accept as fact, is there anything we can do if the parties are stuck on the Issues (positional bargaining) or on the Interests (principled negotiation) or on both (traditional negotiation)?

The absence of a third-party mediator in a deadlocked negotiation requires that one of the parties considers taking over that role – at least attitudinally. This is not easy, not least because the idea incorporates a number of serious contradictions.

Mediation:

Intervention by an acceptable, impartial and neutral third party, who has no authoritative decision-making power, to assist the disputing parties in voluntarily reaching their own mutually acceptable settlement of the issues in dispute.

This definition of mediation shows that it does not take much experience of negotiation to know that neither of the negotiators fits the definition. For a start, as a negotiator, you are neither 'impartial' nor 'neutral', which is why you have deadlocked! Together, you certainly have 'authoritative decision-making power', provided your power to decide is exercised jointly and not singly. The notion that one of you would knowingly permit the other to 'intervene' in the manner prescribed for mediation is most unrealistic.

In summary, when there is no third party available, what is proposed by the notion of the negotiator as mediator involves one of you acting as a surrogate third party without the knowledge or awareness of the other. But can you perform the role of a mediator while remaining one of the negotiators? On the surface I would doubt whether you can.

Bill Ury makes a thought-provoking point that, when in a deadlock, you should 'go to the balcony'. This is like taking the age-old advice of 'putting yourself in their shoes' but with an added twist. From your mental balcony, you are enjoined to look 'down' at both of you and not just across a table at the other negotiator from the same level. Behind this idea is the observation that people who are in the thick of a dispute see the issues differently to those who are looking at it from the outside. When involved 'eyeball to eyeball', so to speak, you are more emotionally committed to what is going on, and what you believe is likely to happen, than when you are not so emotionally involved. The mental act of 'going to the balcony' may weaken that emotional involvement just enough for you to glimpse what is blocking progress both on your side and theirs.

Attitudinally, you should accept that other people have Interests that are as important and valid for them as your Interests are important and valid for you. This does not mean that you have to agree that their Interests necessarily override your own – this is not about becoming a Blue submissive! But by reminding yourself of this you might want to explore ways of meeting their Interests in the course of meeting your own. The deadlock is caused by the proposed solutions of the problem not meeting enough (or any) of the Interests of each party, and the act of reviewing the shortfall should itself produce some new thoughts on how to correct the current weaknesses in the existing proposals.

The fact that Interests may be traded implies they can be prioritised in the same manner as Issues. What are the other party's priorities among their Interests? To prioritise, you must first identify their Interests. Remember, their Interests are uncovered by asking 'why?' they propose this or oppose that proposal or position. From the balcony, you may be able to 'see' what it is they are concerned about, whereas, at the table, you may be so engaged in the inconvenience of their opposition that you cannot 'see' what lies behind their contrary stances.

A third-party mediator would explore this agenda in private meetings with each party, but as one of the negotiators you do not have licence to access them in the formal role of an agreed mediator. The more convincing you are in the role of trying to see the world through their eyes – the more you 'disarm' them – the more you will learn about the game they think you both are playing.

Understanding the other party's deeper Interests and their perspectives of the world should enable you to make changes to your proposals by reframing them to accord more with their aspirations and to lower their threat perceptions of what you are about. They are more likely to say 'yes' to movement if you address their Interests than if you irritate their inhibitions. The latter deserves what it usually gets – a resounding 'no'.

In the role of a negotiator as mediator, you try to 'rise above the fray', to search productively for agreement without compromising your role as one of the participating negotiators. Nothing outlined above should suggest that this is going to be easy or that it will necessarily work. It is only indicative of a line of approach when faced with the alternative of persisting in deadlock.

Conclusion

Principled negotiation is an insightful process, but it is not the alternative to traditional negotiation that its proponents celebrate. As a sub-set of traditional negotiation, principled negotiation makes a valuable contribution to negotiating practice and especially to dispute resolution and problem-solving. Abandoning traditional negotiation methods, however, in favour of the exclusive use of the four prescriptions of principled negotiation could be a serious error.

Principled negotiation is largely about the conduct of mediation, conciliation, counselling or joint problem-solving, and it provides several useful insights into the avoidance of negative outcomes by applying its four main prescriptions. Closely allied with rational problem-solving methods, principled negotiation is mainly about uncovering the layers of distrust and other inhibitions of the parties in dispute by using these methods, rather than the Purple conditional exchange principle. In this one sense, it is an alternative to traditional negotiation but it cannot replace it.

It is preferable to see principled negotiation as another decision-making technique, appropriate in some circumstances but not in others, neither superior nor inferior to traditional negotiation, and one of several ways of making a decision. It is not a panacea for the failings of other decision-making processes, nor is it guaranteed to resolve all of the world's intractable problems. Where principled negotiation is able to make a contribution to solving certain problems, it must be welcomed, but we must also recognise its limitations for resolving many negotiating problems.

Much of the influence of Fisher and Ury has been on the broader, macro, world political issues. They are very popular among liberal radicals who have prescriptive views on how the world should be reorganised. The fact that they have a highly plausible and well-presented model for how negotiations should be conducted adds much to their certainties that, if only the world were different (i.e. shaped according to their own perceptions), it would be much easier to get from the lose–lose square in the dilemma game diagram to the win–win square.

Interestingly, both Fisher and Ury, in separate and subsequent books to *Getting to Yes*, have co-authored with other people extensions of their theme of principled negotiation to address the problem of relationship building (Fisher and Scott Brown, 1989, *Getting Together: Building a Relationship that Gets to Yes*, Hutchinson) and dispute resolution (Ury, Jeanne Brett and Stephen Goldberg, 1988, *Getting Disputes Resolved: Designing Systems to Cut the Cost of Conflict*, Jossey-Bass). This indicates that a large investment in restructuring the context of a negotiated relationship might be required before principled negotiation can be applied generally, and somewhat restricts its applicability to the relatively unstructured context of business negotiation.

Checkpoint 8

8.1 *Why are John Nash's assumptions on bargaining so unrealistic?*

8.2 *Fisher and Ury suggest that their principled negotiation is suitable for all types of negotiations. Do you consider this to be true?*

8.3 *What does BATNA stand for, and what does it mean?*

9 Ploys and tactics

Introduction

> *'It's not the most profitable deal'*, moaned Jeff.
>
> No, but once we have their agreement to buy the Digg200, we can easily get them to spend more money by pushing the extras. For example, they will need the purpose-built DiggItTool to help with maintenance at an extra £400, also delivery charge of £150, not forgetting extended warranty at £250 for 3 years and, if they really want to keep it looking good, there is the CarePack for an extra £399. Before they realise it, we will have doubled the order value. And that, Jeff, is how we make money,
>
> explained Archie.
>
> *'Won't the customer complain or go elsewhere? It seems a little underhanded'*, said Jeff.
> *'It happens occasionally, but mostly we win the business, and it's so much more profitable when we do'*, replied Archie.

If this sounds a little unethical to you, you might be right, or if you are dealing with a Red negotiator, you might be seen to be a little naïve. The practice of manipulative ploys is common. The users aim to manipulate the outcome of a deal in their favour by changing the natural flow of the negotiation.

Learning about ploys

Most repetitive interactive activities, such as negotiation, develop a 'rules-of-thumb' approach to the induction of new entrants to the activity and to the learning process. What works and what does not work are expressed in the accumulated knowledge of experienced, hard-bitten, old hands in the business. New hands usually learn by 'sitting next to Al' and watching what Al does. Those who survive to become old hands in any activity do so because of their innate, or learned, skills and because they have adapted quickly to the exigencies of their craft. This is true of footballers and of business negotiators.

It is possible, and indeed it has long been the norm, for a person to become an experienced and effective negotiator in his chosen field without any formal induction into, or analysis of, the business. Even today, for example, the majority of solicitors have no formal training in negotiation, yet this probably takes up more of their time outside formal legal work than any of their other non-professional activities. Indeed, it is hard to imagine a competent solicitor who cannot negotiate.

For practitioners, there is a demand for 'streetwise' advice on how to cope with their daily work. At one of my workshops, I asked if there were any areas I had not covered in the session, and a voice from the back said: 'Give me some dirty tricks, that's what I need right now'. My message about styles of negotiation had obviously not got through to him!

The market for streetwise advice, however, has been addressed by several presenters of highly polished and professional seminars over the years, and to some extent, they convey the impression that negotiation is a form of gladiatorial contest in which the strong thrive and the weak go to the wall (unless the weak attend one of their seminars first!). Many extol the virtues and benefits of using ploys and tricks to 'win' the negotiation, some have elaborate tales that prove how well they did when using them and others build their entire workshop on the premise that manipulation can benefit the outcome. What many will not discuss is the reason why the use of any ploy is not a long-term strategy, but (perhaps) a short-term gain. Once you are known for using a ploy, its value is removed.

The buying team from a large national retailer were well known for their tactic of walking out of a negotiation if they didn't get the price reduction they demanded. After a few iterations of this ploy, the selling team started to pad their prices to allow for discounting to bring the buying team back in, after they had walked out.

So knowledge of ploys is not discussed in this book to encourage you to use them – far from it. There is a hugely positive value that a knowledge of ploys can have for a negotiator: a ploy recognised is a ploy disarmed, and, in the fortunate context that almost every ploy has a counter, it is incumbent on you as a negotiator to know how to handle yourself when face to face with another negotiator who thinks he has got your measure. A purely ploy approach to a negotiation – which is how some workshop delegates narrow it down – is foolish and short sighted.

> **Learning point:**
>
> *We learn about ploys to understand them and how to counter them, NOT so that we can use them.*

Negotiation has always had associations with devious and manipulative ploys that vary from the secretively sly through to openly barefaced rip-offs, so negotiating with 'streetwise' manipulators is risky. Hard-pressed sales and purchasing

184 Ploys and tactics

people, who are out to do better, or do just well enough to keep their jobs, learn how to deal with tricksters. And if they can't see the particular ploy you are using at this moment, that is only because you are so devious that they haven't spotted it – yet. Before long they become convinced that every seller is a manipulative trickster.

Hence, becoming 'streetwise' is another approach to negotiation, both for students and for practitioners. A genre has grown up where manipulation is discussed, dissected and, in extreme cases, recommended to negotiators without reference to the competing approaches of negotiation as a phased process, or to the prescriptions of principled negotiation.

Students of negotiation are in a bind: we must study ploys because, like influenza and sore throats, they are a fact of life. Ploys are common enough in negotiations for you to need to be aware of their consequences for your interests if the other negotiators who use them are 'successful'. The danger is that in your disappointment about manipulative conduct, when you feel cheated, you are tempted to replicate on others the same moves that resulted in what you suffered. Those negotiators who express a preference for manipulative negotiation claim that they manipulate others because others manipulate them. They claim they manipulate only to protect themselves (does this sound familiar? 'I play Red ploys not because I want to, but because I must!'). All manipulative players, however, attempt to exploit you and you should heavily discount any excuse you hear about their desire only to protect themselves. What is more, their excuses are irrelevant. What they do – how they behave – is more important than uncheckable claims about their intentions. Bad behaviour only looks good to somebody with a proclivity to avoid looking in mirrors.

All ploys aim to influence your expectations of the negotiated outcome. Your expectations of a negotiated outcome derive from your perceptions of the other party's power over you. Briefly, if you believe that your power over me is high, you are likely to be bullish about the outcome. You expect to do better than in the opposite case, where your perceptions of your power over me are low. The more powerful that you feel I am, the less well you expect to do. Figure 9.1 illustrates the relationship. Power perceptions run left to right, from low to high, and your expectations of the outcome run right to left, from low to high. It is in practice an inverse relationship: the less power you believe that I have, the higher your expectation of the outcome in your favour.

Your perceptions of power are subject to all kinds of influences, some mere whims and fancies, a few with substance. Observation suggests that people make assessments of relative power on the flimsiest of data. The ploy merchant takes advantage of your neglect of real evidence. They manipulate the context and the environment to portray their power over you as greater than it is.

For years, in seminars all over the world, I have asked my father's 'Camel Question', including in countries where camels are a common bargaining currency. Most negotiators get it wrong the first time. Try it now by marking the answer you think is closest to your immediate reaction.

Figure 9.1

```
                Your perceptions of their power
Low  ┌─────────────────────────────→─────────┐ High
     │╲                                       │
     │ ╲                                      │
     │  ╲                                     │
     │   ╲                                    │
     │    ╲                                   │
     │     ╲                                  │
     │      ╲                                 │
     │       ╲                                │
High └────────←───────────────────────────────┘ Low
              Your expectations of the outcome
```

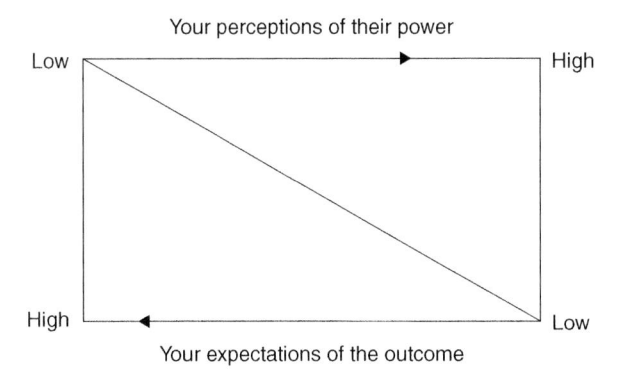

Figure 9.1 Relationship between your perceptions of power and your expectations of the outcome.

Exercise 9A

A man with six camels approaches an oasis in search of water, where another man stands beside a sign: 'Water, all you can drink, price one camel'.
  Who has the power?

a) *the man with the camels?*
b) *the man with the water?*
c) *impossible to say?*

(A similar version of this question was originally published in Everything is Negotiable, *by Gavin Kennedy, 1982, Random House.)*

Answer: Neither (a) nor (b) is a correct answer. The additional information that imaginative participants at seminars sometimes invent and rely upon to make their decision is absent from the 'Camel Question' question.

This is the point. Without more data, you cannot sensibly make an assessment of the relative power of the two men. Yet the majority who choose answers (a) or (b) do just that! And from observation, and not a little introspection, I think we all fall into the error of judging who has power on severely limited data from time to time. You often accord greater relative power to other negotiators than the context warrants, and you lower your expectations accordingly. In short, you end up negotiating with yourself. You accept less than you might because you expect less than you could realise, if only you approached the negotiation in a different frame of mind.

No wonder manipulative behaviour exploits this very human weakness! It would require a mass resistance to temptation not to exploit opportunities to influence other peoples' expectations. If an opportunity exists to gain from behaving in a certain way, somebody will behave that way. Power is the ability to get someone to do what they otherwise would not do, and manipulative ploys and tricks are about making people do more than they otherwise would. In short, manipulation coerces you to concede more.

Three types of ploys

All ploys belong to one of three main types: dominance, shaping and closing.

Achieving **dominance** from an early stage enables one party to set the tone and the tempo (not to say the temper) of the following sessions. It coincides with the most conflict-ridden phase of negotiation because the struggle for dominance involves conflict-enhancing behaviours.

Characteristically, dominance behaviour is about defending extreme positions, appearing to be intransigent by design, revealing narrow grounds for manoeuvre – if any – and generally bullying 'opponents' (which accurately describes how manipulators see and portray the other negotiators) into early concessions, or into revising how far they will have to move to get a settlement.

In the middle phases of negotiation, with the concentration of the parties on debating the parameters of a possible settlement (signalling, proposing, packaging and bargaining), numerous opportunities appear that can **shape** the deal. This is where ploys flourish, and the literature abounds with ploys to shape the perceptions of what is possible and to shape expectations of what is likely. Some are outrightly dishonest and do not have any ethical justification whatsoever. They are about cheating in its crudest form, and negotiators who use them are using disreputable methods – true 'dirty' tricks.

Certain ploys flourish in the end game, or the **close**, of the negotiation and are about *pressuring* the opponent to settle on the last offer. Some of them are well known and obvious but still work in the right circumstance when used against those who do not notice what is being done to them.

Ploys range in sophistication from the subtle to the obvious. Most are well known, but what is more important, they all have counters, which you can use to defeat the ploy's purpose of tricking you into giving far more away than you intended. To combat the use of ploys, you need to neutralise their effects. That begins with understanding their purpose and the intentions of people who rely upon them. A ploy neutralised is a ploy defeated. To neutralise a ploy, you must first identify it. Your options from then on are to expose the ploy or to counter it. Exposing a ploy risks embarrassing the perpetrator, which may concern you if you wish to maintain the relationship and because the outcome is more important to you than 'winning' an ego contest. There is another risk worthy of consideration. Exposing what you believe is a ploy could be disastrous if it is not a ploy. Instead, it could be that it was a genuinely unintentional and fair move as seen by the other negotiator. Accusing people of 'crimes' they have not committed, or crimes they plausibly can deny, are short routes to interpersonal disasters.

Neutralising a ploy seems by far the better response, with some slight risk that they interpret your neutralising move as your ploy. Fortunately, to neutralise a ploy normally only requires that you identify it, which you can keep, of course, to yourself. How can you recognize it? You don't have to be able to identify which ploy it is; rather, if the course of the negotiation is going quite differently to how you thought it would, stop and ask yourself, 'Am I being manipulated?' It can be as simple as taking a minute to think before being drawn in to the ploy; it gives you the space to consider and act to counter instead.

A survey of all the known ploys would be exhausting to tabulate and probably would not be exhaustive enough to cover all their possible variations. Chester Karrass comes close with an 'A to Z' listing (1974, *Give and Take: The Complete Guide to Negotiating Strategies and Tactics*, Thomas Y. Crowell), which is worth dipping into for elucidation of the craft of ploys from a major contributor to the teaching and practice of negotiation.

Dominance ploys

Those of a bullish disposition feel the need for **dominance** in the opening debate phases of negotiation. They need to dominate to control the situation. This goal of control also inspires another group of people who need to dominate. Their inexperience of handling tough (for them) decisions, in which there is a real prospect of other people saying 'no' rather than 'yes', fires their need to dominate. They push for dominance to limit the prospect of any other decision than the one they want, just in case you are awkward enough to say 'no'.

Props

Many of the plays for dominance begin before the negotiations really get under way. Of course, ploys are not always verbal; some come in the fashion of 'props', which can be used to scene set. These include all those symbols, signs and stage settings that create an image of the power balance between you and the other party, aimed at softening you up to induce you to move the most.

Sales negotiators are familiar with the props deployed by buyers to intimidate you into negotiating with yourself. In business, they use props on a grand scale. Dominance is intimidation, and while the props are less active and obvious than the verbal versions, nevertheless, they are as powerful on your perceptions and can be even more powerful for being so subtle.

Have you ever been to a meeting to find yourself sitting in a (slightly) lower chair across from the other party? It can have the effect of leaving you feeling intimidated, perhaps taking you back to your school days when you also sat on very small chairs in front of the teacher. Subtle, but effective. The remedy? Understanding why the props are there is a good place to start. They are there to make a statement about them to you. You are visiting them and they have all this splendour around them. What do you have in contrast? If the comparison is unfavourable, and you notice this enough to covet their surroundings, it's a 'gotcha'. You have taken the first step to lowering your sights.

Better to remind yourself that splendid foyers, complete with fountains, atriums and super-silent glass lifts, are the early signs of insolvency (followed closely by company jets and helicopters, yachts and a penchant for the fast life). Overcome your envy with pity and determine that such props are an incentive for you to up your prices and to insist on cash up front.

Pre-conditions

When face to face, or just before it, the verbal dominance ploys begin, as if on cue. The **pre-conditions** ploy sets the scene between you. Either you meet the conditions and comply, or there is no purpose in meeting. Their pre-conditions include insistence on 'vendor's contracts only', 'assignment of intellectual property rights', 'prohibitions on working for competitors', and such like. These are tricky ones. Pre-conditions are tried in extremely difficult negotiations where the parties have a history, often a bloody one, and each side demonstrates its reluctance to negotiate their differences by attempting to impose a pre-condition.

To be sure, some pre-conditions enable the parties to accept negotiation as the solution to their problems. Distinguishing between blatant ploys and trust-building measures is a matter of circumstance and context. 'No negotiations under duress', or 'No negotiations with terrorists', can be ploys to stop negotiations beginning by creating insurmountable barriers between the parties, thus adding another problem to the one that causes them to be under duress. This pre-condition ploy demands the (unlikely) surrender of the strikers or the terrorists, which is OK only if you can break the strike or defeat the terrorists.

As confidence-building measures, some pre-conditions and the willingness of the parties to accept them create the right conditions for a negotiation to begin. Those pre-conditions that are part of a propaganda war between the parties are not about confidence building. They are simply part of the wider conflict between them. Negotiating the release of some hostages – the sick, the young, the aged, etc. – is a useful pre-condition to build confidence between the terrorists and the authorities for the more difficult negotiations that must follow. In business, similar pre-conditions can be a useful test of intentions.

Non-negotiable

Closely aligned to the pre-conditions ploy is the assertion that some issues are '**non-negotiable**'. This widely used ploy prohibits re-negotiation of the fixed terms and conditions insisted on by powerful vendors and buyers. Taking vendors first, included in the non-negotiable issues are their 'standard terms of sale', often printed in closely set type (I have seen them printed in grey ink, making them almost invisible!). Whether you accept that they are non-negotiable depends a great deal on how you perceive the relative power balance.

Before mainframe computers became a commodity item, the big vendors, such as IBM, Digital, SUN, etc., imposed vendors' contracts on their customers. As substitution into other forms of computing power became prevalent, the major customers of these suppliers, often large public utilities and government departments, insisted on contracts that included *emptor* clauses, and, in time, they insisted on buyers' contracts only. Now the buyers play the non-negotiable ploy on the vendors.

Many will argue that non-negotiable terms and conditions are merely prudent business and are not the same as negotiating ploys. Yet every contract is the written expression of the distrust one party has of the other, and much of this distrust arises not from a specific concern with the person with whom you are about to do business but from unfortunate experiences you have had with others in the past. Given the billions of transactions across the globe, it is no wonder that solicitors add more clauses to what should be fairly simple contracts to cover this or that obscure possibility that might occur because of reported experiences of it elsewhere.

Demands that issues are non-negotiable are a well-known dominance ploy. They aim to weaken your negotiating stance by taking away the possibility of you weakening theirs. Sometimes they are emotional, sometimes logical. Such is the emotion that clouds judgement that they will not discuss other issues unless you agree to certain issues being set aside. You can accept this in total or you can bend partially by suggesting that, for the moment, you will set aside the forbidden issues and see what progress you can make on the others, while reserving, or at least intimating, that the whole deal depends on all the issues being aired. If the demand for items to be non-negotiable covers items of great importance to you, it could be a deal blocker until you overcome the obstacle. Context will determine the best way to move on.

The brute fact remains that, if they have enough power to enforce on you the non-negotiability of anything, they will probably get their way. It depends how much you value a negotiated outcome, what cards you have left to play, how much you fear what they threaten if they do not get their way and what time you have to reverse their demands.

Rigging the agenda

Similarly, they could attempt to rig the agenda, either by rigging the content or by rigging the order of business. Generally, unilateral determination of either the agenda or the order of business is not compatible with normal negotiating practice. Both parties have a veto on what they negotiate about – if they won't attend your meeting to discuss whatever it is you demand, you cannot negotiate for them – and they have a veto on the order in which you go through the agenda. In some circumstances a party tries to gain advantage by trying to separate issues into a particular order, which suits them because it presupposes hidden constraints on what follows. If you agree to a total budget before you cover your expenses, you are under the gun to cut your necessary expenses. This squeezes your profitability.

Anchoring or high initial demand

Your initial entry position acts as an anchor upon which the changing pressures in the negotiation pull you towards a settlement or deadlock. The anchor influences perceptions of the other negotiator about what is possible. Chester Karrass advocates that you open 'high', which is another way of saying that you should strongly anchor your entry point. I have heard many a negotiation tale, from proponents of the anchor, suggesting 'much better prices' are agreed, or 'exceptionally high profits', etc.

The problem arises when you decide on where to open. Upon what information is your decision based? The irrationality of anchoring on non-relevant information leads to entry points that deter negotiation when they appear to be unrealistic for the other party. Certainly, outcomes are influenced by opening positions because your entry point can structure or influence their expectations, but they can also influence the outcome negatively – they cause the other negotiator to walk away when they believe you to be too extreme.

If you remember that an entry offer is only a first offer and that you should challenge the first offer, you have an antidote to overreacting to initial stances. If anchoring is unrealistic, so is walking away when they first reveal their aspirations to you. You can counter-anchor too. This might set a large gap between you, but what works on your expectations also works on theirs. You both have, perhaps, a long way to go before it is appropriate to make a definitive judgement that the anchors are too entrenched. If too early a reaction is irrational, so is collapsing towards the other's extreme position, and so is taking too personally what they are doing.

Shaping ploys

The early (too early?) shaping ploy warns you of their intentions. The most fatuous one of all is the '**final-offer**' ploy in the opening exchange before much has been said by either party. 'That's my final offer' is so crude it is a wonder anybody takes it seriously. How can an opening position be a final offer, unless you have the absolute power to enforce it? If you have, why are you bothering to negotiate? If you haven't, why should they take you seriously, except perhaps out of embarrassment for the hole you have dug for yourself?

Publishers often try the intimidating ***fait accompli*** ploy of sending a signed contract to the author with an implication that it is best for them to sign and return it, without resorting to the 'messy' business of challenging any of its clauses, because delays and troublesome queries might induce the publisher to quit the deal and withdraw their 'generous' offer to publish your precious manuscript. Many an author has meekly signed a publisher's contract so as not to 'antagonise' him with querulous detail.

Shaping ploys shape deals in their favour. Every deal can be cut several ways, and the manipulator aims to pick up concessions here and there, often without offering much, if anything, in return. Remember, identify a ploy and you neutralise it.

Tough guy/soft guy

Probably the most famous ploy is that of '**tough guy/soft guy**'. Almost everybody sound in body and mind knows of it, so I wonder why it still works? I know of no book on negotiation 'ploys' that does not mention it.

In negotiation, you meet the players of this ploy in many guises. They can appear as two people, ostensibly different individuals but in reality working as a team. This helps you to identify the game they are playing. Or they can be a single person, using the device that, while they are amenable to your position they have a distant committee, or an unsympathetic boss, and unless you help them by making concessions, they will be unable to help you. If you fall for the line, you go out of your way, even beyond your budget mandate, to 'fix' the deal with them, and you wish them luck when they negotiate for you with the, probably fictional, superiors they created to play the tough/soft guy role against you.

Good cop/bad cop

An easily irascible cop interrogates the suspect; she shouts a lot, physically intimidates, perhaps slaps the guy around a little, threatens dastardly outcomes and leaves the room after a while, leaving the suspect cowering and whimpering. In comes a nicer cop. He oozes humanitarian sociability. Off go the lights in the eyes, he releases the cuffs, and produces cups of coffee and a sandwich. Your gratitude to be reunited with the human race is such that you cooperate with him, as long as you avoid dealing with his partner.

The 'Mother Hubbard'

The 'Mother Hubbard' comes from the nursery rhyme of the same name. It is very effective and simple. It consists of convincing the seller that you 'love his product' but you have a strictly limited budget (the 'cupboard is bare' analogy), and that if he wants to sell his product he must come down in price. Depending on the seller's reaction, a new, better deal is possible. The Mother Hubbard does several things. It can be used to test the credibility of the seller's price.

The seller might react positively as it's often convincing enough to encourage the seller that you really love his product, and how can anybody be seen negatively when they love your product. He might be willing to reveal information about the details of his costings, such that you are in a better position to force his price downwards. On the other hand, it might provoke the seller to look at your 'real needs', and enable him to trim down the costs appropriately. This, somewhat wishful, Blue outcome, however, is less likely than the more common one of simply confirming the Red buyer's suspicions that all prices are padded, and the Red seller's belief that all prices should be padded in self-protection from a buyer's ploy.

There are, of course, alternatives, and they all involve the seller blocking the ploy with Red-style counters:

- He can test the ploy and seek flexibility.

It is a typical Red response to assume that all budgets are flexible upwards.

- He can be ready to offer an alternative (cheaper) package that meets the budget.

This is the Red ploy of switch-selling from what the buyer wants to an El Cheapo version. (Car sellers do it all the time – they show you the rock-bottom standard model before they show you the deluxe one, as if this is all the choice that you have. The contrast in quality is supposed to frighten you into paying the higher price for the deluxe model.) This Red ploy is called the **Russian Front** – present someone with two awful choices, but one that is absolutely more awful than the other, and they plump for the less awful, echoing the Second World War preference for German soldiers to go anywhere but the Russian Front.

- He can escalate the decision to another level – find out who controls the finances for the deal.

This is a highly provocative Red ploy as it risks offending the other negotiator who is usually in his position because he carries out his financial boss's instructions to squeeze the seller's prices.

- He can also come prepared with Red blockers, such as minimum order value, minimum quantities, compulsory joint purchases, fixed warranties, high volume discounts, exclusive supply clauses, special prices for special specifications, charges for redesign and advance payments, etc.

All of these are Red ploys and are frequently included in the seller's conditions of business by his company to prevent him giving away the store to Red-style buyers. They are also vulnerable to Red-style demands for special cases and exceptions 'if you want any of our business'.

The nibble

In some contexts the nibble works, and in others it is a constant source of strife: a demand for a relatively low-cost/small-value concession in a much higher value contract. Its effectiveness relies on its underlying psychology: who wants to make a fuss over a small concession, which might in turn jeopardise the whole contract? It is tried in too many instances for good business relations and is the single greatest cause of loss of your competitive advantage in favour of those firms that avoid the nibble and deliver what they promised. Buyers nibble on sellers and sellers nibble on buyers. All of this is Red play and it is ultimately self-destructive.

The audience of business executives at a seminar propounding this streetwise description of the real world are easily wound up into indignation – has not some of the above happened to you in your dealings with a buyer or a seller? It certainly has to me and it gets me angry to think about it. Having been worked up, I am now in a mood to get back at them and there are loads of things I can do to get revenge – the presenters have shoals of ploys available in books and tapes that will help me fight back, and with justice too! But hold on. Is this not where we came in? In what possible sense can there be a winner and a loser in a lasting relationship? The central question posed by a knowledge of the nibble is surely: how do we stop the cycle of Red–Red behaviour in two parties trying to do business together? The answer lies in looking at the negotiation game as a whole and not in staring myopically at individual components of it.

A purchasing department, for example, divides its time two-thirds/one-third between negotiating prices and clerically correcting botched-up invoices and despatch notes that are irreconcilable with reports from Goods Inwards (I speak from experience of several major company purchasing departments in this sort of bind). Heads of departments who attend a ploy seminar will find plenty of ammunition to go to war on delinquent suppliers. However, their better course of action is to review the purchasing policy that lets loose its buyers on hapless sellers from these few delinquent companies, and that endorses the view that its staff are doing their job well when they drive down prices by reflex action and impose onerous conditions for the sake of them, which get more onerous as they try to fight back against more subtle, and persistent, supplier failings. It is a vicious circle and one you should be familiar with in your knowledge of the argument trap of the debate phase.

Miscellaneous ploys

The **salami** ploy is similar to the nibble. Salami comes in slices. Unable to get agreement to a major change – such as a company pension scheme – the negotiator attempts to salami by trying for agreement, a thin slice at a time. He suggests that only the longest-serving employees qualify for company-paid pension contributions, not everybody. Facing a couple of dozen people qualifying against a couple of thousand, the employer's representative feels able to justify committing to the smaller expense.

Of course, next time the contract is re-negotiated, and every year thereafter, the union negotiator seeks new salami deals to widen eligibility among the employees until, in due course, the entire workforce is covered by a company pension scheme. The employer, meanwhile, saves pension contributions for the diminishing band of those not yet eligible. In like spirit, the employer could pave the way for agreement on a company pension scheme by rejecting the union's claim for everybody by disqualifying all but a few employees in a reverse salami, hoping to postpone the cost increases by dragging out the timing of changes in the eligibility criteria.

The **sell cheap, get famous** ploy is legendary in the world of entertainment and in any circumstance where you are pitching for business for the first time. It is also controversial, or at least the appropriate response I recommend is controversial among some people at our seminars. So many people think unlike negotiators that I am not surprised that they get worse deals than they need to. The power of the ploy is founded on the sheer determination, nay desperation, of its target victim to get a foot in the door that they will consider almost any pricing proposition put to them by a buyer with a plausible line in having some 'golden key' to their future.

The producer, for example, tells the young actor that, as she is unknown, she cannot get the top rates she wants – probably deserves – but if she does this film on the 'cheap', she will get so famous that 'trainloads of money' will be hers from then on. Its use is not confined to film producers. I have lost count of the corporations who have told me that just having them as clients will do 'untold good to my reputation'.

We are all familiar, I hope, with how advertisements refer not to 'low wages' but always to 'good prospects', and how buyers speak not of 'one-off low-priced orders' but vaguely of 'the possibilities of high-volume purchases'. The 'Chinese widget deal' is an extreme example of the 'sell cheap, get famous' ploy. In this version, the Chinese buyer places his demand for a low price in the context that there are a billion people in China. True, but the two facts of a low price and a large population are not necessarily connected. My advice is that if you sell yourself and your products cheap, you will get exactly what you demonstrate you think they are worth.

Sellers use the **add-on** ploy in the often successful attempt to raise the final price paid by the buyer for the product. You negotiate what you think is the actual price for the product or service. Once this is agreed, the seller interprets your agreement as a signal to charge for extras. What you bought was the standard product or service and not the full one.

It is essential, therefore, to know what it is you are buying by asking insistently: 'What do I get for my money?'; 'What does your offer include and exclude?'; 'Let me be clear, if I buy the all-inclusive package at the price you have quoted, what is meant by "installation", "training", "access to helplines" and "upgrading"?'. Until you are satisfied that everything you want covered is included in the price, do not agree to anything. If you do agree too early to an unspecified package, you might regret it when the full bill comes in for payment.

Limited authority gives the ploy-maker a power he is not entitled to, though he is entitled to claim it if you are willing to acquiesce in his deception. If he tells you his authority to vary a deal is strictly limited, and you are already at that limit, you have a problem if you want the deal (he has a problem if you don't). He is not refusing to move, and it is somebody else (echoes of 'tough guy/soft guy'?) who is the cause of the problem. How can you argue against that?

If company policy declares minimum order quantities, maximum volume discounts, large pre-order deposits, strict 'taken into use' provisions and delivery charges, it is difficult to expect the seller to overturn company policy on your behalf. If he does not have discretion, he cannot use it. You either accept the deal within the parameters of his limited authority, or you start again with somebody else.

Akin to limited authority is **higher**, or **escalating**, **authority**, in which the deal has to be referred to the next most senior person in the organisation, and the next, and perhaps the next above him. Union representatives explicitly require endorsement of what they agree with you from their members, and, to be frank, deals may not be worth much if the representatives are not allowed this facility. Of course, you are dependent on how they report on the deal – with enthusiasm, or by them just going through the motions – and it can provide an excuse to come back for more because the members 'won't agree to what is on offer'.

Many deals are also agreed 'subject to Board approval', giving the negotiator a passable excuse for coming back with a couple of yes, buts, and at least one quivering quill. Of course, having to get a deal passed by a higher authority could well be a genuine situation, as seen with recent Brexit negotiations, which could only be agreed once passed through Parliament. This caused no end of blocking and delays, some for political gain and nothing to do with the deal, but perhaps giving some leeway for renegotiation, as several rejections left little other viable options – no one really wanted no deal. I don't think the government could be seen as using this as a ploy, but they certainly took advantage of it once it occurred.

Closing ploys

Closing ploys tend to be pressure ploys. Momentum builds towards agreement, and the final shape of the deal looms. Careful pressure here by a manipulative negotiator pays him dividends at your expense.

Quivering quill

It is often observed that the most dangerous time in a negotiation is when the euphoria of agreement is building up, the more so when the negotiations have been difficult and time-consuming and you are ready to go home. Extra concessions can be extracted by the **quivering quill** (named thus by me because 'quivering biro pen' does not quite sound right!). It relies on your enthusiasm for a settlement overcoming your judgement. The deal is close, they have their writing instrument in their hand, hovering above the page, and then they spring it. 'I'm still not happy with clause XI', he says, laying down his pen, 'for reasons I have already stated. It leaves me vulnerable to price swings. If you could agree to cover them, then I could sign now and we could get on with the deal.' If you are desperate to sign and the concession is palatable (too high a demand and they would interrupt your drift into euphoria), the chances are you will move enough to get their pen over the page again. And if you do, it is not unthinkable that they might try another quivering quill ploy to keep you moving.

Yes, but

A more blatant quivering quill is the **yes, but** version of the ploy. Here, she tells you directly, euphoria looming or not, that there is this or that minor difficulty in the way of a deal. It can be infuriating to deal with a 'yes, but' player. No sooner do you resolve one 'yes, but' and another one pops up. But you only have yourself to blame.

If you only moved conditionally and kept the deal as a package – 'nothing is agreed until everything is agreed' – you could insist that all of the remaining 'little difficulties' were identified before you responded to any one of them. You could also insist that these new items could be discussed only if they were taken care of within the present package limits, otherwise you would have to re-open the package to make adjustments across the other items which you had put forward as a basis for your solution. This places the 'yes-but-er' in the uncomfortable, for her, position of having to move to get concessions from you, instead of getting them for nothing. Therefore, check for all the 'yes, buts' she has and never take them one at a time because she will likely think up as many as she can get away with as long as you appear willing to accommodate her.

Now or never

The **now or never** closing ploy is usually foreshadowed by hints of a pending deadline. The hints become more explicit as you near deadlock over some of the issues. If the deadlock is right across every issue, now or never becomes an ultimatum and it is less effective. It is the gentle hint of a 'natural' termination of the negotiations that works most effectively, particularly if the deadline has some apparent, though spurious, credibility.

The pressure intentions of now or never are obvious. It works when you accept that you are under time pressure to take what is on offer and, though you are dissatisfied with aspects of the offer as it stands, you are more concerned that prolonging your search for better terms might jeopardise the deal if it runs into a credible deadline imposed by the other party. Deadlines are always questionable. Some are serious, many are dubious, which is hard to determine in advance. If the deadline bluff is called and it is a bluff, all well and good. If it isn't a bluff, you end up without a deal.

You test a deadline by running right up to it to see what happens when it looks like it will not be met. You can also turn the deadline against the person who has introduced it by asserting that 'this is the best I can do . . . in view of the deadline'. Deadlines are like threats and, in my experience, are best ignored. Responding to them, or looking as if you accept them, only legitimises them.

Take it or leave it

In a similar vein, **take it or leave it** is an ultimatum pressure close. It is the antithesis of negotiation, hence, the earlier it is tried in the negotiation, the less credible it must be, but the later it is tried, the more credible it becomes in the sense that they probably mean it. Your choice is to do exactly what they demand: take it, if you believe this is the best you can do, or leave it, if you can do without whatever they are offering. It is not just your problem, of course. They too have to cope with the consequences of you leaving it.

Presumably they prefer you to take it, though the ultimatum suggests they are indifferent, and that is the significant deciding factor for your reaction if you are at the receiving end of one. Only context can inform you of the likelihood of it being a bluff, though you always have the choice of rejecting a deal that is less than satisfactory to you. This is a major part of the case for developing what Fisher and Ury call your BATNA (best alternative to no agreement). If your BATNA is better than taking the deal, you can opt to leave it.

Split the difference

A seductive closing ploy, masquerading as a fair and sensible compromise, is the old stager, **split the difference**. It seems so reasonable and equitable. A difference is proving difficult to bridge, so she suggests that you split the difference with her. This is tempting, sometimes too tempting, and so you agree. In doing so, you have moved 50 per cent across the remaining gap between you and her. Fine, if you can afford to do so. But you have also missed the point that by making this suggestion she has revealed her own willingness to move at least 50 per cent of the way towards you. This leaves her vulnerable to you insisting that while she obviously can afford to move, you cannot. You can now acknowledge that the gap has been halved by her unilateral offer. Splitting the difference, while attractive, is deficient as a bargaining move because it is unilateral, unconditional and vulnerable to rejection. What next? Split the split difference?

Most closing ploys are obvious, though they consistently work if you bring to the table a state of mind susceptible to them. In long-distance negotiations, being away from home for long periods or the influence of pressing social engagements on timetables for your departure, can work against your resolve. With modern air travel you now have an alternative to waiting for days or weeks for further meetings, though you must be careful that you do not leave merely because your patience is driven by the pace at which business negotiations are conducted in your own culture. Expecting strict timetables to be adhered to in cultures less driven by clocks is going to end in tears unless you adjust your pace to theirs. While waiting for answers, why not go home and return when they are ready? You'll probably save more than the airfare by doing so.

Conclusion

The side effects of a purely ploy approach include an overexcitement of the Red style latent in all negotiators and a narrowness of vision limited to the blow-by-blow interaction taking place momentarily at the negotiating table. The negotiator who is fixated by his relative prowess at ploys and counters and who is detached from the overview necessary to see through a complex deal involving many people at different levels and with different interests, is severely handicapped. It is not Red ploys that determine their interests, but their interests that should determine their behaviours, and their interests are seldom served by a Red–Red confrontation. Only by addressing each party's interests, through debate and proposals on issues and positions, is it possible to secure a lasting and implementable deal.

This last observation is illustrated by the nibble, for what else is the nibble, but a clear example of a Red-style deal that is non-implementable? The purchasing departments alluded to above were in fact spending a full third of their expensive time patching up those deals that failed to be implemented and were thus cutting down on the time they had available to prepare fully for their upcoming purchasing negotiations, which forced them to rely on good old Red-style ploys, such as playing one supplier off against another, to bash their sellers, when what they really needed was time to reflect on what sort of long-term relationship they required with their (fewer) suppliers and which was the best Blue way to achieve it.

An approach that relies too heavily on ploys causes interests to fade from consideration, despite some admonitions to the contrary that the presenter of a ploy seminar might slip in for completeness, and once Interests fade from view, Red battles can only be engaged on Issues and Positions, with each side taking his revenge for losing on a detail by failing to deliver what was promised, or more correctly, enforced, under the duress of the other's Red ploys.

The man who asked me for some 'dirty tricks' needed them like he needed a hole in his head. If he perceived of negotiation in those terms, he was on to a losing play to start with. Clearly somebody in a recent negotiation had upset him greatly – perhaps he was the victim of the Mother Hubbard, the nibble or the quivering quill, or some other of the hundreds of ploys that have been identified. Perhaps, too, it would make him feel better if he was able to shoot from the hip at Red-style negotiators who give him a hard time. But, like the 'fastest gun in the West', there are always faster ones somewhere who are ready for a showdown. The life of gunslingers was short and only glamorous to those who fantasise about the Wild West in the movies. Those hankering after a Red lifestyle as a negotiator should contemplate the thought that no matter how smart or Red they are, there will always be someone smarter, and Redder, about to join them at the table.

As with all ploys in negotiation, what you think is a ploy isn't a ploy on occasion. Admittedly this is a rare scenario, but it is just possible that she does have a tough guy in the wings and he is giving her a hard time over the deal with you. There is no sure way of finding out whether it is a very good play of the ploy or whether it is just the plain truth. The least you should do is block it with your own tough-guy pitch, but be careful of overdoing the humorous counter if you suspect she is being truthful. Nothing in this situation, however, implies that you must make a unilateral move to soften her tough colleague with concessions. If you only offer to move conditionally – as you always must – you protect yourself from falling for the phoney tough guy/soft guy ploy and from the, albeit rare, genuine plays of its truthful cousin.

An engineering company was having problems recruiting and holding programmers for its online operations. The basic problem was that its pay rates for technical staff were substantially below what programmers could achieve in the local market for their services. In preparing for the forthcoming annual wage negotiations, senior management decided that a substantial increase in programmers' pay was needed and that this would be covered during the negotiations.

At the negotiations, conducted by junior personnel managers, the usual contest of wills was evident. The union pushed on the management's offer, and the management pushed for some changes in working practices. The personnel managers, caught up in the cut and thrust of the debate phase, thought they saw an opportunity to implement more of the changes than had been expected by their seniors, and they worked very hard at squeezing the union's resistance in exchange for a below-target wage increase. On concluding an agreement, they reported back to senior management, expecting acknowledgment of their triumph. But as their ploy success on wages still left the programmers' pay out of line with the local market, they had not resolved the strategic issue of retention and recruitment of these skilled employees. This left, in consequence, the IT department understaffed.

In short, a brilliant ploy can result in a strategic defeat.

Checkpoint 9

In the following scenarios, name the ploy and suggest a counter.

9.1 You are Sales Director of a company that supplies coaxial cables to a major telecoms customer. They spend £10 million per annum with you on this product, which represents about 20 per cent of your total turnover. You have received in the post today a letter from their Finance Director stating that, as from the first of next month, they are extending their payment terms to you from 30 days to 90 days. You are not only angry about the lack of consultation on this matter, you are equally surprised to find out from the customer's Supply Chain Director (your normal contact) that he knows nothing about the decision either.

9.2 You have been approached by the Training Consultant of one of London's top stores to provide your three-day Essential Management Tools course for a group of their senior managers on an in-house basis. However, due to a cutback in budgets, they are not proposing to pay you for this programme. The suggestion is that you see it as a selling opportunity that, if successful, will mean that you will get next year's contract of four three-day courses when the contract is let.

9.3 The Sales Executive of the local BMW dealership is just completing the sale of a 318i model to a well-known customer, with all details (price, delivery, trade-in and finance arrangements) having been agreed. As the confirmation order is being written out, the customer says 'oh, just one final point: you will provide fitted carpets just as you did on the previous car, won't you?' This 'request' sounds more like a statement than a question, and fitted carpets are an optional extra priced at £175. This is an important sale to meet this month's budget. The car retails at £39,500.

9.4 The lease on your office equipment (printers, telephones and photocopiers) expires in 1 month. Yesterday you had a meeting with the current supplier to discuss a new deal involving the latest models to replace your ageing equipment. Your local representative unexpectedly brought her area manager to this meeting, and he stressed the need for you to act immediately. Two proposals were mooted: either avoid an imminent price rise by signing up to a new deal straight away, or incur higher equipment charges together with a review of both maintenance and call-out costs.

10 Culture and negotiation

A negotiating tale of two cities

> *A Londoner was sent to Tokyo to negotiate and close a deal with a local corporation. She was faced with a team of Japanese (male) managers on one side of the table, with herself, alone, on the other. She answered their questions, addressed their previously expressed concerns and then made her final pitch. She spoke slowly, as her words were translated and, having covered all the points including her prices, she finished, only to be met by silence.*
>
> *Nervously, she took this as a rejection of her proposal (first mistake) and started speaking again, signalling that her company was not rigid on the prices she had quoted (second mistake). Still silence. So she became specific, identifying the prices that could be improved (third mistake). More silence. So she spoke again (fourth mistake) and no doubt would have gone on for longer but was saved from further price concessions by the Japanese chairman intervening and suggesting that the meeting be terminated while they considered what she had said. Her company did not get the business, despite her lowered prices.*

How might the Londoner's behaviour be explained?

A professor commented that the Londoner had made a major *cultural* mistake. Allegedly, the professor claimed, she had not allowed for the cultural fact that the Japanese side would want to reflect on the implications of her proposal and would normally withdraw politely at an opportune moment, or simply retire to a corner for a quiet discussion.

But was this a result of her cultural ignorance or a major negotiating mistake on her part? It could be both, of course. Correcting the cultural error for a Japanese negotiation, however, would not help her to avoid the same negotiating mistake elsewhere; correcting the negotiating mistake would help her wherever she negotiated.

With even a minimum of negotiating skills the Londoner would have known that whenever you make a proposal, you do not follow a silence with an elaboration of your proposal and certainly never follow with 'improvements' (i.e. unilateral concessions) to it. That is true for negotiators in both London and Osaka. The professor apparently assumed that negotiating skills are different outside London. They are not. Perhaps the professor should consider whether the negotiator made the same negotiating mistakes in London? If she did, her company had a more serious problem than how to correct her mistake in Japan – she needed help to correct her negotiating mistakes wherever she negotiated.

Having stated her proposal, she should not speak again until the other party has responded. Silence in negotiation can be a powerful signal and is only intimidating to inexperienced negotiators from any culture. Basic negotiating training would show her that she should not move from her proposal until she has heard the other side's alternative proposal. If she receives criticism, including a rejection, of her proposal, she is entitled to ask: 'Well, what would you suggest in its place?' And she should await the answer.

Her negotiating 'mistakes' would not be corrected by culture training and, by definition, whatever training she received in the specific cultural norms in one country may be inapplicable in other countries. She is now cleared to negotiate in Japan but what of elsewhere? Until she has corrected her negotiating mistake, it would be unsafe for her to negotiate anywhere, including London.

Cultural relativism

The cultural relativist believes that, if you want to do business with people the world over, knowing about the differences between them is an obvious, necessary – indeed essential – advantage. However, the cultural universalist (that is, someone who challenges the assertions of the relativists) believes that, while awareness of the cultural norms of the people you visit may be beneficial, your competence in negotiation skills is more important.

The process of negotiation is universal across all cultures. Different cultures may exhibit different nuances of Red, Blue and Purple behaviours, much as the world's different languages use different sounds and rules of grammar, but the core intentions (Red players take; Blue players give; Purple players trade) driving these negotiating behaviours are the same.

Culture, like personality, influences behaviour, but neither fundamentally changes the universal negotiating process of 'obtaining what we want from someone who wants something from us'. Culture defines a group and personality defines an individual, but neither culture nor personality defines negotiation as a phased process. I assert that there are no such phenomena as 'Western' or 'Eastern' negotiating *processes*, though there are many different Eastern or Western 'cultures'. Undoubtedly, there are differences in manners and courtesies and in the articulation (in different languages) of interests, values, wants, positions and expectations. These differences, while partly culturally determined, co-exist within the common four-phased process of negotiation (prepare, debate, propose and bargain).

A stereotypical Chinese negotiator's exploration (and exploitation) of his relationship with the other party is not totally alien to an American negotiator's alleged preference to 'get to the point'. Competent American negotiators also explore and exploit personal relationships (as the vast US literature on the lives of prominent American business leaders testifies), and some Chinese negotiators are just as keen to 'get to the point' as their American counterparts – witness Chinese money dealers. American-trained negotiators would be surprised if a co-American jumped straight to her sales pitch before she explored whether her product was needed and whether she wished to deal with the buyer. How many times are the words used in US proposals that a deal is 'subject to status' (i.e. the buying party must, among other criteria, prove its consistent record of paying its bills)?

In very large markets, such as in North America and Europe, the intense division of labour precludes personal knowledge of every player by every other player. Only relatively small markets with high levels of vertical integration and close-family and near-family ties are conducive to dominance by traditional personal relationships, making negotiation outside the favoured few players a game of reducing mutual suspicion and building trust. What the cultural relativist sees as highly significant in a specific culture or country appears to be less so to a universalist who sees commonalities between countries with similar socio-economic levels of development.

For example, traditional personal relationships are cemented by continuous, often life-long, reciprocal favours in Chinese business, administration and politics. This is called Guanxi (pronounced 'Gwanshee') in Chinese, and cultural relativists have contributed a vast amount of information about this phenomenon, almost giving it the mystique of something uniquely Chinese.

A contrary view asserts that the existence of Guanxi reflects limited resource allocation by market prices in China until relatively recently. In the absence of impartial and anonymous market prices as the chief tool of resource allocation, the alternative of allocating resources, including official permissions and licences through Guanxi networks, is not surprising. To get things done in Guanxi networks, the rule becomes that it is not 'what you know but who you know'. In the absence of price allocation, personal relationships are more valued than market efficiency. While officially disapproved of, Guanxi allegedly permeates all business and public life. The obverse is that an anonymous rival's quiet but powerful Guanxi relationships may mysteriously block your project – you have chosen the 'wrong' partners since they don't have the right, or enough, Guanxi!

Rising commercialism and growing reliance on markets in China explain why Guanxi is reported to be in decline, particularly among younger, more market-oriented Chinese. What was until yesterday the epitome of Chinese culture is ceasing to be so today. Cultural relativists are left stranded as the exponents of special cases. Negotiators, as exponents of the enduring and universal phenomenon of negotiation as a four-phased process, are not required to revise their concepts as economies develop.

Do people negotiate using different processes?

It is understandable but misleading to assume that people from different cultures negotiate by means of different processes. Nobody to date has reported evidence to sustain the cultural relativist's assertion that there are different negotiating *processes* at work. Some, however, assert that culture must make a difference, apparently because cultures are, well, different. Yet, if culture is partly formed by history and history, of necessity, changes, then culture itself will change over time and the absolute certainties as to how to behave in negotiation with different cultures will dissolve.

It is not only culture that attracts sweeping assertions and intuitive truths. Allegedly, for example, women are inherently cooperative (Blue) and men are competitive (Red), yet the evidence for these assertions is of the 'it must be true' kind; men and women are different, ergo, they negotiate differently. Long runs of plays of the Red–Blue game show no tendency for women as a group to play differently from men as a group (a three-year study showed only a 0.03 per cent difference). You cannot predict how the women in a group will choose between Red and Blue in round one, nor can you predict the sex of those pairs (about 8 per cent) of the group who will achieve a Blue–Blue maximum score. To assert, therefore, that the conduct of a negotiation is changed by sex differences is as mistaken as to believe that, because an individual's conduct is different in some respects, it must be different in all respects. Some women are 'Red' players, others Blue, and some men are Blue players and others Red. And women and men trained in the distinctions between Red and Blue behaviour can become consistent Purple players.

It is important, however, to recognise the existence of cultural diversity, and it is advisable to acquire knowledge of the relevant cultural imperatives and how they interact for working in, or managing, a group of culturally diverse employees. Ignorance is never bliss, and it can be positively disastrous in certain circumstances. Cultural knowledge has the same significance as that of language fluency but fluency will not save you if your negotiating skills are primitive. It is more important, therefore, that negotiators understand the universality of the negotiating process if they are to make sense of the cultural conflicts sometimes evident in their negotiations. Cultural relativism misses the target.

What is culture?

There are many definitions of culture and most of them are unsatisfactory. Because culture might orchestrate behaviour, it may be worthwhile for negotiators to consider whether or not the values, beliefs, shared meanings and attitudes of a group determine in significant ways their negotiating behaviours. There may be other explanations for variations in people's behaviour. Understanding what causes certain behaviours is always helpful. Moreover, if the influence of culture on behaviour is ignored, we might act on irrelevant but biased cultural assumptions and thereby frustrate our efforts to secure important agreements.

Culture is about those values, beliefs, self-justifying assumptions and 'world views' of members of the distinctive groups with whom we deal. Culture encompasses their histories, received experiences, accounts of events, political perspectives, myths, folklore, collective memories, religious or mystical ideas, philosophical outlooks, rituals and social preferences. This is quite an agenda if you are from another culture, even assuming you could learn much within the time that you have available.

All of us put our different 'cultures' on display to suit circumstance. The language and subjects we discussed in the school playground were different from the 'language' we might have used or the subjects we might have discussed in front of our teachers, or in front of our parents and grandparents at home. We speak about different subjects with our work mates from those we discuss at home with our families and our children, and the conversations and the views we share with colleagues are not the same as those we have with our bosses.

Only in the most general and nominal sense, therefore, can outsiders access another culture's imperatives unless they are able to devote considerable time and resources to its study. You can become superficially 'fluent' in another culture's imperatives but, except for a small minority of exceptionally gifted people, you are unlikely to become a cultural 'polyglot' in more than a very few cultures. And if you are a cultural polyglot – or remarkably 'fluent' in a particularly important culture – you have a commercial interest in endorsing the concepts of academic cultural relativists.

Consider your own culture in which, presumably, you are 'fluent'. Your understanding of what it means to be a member of your culture is controversial, particularly with people who nominally share your culture. All cultures to some degree are riven with controversy and, though their members have common experiences, they do not necessarily interpret those experiences monolithically. Undoubtedly, you share certain cultural imperatives with others in your group, but it is doubtful that you share everything conceived as defining your culture. Your differing views are part of the rich tapestry of your shared cultural life!

Differences between a country's sub-cultures are likely to be too subtle for visitors to recognise on short visits. Do you recognise, for example, the cultural differences between citizens of Glasgow and Edinburgh, cities only 45 miles apart? And what of the differences between Scottish and English citizens? Yet as citizens of the United Kingdom they would be lumped together by cultural relativists (from distant cultures) as sharing an identical culture. But the constituent nationalities of the UK (the English, Scots, Irish and Welsh), plus several generations of ethnic minorities who are British by birth and upbringing, do not act culturally in the same manner in business, community and family matters. Extending this phenomenon to other countries larger in population and territory (e.g. China, the United States, Russia, Nigeria and so on), we cannot be sure that the negotiator across the table from us conforms in any reliable way to the norm a cultural relativist would impute to her just by identification of her nationality.

Anthropologists warn rightly against ethnocentric conclusions about other cultures. Each cultural identity has several 'dialects'. And just to complicate the problem, other factors (beliefs, attitudes, experiences), which always remain invisible to those ignorant of them, influence particular behaviours of individuals, either by countering or reinforcing their cultural imperatives. Not all Chinese, or Swedes or Americans behave the same in similar circumstances. In addition, personality may intrude to some extent in negotiation, as may the type of organisation (a capital-intensive business operates differently from a labour-intensive business) or state structure (the norms in an Islamic state may differ from those in a secular democracy). It becomes close to unmanageable to predict negotiation behaviour from a person's cultural identity when varying shades of personal awareness of ideology, politics, theology and history are brought to the table in a complex mix of what influences that particular individual.

Kevin Avruch (1998, *Culture and Conflict Resolution*) put the difficulties of this problem in perspective when he wrote that knowing an individual's culture (he is Mexican) does not permit you to predict his behaviour. He may have many 'cultures', and even if you know that he's a US-educated engineer, of southern Native American background and an evangelical Protestant in Catholic Mexico, etc., you could still be wrong in your predictions. And even when you know him fully as a person you still cannot predict his behaviour.

> **Exercise 10A**
>
> *Would you say that you conform to the norm for people from your country? Try to define the 'norm' for your country. How many people do you know who are members of your own culture who do not conform to the norm of that culture?*

In studying the role of culture (and any other influence on negotiating behaviour) you embark on a vastly complex field, much of which is still tentative, deeply controversial and weak in applicability, even after 40 years of earnest endeavour by hundreds of researchers and thousands of practitioners.

The cultural relativist's challenge

Richard D. Lewis (1996, *When Cultures Collide: Managing Successfully Across Cultures*) persuasively argues for the significance of culture in international negotiations. He claims that 'the moment people of different cultures are involved, the approach of each side will be defined or influenced by cultural characteristics' because 'nationals of different cultures negotiate in completely different ways' (p. 161). Is this assertion true? How different can we be without being completely different?

The influence of culture on negotiation is analysed on two levels. The impressionistic analysis describes the varying manners, courtesies and curiosities of everyday contacts between people from different countries. Roger Axtell's *Do's and Taboos Around the World* (1990) was compiled from 150 offices of the Parker Pen Company and is the best example of this genre. The other, scientific, level incorporates detailed analyses of attitudes according to national origins. In both these levels, it is common for the authors to equate membership of a 'culture' with the national origins of the people they write about. But a person, who has one national origin, may be influenced in behaviour by many 'cultures' in a lifetime.

In the 1970s, social science discovered data processing. Data were collected, processed and correlated until fascinating associations were uncovered. Reports galore rained down. Mercifully, a finite supply of paper constrained its publication. Simplistically, in the inductive method of data analysis, you collect data, identify shared characteristics (age, sex, social strata, educational attainments, national origin, religion, or whatever) and then exhaustively correlate the characteristics using computers.

Geert Hofstede's work was of an exceptional quality. In 1966, he accessed data extracted from 60,000 employees of IBM, located in 53 countries. A second survey was undertaken in 1971–1973, covering 30,000 of the original employees and 30,000 new ones, or, in all, 90,000 people. He published his results in his classic *Culture's Consequences: International Differences in Work-Related Values* (1980) and showed that attitudes and values varied with the nationality of the respondents (presuming nationality is a surrogate for culture). He defined culture as the 'collective programming of the mind which distinguishes the members of one human group from another' (p. 21) and initiated the scientific study of the impact of culture on business behaviour (see Table 10.1).

Cultures with greater power distance tolerate unequal power distribution. Hofstede included in power distance such inequalities as exist in physical and mental characteristics of individuals, their social status and prestige, their wealth, the exercise of political power, and how laws, rights and rules may operate in their favour. He used the concept of power distance to measure the interpersonal power or influence of bosses over subordinates in 40 countries. Strong individuals strive to increase their power distance over others. However, the weaker the power distance between individuals, the stronger is the tendency to reduce power distance, and the weaker is the tendency to display deference to 'superiors'.

Table 10.1 Hofstede's cultural differences using four indices

Dimension	Measure	Examples	
		High	Low
Power distance	Tolerance of unequal power distribution	Philippines India	Denmark New Zealand
Individualism vs collectivism	Degree to which the individual is the focus	Australia USA	Venezuela Pakistan
Masculinity vs femininity	Extent to which values are masculine	Japan Austria	Netherlands Sweden
Uncertainty avoidance	Extent to which they are comfortable with ambiguity	Greece Portugal	UK Canada

Source: G. Hofstede, *Culture's Consequences: International Differences in Work-Related Values*, 1984, Sage; extracted, summarised and re-arranged from Figures 3.1, 4.1, 5.2 and 6.1.

Hofstede found that there was a high tolerance of unequal power distribution in the Philippines and India and markedly less tolerance of power distance in Denmark and New Zealand. Since the 1960s, there may well have been a decline all over the world in tolerance for power distance, which relates to the sustained growth in the world's economies and is reflected in the collapse of Soviet communism and the spread of various degrees of democracy in Latin America, Asia and South Africa. In the traditional democracies, too, there has been a noticeable decline in social deference. These findings again suggest that cultural imperatives are fragile.

Four methodological questions arise from Hofstede's data.

- Is the absence of domestic tension a reliable measure of the degree of tolerance of the status quo, and how stable over time (a few decades) is a particular status quo?
- What happens to the index of tolerance when a country with high inequalities in social status and prestige, wealth and political power experiences social turbulence?
- To what extent is the index of tolerance influenced by an absence from the 1960s sample of IBM employees of, say, the Muslim minority in the southern Philippines, or the Dalits ('Untouchables') in India or the Maoris of New Zealand?
- How might the indices of these measures change through time?

Of the 20 countries in the sample with the highest tolerance of power distance, five were secular democratic and 15 were, to varying degrees, authoritarian. It may be, therefore, that an index of toleration reflected (transient) political controls in 1966–1967 rather than a lasting 'cultural' difference, particularly as 13 of the 15 are now (2001) classifiable as secular democracies. Negotiators cannot rely on cultural attributes that change on this scale within 20–40 years. These attributes appear to be political and not cultural and, far from following unique cultural influences, also appear to follow similar socio-economic trends associated with development and experienced by many diverse countries.

Hofstede asserts that individualist results-oriented cultures (e.g. USA) focus less on relationships than collectivist cultures (e.g. Pakistan). The relationship between individuals and the collectivity of their society, he suggests, influences the norms, or values, attributed to that society. Hofstede noted how China (then under Mao Tse Tung's political influence) was hostile to individualism, while American society valued individualism highly.

How much of this is a political consequence of each country's economic structure and how much can be attributed to its 'unique' culture? China has long been 'collectivist' on this index because it has a long history of authoritarian governance. The United States, since 1783, has been a secular democracy following a couple of centuries as a colony. It has not had a 'collectivist' political structure or an authoritarian government. Change either of these influences and the index of individualist versus collectivist rankings would change too.

There is a timeline suggesting a linkage of this dimension to changes brought about by commercial development, a movement towards secular democracy and pluralism and the legitimisation in law of concepts of human rights. That this is the case can be seen in the gradual opening of China towards the global economy; we would expect this to accelerate 'cultural' changes as China's membership in the World Trade Organisation (WTO) takes effect in the next few decades.

Traditional collectivist societies that move through commercial development (globalisation) towards individualist societies (what Hofstede describes as the difference between *Gemeinschaft* and *Gesellschaft*) will dramatically alter this index. Because such changes will alter their 'cultures', how deep or shallow are cultural differences? Also, and thankfully, because negotiation processes are universal, there will be minimal, if any, requirements to change either party's negotiation behaviours.

'Masculine' cultures, according to Hofstede, are more competitive than more caring 'feminine' cultures. This is the least convincing of Hofstede's indices. It reads somewhat dated 50 years after the data were collected. Hofstede reports his difficulty in collecting statistically significant data for calculating the index because of the relative paucity of female employees in many of the occupations he studied in IBM in the mid-1960s.

Exercise 10B

To what extent would you expect the index to change if the data were re-run today following the substantial changes in the sex composition of the workforces in developed economies in recent decades?

Given that proportionately many more females have joined the workforce – in some occupations, females account for 50 per cent or more of the employees (e.g. law, education, professions allied to medicine and magazine journalism) and females are now sizeable minorities in other occupations, including higher management, senior public servants, police and the armed forces – we should expect such indices to change substantially.

Hofstede introduced masculine and feminine characteristics – broadly against a 'nurturing' versus 'achievement' dimension – that conformed to traditional stereotypes of the roles of the sexes in society, work and management. The data were stretched to determine a 'masculinity' index that, interestingly, shows that 'masculinity' favoured larger over smaller corporations, individual over collective leadership, and firms that provided welfare support for their employees, all attributes associated with IBM in its heyday and suggesting the prevalence of a company, as opposed to a country, culture. Hofstede also identified employees' beliefs that promotion is based more on 'influence' than on 'ability', which is a common enough view in large organisations.

Hofstede's uncertainty avoidance refers to the extent to which employees are comfortable with ambiguity. Everybody feels the pressures of uncertainty – because we cannot predict the future accurately – and in so far as we rely on uncertain future events for our future daily necessities, and rely on our ambitions to access future power and prestige, we react with varying degrees of stress to uncertain guarantees that we will get what we want. As individuals, we do not accept with identical equanimity the gap between 'getting what we want' and only 'getting whatever we get'.

Hofstede used an index based on the extent to which employees in 40 countries adhered to company rules and procedures, their preferences for stable employment prospects and their attitudes to stress. These indirect data were illustrative of Hofstede's claim that the more uncertain we feel about our future prospects, the more we try to avoid future uncertainty, and his index of 'uncertainty avoidance' purported to measure our culturally derived attempts to avoid uncertainty. He found Greek and Portuguese employees scored highest and Danish and Singaporeans scored lowest on the uncertainty avoidance index. And those most comfortable with ambiguity (Greece) were more laid-back (manana, manana?) than those (UK) so uncomfortable that they fretted over it.

There is a relationship between the three overlapping boxes illustrated in Figure 10.1 that are labelled behaviours, attitudes and beliefs and values. 'Behaviours' is shown at the front as a complete box because behaviours are the most visible of the three elements. You can see, hear and feel other people's behaviours, while you cannot be sure of their private attitudes and beliefs. People are aware of your behaviours when they are affected by what you do. Even if they cannot identify you individually as the perpetrator, because perhaps you are a 'faceless bureaucrat', they will know that something has been done to them, particularly if your behaviours affect them negatively. Negotiators are likely to know

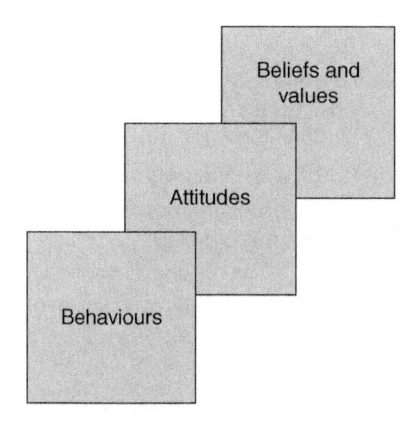

Figure 10.1 A simple model of the relationship between behaviours, attitudes, beliefs and values.

when they have been cheated or threatened, or when somebody has taken advantage of them.

With attitudes it is significantly different. Attitudes can be hidden even in confidential surveys. Attitudes that you choose to reveal to others are less reliable indicators of your true intentions than is your behaviour. In the Red–Blue dilemma game, nobody misses your behaviour when you play Red to their Blue. Subsequent explanations for your playing Red – a 'mistake' or to 'protect' yourself, etc. – are less reliable than the fact of your behaviour and its result: they lost and you gained points at their expense.

It may be convenient to express a certain attitude to acquire (undeserved) moral approval. It might also be dangerous in some circumstances to express attitudes that are contrary to those in a position to hurt you. In such an unhappy case, rather than risk harm by expressing your true views, prudently you show only the approved attitudes.

Negotiating experience shows that some practitioners express attitudes that bear no resemblance to their intentions. They speak of trust but they intend only to deceive. While negotiators do not always, or predominantly, act with deceitful intent, you have no way of knowing for certain if you can rely solely on what they say. This makes people's professed attitudes an unreliable guide compared to their behaviour and compromises, and to some extent, surveys are based on the professed attitudes of respondents.

Behind your attitudes stand your relatively firm beliefs. Where attitudes can be thought of as short, coded guides to instant behaviour – 'leave the tidying up to my sister', 'be polite to elderly people', 'never give a sucker an even break' and such like – beliefs are more robust and much more complex. Belief systems take longer to form than specific attitudes. They tend to form in your early and formative years and, because of the relative ages of those who pass on the beliefs and value systems of a community and those who receive them, beliefs tend not to be challenged in the early years. They are handed down from generation to generation and sometimes are forged in the rebellion of one generation against another, which the older generation regards as a degeneration in society's moral values, and the younger one regards as a liberating influence of them.

Behaviour can be arbitrary, attitudes can be contradictory and beliefs can be hypocritical in practice. Much of the human treasure of its literature and art is about these very human characteristics – what else would be as interesting to dramatise? Drawing conclusions from attitude surveys and belief statements is risky if these are interpreted as synonymous with how negotiators behave. As misleading as it is to explain particular behaviours in terms of the professed attitudes or beliefs of a particular 'culture', these behaviours may be completely explained from within the universal paradigm of negotiation and do not require tenuous connections to specific sets of local attitudes and beliefs.

Note that Hofstede's model did not research the impact of culture on negotiating behaviour. His was a study of attitudes and values, not behaviours, and it is vulnerable to the above comments on the reliability of their relationships. This qualification has not prevented brashly confident inferences being made by others that the impact of culture on negotiation is 'obvious'.

Take Hofstede's power distance, for example. The fact that high tolerance of power distance is found in, say, Mexico, does not make it a uniquely Mexican characteristic. Power distance is found to varying degrees in all cultures but is especially prevalent in authoritarian examples. Hofstede's method is no more than a sophisticated analysis of attitude surveys. It is possible for a significant minority of the Mexicans in the sample to have as low a tolerance of the prevailing power distribution as the majority of Danes, without compromising the finding that proportionally more Mexicans have a higher tolerance of power distance than most Danes. But a negotiator may not know for certain with which part of the sample labelled 'Mexican' or 'Danish' she is negotiating.

Likewise, a particular culture may demonstrate a high incidence of Red negotiating attitudes and behaviours, with a significant minority demonstrating a high incidence of Blue attitudes and behaviours. But in negotiating with members from a particular culture, it is more beneficial to be trained to deal with Red and Blue negotiating behaviours than it is to be trained to identify ascribed characteristics according to national identity, leading negotiators to assume mistakenly that the individuals who happen to be at the table share these ascribed cultural imperatives. Knowledge of alleged cultural ascriptions does not enable a negotiator to deal with people practising Red or Blue behaviours. Indeed, anticipating incorrectly a cultural ascription and confronting universal behavioural traits without knowing how to deal with them is worse than ignorance of the alleged cultural differences.

Sloppy attribution by implied association is common when linking culture and negotiation. That some authors have immense knowledge of different cultures is not challenged – their books are fascinating – but they mislead practitioners with their assertions that cultural characteristics, such as when a member of a particular national group is driving a motor vehicle, are also exhibited when that person is engaged in the altogether different activity of negotiation.

An allusion, for example, to prolonged adjournments while Japanese negotiators consult with superiors is presented as if, stereotypically, the impatient American is driven to distraction waiting for an answer. How familiar are these authors with business negotiation? People negotiating at senior levels on high-value projects do not expect immediate answers. If they do, they will be disappointed no matter what their culture. The lengthy delays that occur while seeking confirmation from levels of authority not present in a negotiation, as with the Japanese example (if that is the real cause of the delay) is not so unusual for experienced negotiators as to be alien or stressful. They do not have to learn about Japanese culture to cope with these delays; among other things, negotiators should learn the elementary virtues of patience.

Cultural relativism's main weakness is that it makes its assertions without direct evidence from negotiations. A selective example of difficulties when different cultures interact does not show that their interaction has significance for the question of whether culture determines negotiation behaviour, or whether the outcome of poor negotiating behaviour is the same in all cultures.

Culture and negotiation 213

An American cultural awareness speaker drew attention to an experience of a European beer company invited to Vietnam to negotiate the setting up of a brewing capacity for its famous beer brand. After several meetings, the Vietnamese officials contacted the brewer's European head office and stated they would not deal with its representative anymore. He had 'offended' them. As a result, it took five years to get the negotiations under way again and conclude them to the satisfaction of the officials (and no doubt, to the joy of their thirsty citizens). The speaker claimed that the (unspecified) offences of the representative demonstrated the need for European exporters and joint venture seekers to undertake cultural awareness seminars to avoid cultural errors.

Officials in authoritarian regimes are not used to people failing to conform to their wishes (that is why they are authoritarian), and there is a veritable minefield of potential errors awaiting visitors more used to challenging offers and demands in freer societies that may prompt claims that a negotiator has offended the officials' need for due deference. In some Chinese negotiations, for example, the charge that you are 'not a friend of China' might arise because you did not agree to an official's demands for unilateral concessions. If the charge does arise in a negotiation, your chances of concluding the deal become more remote than if you cave in and comply, for which you may be awarded the high status of being a 'friend'. I suspect that what lay behind the demand that the beer company replace its representative with somebody more 'culturally aware' (i.e. more compliant) had much more to do with his refusing to comply with demands for unilateral commercial concessions than any offence he might have caused to their national sensibilities.

There are many other explanations for deadlocks in international negotiations that have little to do with cultural ignorance, though they are unfortunately and mischievously presented as such by cultural relativists.

Exercise 10C

A joint venture negotiation between an Italian and a Scottish business illustrates the error of assuming cultural insensitivity whenever a negotiation runs into difficulties. The discussions in Edinburgh went well, but at a reconvened meeting in Genoa they collapsed. The Scottish firm had sent out its senior negotiator, but she and the owner of the Italian firm argued during a late-evening social engagement. Afterwards, the Italian insisted, haughtily, on dealing with the Scottish 'boss' and not a 'junior' manager.

On the basis of the above, would you say that the Scottish firm made a cultural mistake in sending a manager who was clearly junior to the owner of the Italian company? Should they have sent out their Managing Director instead? Or might there have been another reason for the collapse in the negotiation?

If you are told that the Senior Negotiator from the Scottish firm feigned (public) ignorance of what had upset the Italian owner, would this cause you to pause before jumping to a cultural conclusion? I would hope so because the full circumstances of what caused the late-evening dispute, like an iceberg, were left diplomatically below the surface – and it had nothing to do with 'culture'.

Conclusion

First-time negotiators switching jobs to a new business learn in time to cope with a new sector's idiosyncrasies because few people easily transfer from one to another. Businesses are not all alike. For example, negotiating oil and gas agreements for the first time introduces 'take-or-pay' and 'send-or-pay' regimes; negotiating lease agreements includes 'time is of the essence' clauses; negotiating construction contracts uses 'performance bonds' and 'liquidated damages' clauses; negotiating personnel contracts includes 'termination for cause' and 'termination without cause' clauses; and go-between deals have 'non-circumvention' clauses. Becoming acquainted with the many idiosyncrasies of national and international business practice around the world is necessary for negotiating the outcome.

Cultural relativism reveals relevant and interesting 'things you should know' about the habits and manners of other societies (as well as travel guides for visitors). There is a large literature on doing business 'over there', and regular public seminars are offered. And many of the 'things you should know' are in the same category as those that all competent negotiators must become familiar with if they really want to do serious business.

Flying from Edinburgh to Bradford, or New York to Houston, without knowing something of the way the people at your destination are likely to want to conduct their business would be lax to say the least. Flying from one country to another only compounds such laxity. In Spain, it is useful to know, for instance, that a business meeting over dinner is not likely to be underway until after 10:30 p.m., or that breakfasts in France are not of the hearty American kind. Though late dinners and skimpy breakfasts won't change the negotiation process, they might affect your blood sugar levels while you endure them!

Travelling many thousands of miles into distant time zones without any knowledge of the cultural, climatic and geographical differences – the way they do and perceive things over there – is to climb a very steep learning curve on arrival. Thus, the 'things you should know' about other peoples is a vast and valid area of study. Likewise, doing business within your own borders requires more than a passing knowledge of the similarities and differences between firms and people in your business sector, and other sectors you might operate in over a long and, hopefully, distinguished career.

Purchasing procedures in different firms and business sectors in the same or similar cultures can be very different, as are the influences of the sheer scale of operations. Selling small-value items to single decision-makers (a dozen bars of chocolate to single-proprietor 'mom and pop' corner shops) is different from selling through multiple layers of decision-makers a year's supply of expensive high-value components to volume car plants. Confidence that there is a peculiarly American 'wham, bam, it's a deal Sam' negotiating culture is only credible to people who have never tried to sell anything to General Motors! You will not find the negotiating process all that strikingly different when selling to US-owned Hess Corporation (oil) or to Japanese-owned Honda (vehicles).

To expect to walk into the purchasing office in a large US company and lay out your wares for an instant decision is naïve. It just does not happen. It might in 'mom and pop' stores in America and Japan. In Japan, for example, being surprised at the time taken by local managers in 'getting to know you' activities as if it were a totally new experience cannot be taken seriously. Try negotiating in the American 'boondocks' or the Australian 'outback' (or villages in southern Italy) without 'getting to know you' sessions or favourable introductions from close family. Sure, the factors that might reassure a Japanese firm that they want to do business with you may be different from some of the factors that reassure an American firm making a routine purchase, but that is to be expected. It might also be the case that two American firms value quite different factors as prerequisites for doing business. For you, it's part of the process of learning your business, hopefully, better than your rivals.

For example, a global UK oil and gas firm competed with an Italian rival for a major operating contract in an ex-Soviet, newly independent state, just after the collapse of the Soviet Union. The UK firm's engineers inspected the oil refineries and declared them to be antiquated in technology and grievously inefficient in the use of labour. Most of the processes were of a vintage that pre-dated the 1950s, though it was the most modern plant in the former Soviet Union. Whereas a European refinery would require 1,500 employees, these employed ten times that number! The UK engineers pronounced the refineries a 'disaster' and recommended heavy investment to bring the plants up to standard and an early mass shedding of labour to make them as economically efficient as a UK refinery.

As part of the deal, the local leaders had demanded that the foreign operator provide schools, hospitals and medical services for the local population and also insisted that nobody was sacked. This was estimated to cost several tens of millions of dollars. As far as the UK managers were concerned, these demands were euphemisms for bribes.

How far apart could you get? Who had not prepared properly?

What the UK oil company failed to understand was that the leaders of that new country only held their positions by successfully providing goods, services and jobs for their 'clan' members. In this society, consisting of several clans without a welfare state, their clan leaders were the only source of social services for the population. The obligations of the clan leaders went well beyond the remit of private oil companies in Europe – everything the local leaders wanted for their people, for example, is provided in the UK by its tax-financed welfare state. But the ex-Soviet leaders were judged solely on their abilities to provide welfare support for their people. That is how their clan leaders survived communism and how they intended to survive under capitalism.

The Italian company properly prepared and reframed the local leaders' negotiation demands to reflect their historical interests and clan roles. Its bid included the necessary large sum in US dollars required for schools, hospitals and medical services. Unsurprisingly, the Italian company won the contract.

Now, the motives of the local leaders' requirements had to be appreciated if the oil company was to do business with them. Their Interests (not their criminality) drove the negotiating behaviour of the clan leaders. Interests are drivers of negotiating behaviour in all cultures, and all negotiators always do better by searching for the other party's Interests and constructing proposals to address them. The mismatch of perceptions and values illustrated by this abortive (for the UK) bid suggests a need for induction into the important role of identifying the participants' Interests when examining the content of anybody's negotiable proposals.

A search for a cultural explanation merely because it is another culture is less useful than mastering common negotiating skills. Interests and proposals remain Interests and proposals in all cultures. Different cultures do not have different processes of negotiation; the phases and skills of negotiation are universal.

Appendix 1: Glossary of terms

Adjournment: the negotiator's equivalent to a time-out. In the heat of exchange it can be a huge benefit to take some time to consider your next step.
Adjournment Close: once the deal is almost complete, take a break before firmly agreeing (or not).
Anchoring: setting an unrealistically high entry position to change the dynamics of the negotiation.
Arbitration: the use of a private tribunal or person to adjudicate a dispute between parties instead of resorting to litigation.
Assurances: part of the debate phase, a simple verbal device to show positive feelings to some aspect of the discussion. Used to motivate somebody to work towards your objective, rather than against it.
Bargaining: stage four in the process of negotiation. Making a specific exchange that could conclude the negotiation. If you give me some of this, then I will give you some of that.
BATNA: Best Alternative to a Negotiated Agreement, suggested by Fisher and Ury as a preparation tool.
Behaviours: the way you act when conducting a negotiation. See Red, Blue and Purple styles.
Blue Style: a soft giver, willing to make unilateral concessions to gain the relationship.
Blocking: cutting of an avenue of discussion or negotiation. An unhelpful destructive debate behaviour.
Coercion: an alternative decision-making method, often a two-way process, as each side attempts to force the other with threats or actions.
Collective Bargaining: jointly determined rules for the use of labour in employment. Unions negotiate the rules either directly with the employer or through an agent of the employer.
Concession: a giveaway. Never concede anything, always trade for it.
Condition: the 'what you want' part of the proposal.
Conditional Proposition: using the Purple-style if–then proposal format.
Constructive Debate: positive debate behaviours that have the impact of moving the negotiators forward towards a deal.

218 *Appendix 1*

Cultural Relativism: if you want to do business around the world, it is important that you understand how to behave in respect of the other party's culture, and that this is more important than the negotiation itself.

Cultural Universalism: while awareness of cultural norms can be helpful to the preamble of the deal, your competence in negotiation skills is much more beneficial.

Deadlock: when the negotiation stalls, sometimes permanently.

Debate: phase two of the negotiation, where all the issues are discussed.

Destructive Debate: negative behaviours in the debate phase that hinder rather than help in a negotiation.

Distributive Bargaining: the single-issue haggle. Where the negotiation is only about one thing, usually price, and movement costs without any gain (other than *perhaps* securing the deal).

Entry Point: where you intend to start the negotiation. A realistic, defendable position.

Exchange: how decisions are made by negotiation. You exchange things you value less, in return for things you value more.

Exit Point: where you intend to stop the negotiation, as you can go no further. Accepting offers past your exit point is bad for business.

Fait Accompli: a ploy to shift power to the doer and raise the stakes if counter-actions are applied. For example, a developer demolishes a unique old building, then applies for planning permission on the site.

Facts: often disputed, rarely show anything but what you want them to.

Four Phases: the process of negotiation described in this book: Prepare, Debate, Propose and Bargain.

Give In: what we do when we accept an instruction.

Goodwill: earned but shouldn't be given automatically. Not a tangible item for exchange.

Guanxi: traditional personal relationships cemented by continuous reciprocal favours in China.

Haggle: a street slang term for negotiation. Think of foreign tourist markets, selling trinkets and goods – always worth a 'discussion' on price.

If: the negotiator's most powerful two-letter word. All proposals and bargains should start with 'If'.

Inhibitions: concerns that are preventing you agreeing to a proposal.

Integrative Bargaining: searching for solutions to problems where the negotiators have compatible interests.

Interests: why you prefer some things to others. Your Interests are your hopes, fears and concerns; they motivate your decisions in the negotiation. They are not negotiable.

Issues: what you are there to negotiate. They are the agenda items.

Linking Issues: making exchanges over more than one issue using the conditional language.

Listening Skills: the least successful skill of the average negotiator. A constructive debate behaviour when used well.

Mediator: someone who helps unlock a deadlocked dispute between two parties.
Mother Hubbard: a ploy to put pressure on price.
Negotiation: the process by which we obtain something we want from someone who wants something from us.
Nibble: a ploy employed to eat away at the value of a deal.
Non-Zero Sum: what you gain is not at my expense. The sum of the positive gains is greater than zero.
Not Negotiable: a pressure ploy designed to impose something, for example, credit terms.
Nothing is agreed until everything is agreed: a mantra to stick by in complex negotiations.
Offer: the 'what you are prepared to give' in exchange part of the proposal.
Or-Else Bargain: probably the most risky way to end a deal, with 'take it or leave it' ploy connotations.
Packaging: unwrapping and rewrapping proposals to make them mutually acceptable.
Persuasion: an alternative method of making decisions. The most common type of disclosure when faced with a problem.
Point-Scoring: a cheap dig at the other negotiator's expense. Not advised, but devilishly good fun.
Positional Bargaining: negotiators can get stuck in defending a position, to the detriment of the negotiation. Can lead to attacking destructive behaviour.
Positional Posturing: posturing by refusing to negotiate – 'it's a 10 per cent pay rise or we strike!'
Power: like the wind, felt rather than seen. Don't let perceived power (yours or theirs) affect your negotiation.
Preparation: phase one of negotiation. Getting all the information you require ready to begin the negotiation.
Principled Negotiation: the rational bargaining approach by Fisher and Ury.
Priorities: how much you value each negotiable Issue.
Propose: phase three of the negotiation. Making tentative solutions to each other, for agreement in principle before moving on to specifics in Bargaining.
Purple Style: generally see negotiations in the longer term, looking to make a trade for movement, focused on creating a good deal for everyone involved.
Quivering Quill: a ploy used just as you are about to sign the contract.
Ranges: negotiators think in ranges, not fixed points. The negotiator's range is between his entry and exit point.
Rational Bargaining: theoretical approach to negotiation where decisions and behaviours are rational.
Red Style: a taker, looking to win every negotiation, usually at the other party's expense. All negotiations treated as one-off. Interested in results only.
Russian Front: a ploy to make you choose one unpalatable option over an even more unpalatable one.

Say 'No': to outright reject a proposal. An alternative method for making decisions.

Sell Cheap, Get Famous: a ploy used to encourage a lower entry price for the business in exchange for 'goodwill'.

Signal: a subtle change in tone or language to show there is a possibility of movement.

Summaries: an effective constructive debate tool that helps confirm understandings and keep the negotiations on track.

Summary Close: you summarise what is on the table, what each of you has agreed before closing the deal. It ensures everyone is agreeing to the same thing.

Surplus: the amount we gain in a single-issue negotiation by agreeing to a price that is not our exit point.

Take It or Leave It: ploy to put pressure on getting agreement on the offer on the table.

Threat: unlike a promise, something you'd prefer not to implement. A very poor destructive debate behaviour.

Time Trak,: a tool to note debate behaviours in a negotiation.

Tough Guy/Nice Guy: a ploy to engender you to one negotiator (and their deal) over the other not-so-nice guy.

Tradables: cover anything tangible or intangible that the negotiators have discretion over. They can be used to trade for movement when the deal stalls.

Trade: never give an inch – trade it!

Traded Movement Close: a last-gasp trade to finalise the deal.

Trust: earned not given.

Utility: the value of something to one or both people in the negotiation.

Walk Out: a dangerous tactic, as it's hard to walk back in if you've made a mistake. Always try to understand deadlock before giving up – maybe you've missed something.

Win–Win: the goal of every effective negotiator.

Zero-Sum: one person's gain is the other person's loss.

Appendix 2: Checkpoint answers

Checkpoint 1

1.1 When is negotiation an appropriate decision-making method?
Negotiation is an appropriate method when the people involved need each other's consent to agree to the deal. They both need to want something from the other, whether that is something tangible or intangible.

1.2 What is the definition of negotiation?
Negotiation is the process by which we obtain something from somebody who wants something from us. Negotiation is trading.

1.3 What are the three types of bargaining?
Distributive bargaining, integrative bargaining and rational bargaining.

Checkpoint 2

Exercise 2B:

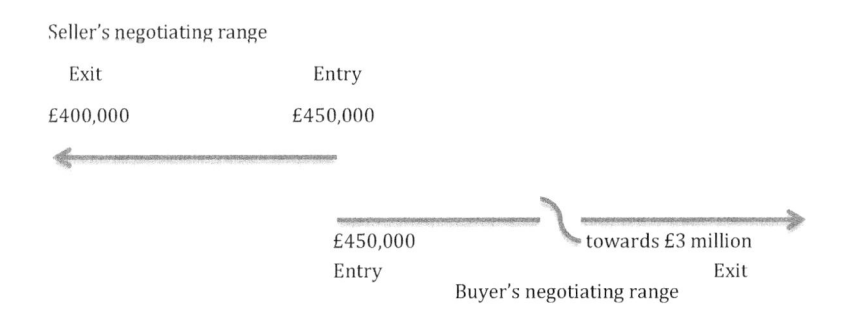

Seller's negotiating range
Exit — £400,000
Entry — £450,000

Buyer's negotiating range
Entry — £450,000
Exit — towards £3 million

2.1 What is the definition of distributive bargaining?
Distributive bargaining is a single-issue negotiation such that when one side gains, the other side loses. It's a fixed-pie, zero-sum type of negotiation.

2.2 What is the surplus, and how is it calculated?
The surplus is the gain made by the negotiator by agreeing to price P* rather than going all the way to their exit point. There needs to be an overlap for a surplus to exist.
It is calculated as follows:
Negotiator's Surplus = Buyer's Exit Point − Seller's Exit point
Buyer's Surplus = Buyer's Exit Point − P*
Seller's Surplus = P* − Seller's Exit point

2.3 When should you stop negotiating in distributive bargaining?
Your exit point is as far as you can go in the negotiation before you have to walk away and say no. So in a negotiation, while circumstances can alter your decisions, the time to stop negotiating is when you reach your exit point.

2.4 You are considering selling your caravan for £12,000. While you are preparing to advertise the caravan, someone offers you £15,000 for it. Do you:
   a) *Accept the offer* – No! Remember, negotiators think in ranges. If this is their opening offer (their entry point), how far might they be prepared to go to get the deal?
   b) *Tell them to wait until the caravan is advertised* – No! You have someone in front of you ready to negotiate; why let them go? They might not come back.
   c) *Negotiate* – Yes! Try to get them to move closer to their exit point.

Checkpoint 3

3.1 In a dispute with a supplier over his failure to perform his contract, the buyer should:
   c) *Collect data on failure to perform.* Data are the lifeblood of any negotiation. Understanding the situation with real data can help shape your preparation and will give you a platform to defend your positions with the other negotiator.

3.2 Negotiators have Interests because:
   b) *They are motivated by different factors to prefer some outcomes to others.* All negotiators are motivated by different factors, and these motivations will affect *why* they negotiate and *what* they eventually agree to.

3.3 An Issue is:
   c) *An item on a negotiator's agenda.* Issues are *what* we are there to discuss/negotiate during the negotiation.

3.4 Which of the following is correct?
   d) *Negotiators can move from any Position on any Issue if it suits their Interests.* Ranges are there for movement, and if it suits the Interests of the negotiator, they will move Position – so long as it doesn't go past their exit point.

Appendix 2 223

Checkpoint 4

4.1 In the debate phase, you should aim to:
   a) *Complete it as quickly as possible to avoid argument.* No. Trying to hurry a negotiation may provoke argument rather than avoid it.
   b) *Discover the other negotiator's interests and inhibitions.* Yes. The negotiator requires information, particularly about the other negotiator's interests and inhibitions. No proposal can sensibly be made without some preliminary exploratory questioning *and* listening.
   c) *Ensure that the other negotiator understands your positions.* No. Your positions are more likely to be revealed in the proposal phase.
   d) *Inform the other negotiator of your interests and inhibitions.* While it is in his or her best interest for the other negotiator to seek information on your interests and inhibitions, it does not always follow that they will do so.

4.2 Negotiators signal in order to indicate:
   a) *A willingness to move.* Yes. Though the movement must always be conditional.
   b) *A desire for the listener to move.* That is the implication of the willingness to move, but hoping for a one-way movement on behalf of the listener could be futile.
   c) *That a proposal is imminent.* No. A proposal may or may not be imminent but could be delayed until you have sorted out whether and how far they are willing to consider movement and on what terms.
   d) *A preference for a compromise.* Not quite, as you could be testing the other negotiator's willingness to compromise.

4.3 The most effective way to handle a disagreement is to:
   a) *Point out where the other negotiator is factually wrong.* Definitely a high-risk response and certainly not the 'most effective' one.
   b) *Ask questions.* Correct. We need to be sure what the disagreement is about before reacting, and asking questions and listening to the answers is the most effective response.
   c) *Explain with great courtesy the grounds for your disagreement.* While courtesy is always recommended, explaining why you disagree before you know for sure what you disagree about is not sensible.
   d) *Summarise the case against the other negotiator's views.* You might eventually be required to do this but this should follow a series of questions rather than precede them.

4.4 Open: 3, 5, 8, 10 and Closed: 1, 2, 4, 6, 7, 9

4.5 Find the signal in the following statements:
   a) I am unable to meet your **current** terms on delivery dates and penalties.
   b) I can't accept an **annual** review.
   c) Before we move forward, we need to discuss **some** discounting on bulk orders.
   d) These timelines are very **difficult** to commit to.

224 *Appendix 2*

Checkpoint 5

Answers from resetting the proposals 1–5 in Exercise 5C:

'If you support our claim for landing rights in Germany, I would seriously consider supporting your proposal for landing and pick-up rights in Singapore'.

'If you accept two persons per room, I could consider providing you with more bed-nights per week'.

'If you look at the manning levels, we will look at the shift differential'.

'If you tell me what would meet your client's needs, I could be prepared to respond with a positive offer'.

'If you accept the changes in the vendor's contract that I have set out in my paper, I will consider the possibility of your becoming a sole supplier to our sites'.

5.1 Your terms and conditions include a protection against consequential loss, and the other negotiator has signalled his unwillingness to accept this. Do you:
   a) *Ask him to explain his objections to consequential loss?* Probably the best response. His objections may be major or minor and it is best to find out what the other negotiator considers to be important rather than to assume that you know the answer. On the basis of his answer you can respond with assurances, amendments to your requirement or an alternative method of achieving your needs. You could also decide, of course, that his objections are more dangerous to you than spurious in themselves (that he is likely to fail to perform and escape his obligations) and that your best response is to insist on protection, even at the cost of not doing business with him.
   b) *Defend the necessity of your business having a consequential loss provision?* This would not assist progress in the negotiations as you do not know yet on what grounds he is opposing a consequential loss provision.
   c) *Ask for a proposal on how he intends to cover your need for protection against a failure of performance?* A close alternative to answer (a) but not necessarily the one to be chosen first. Once you know the basis of his objections you could use this response.
   d) *Tell him that a failure to sign a consequential loss provision means that no business can be concluded with him?* As with answer (b), this is too peremptory and best left until you have listened to his answer to (a).

5.2 False. While a proposal is generally preferred to an argument, it must always depend on the type of proposal to determine whether the proposal assists or hinders the negotiation.

5.3 False. An unconditional proposal is a 'giveaway' and can damage the negotiator's chances of making progress by stiffening the resolve of the other negotiator to stick to his positions. A conditional proposal protects the negotiator from one-way concessions.

5.4 True.

5.5 False. Proposals should always be conditional, but the use of assertive language is not mandatory, though it is advised.

5.6 While answers (a), (b) and (d) might be correct in some cases, in all cases proposals should be conditional.

5.7 Answer (c).
   a) *Avoid proposing a change and wait for the other negotiator to propose a change.* This is asking the other negotiator to take the initiative against his own interests in maintaining the status quo and is therefore likely to be futile.
   b) *Propose a change and not wait for the other negotiator to propose.* Correct. If the other negotiator is happy with the status quo, he or she has no reason to initiate change. To wish for change but not to propose it is a recipe for an argument.
   c) *Avoid proposing a change until the other negotiator asks for a proposal.* This could lead to a long session, certainly longer than answer (i), and might not be arrived at.
   d) *Propose a change only if the other negotiator signals a willingness to change.* This is asking a lot of the other negotiator who might be more than happy to leave things as they are and might never indicate a willingness to change at all.

5.8 Answer (c).
   a) *Say 'No'.* The least helpful response because it tells the other negotiator nothing about your position and usually leads to an argument.
   b) *Stop negotiating.* A futile gesture. The proposal may be a misjudgement on his part, not a fixed position or solution.
   c) *Ask for an explanation.* Correct. By finding out more about the basis for the proposal you will gain additional information about the other negotiator's attitudes and, perhaps, an insight into his interests.
   d) *Counter-propose.* It is best not to counter-propose immediately. Wait until you know more about the basis of the other negotiator's proposal.

5.9 Answer (c).
   a) *Insist on them being linked.* Partly correct, but as it stands it is too abstract an approach. The other negotiator will be wary of your insistence on something for which he is unclear as to its effects on his positions.
   b) *Judge them as separate issues on their own merits.* Dangerous if it means that you lose negotiating room on the remaining issues as each issue is settled.
   c) *Decide upon nothing in finality until agreement is reached on all of them.* Correct. 'Nothing is agreed until everything is agreed' is a workable and sensible rule of thumb for separate issues.
   d) *Be tidy in your approach to difficult issues.* True but not relevant to the separate issues problem.

Checkpoint 6

6.1 What is the difference between a proposal and a bargain?
   A proposal uses vague language, whereas a bargain uses specifics only. A proposal is a tentative solution, searching for possibilities and is vague to protect both parties. A bargain is used to finalise a deal, when all that is left to do is to add specifics to any proposals that can be agreed on and actioned.

226 *Appendix 2*

6.2 List 10 Tradables you could use in a pay negotiation.
This list is not exhaustive, but some examples could be:
Salary, Training, Responsibilities, Performance, Hours, Working from Home, Flexitime, Overtime Pay, Sick Leave, Travel Perks (Extras), Shift Premiums, Medical Benefits, Compensation, Redundancy, Promotion, Re-location, Stock Options, Conferences, Company Pension Scheme, Pay Frequency, Holiday Pay, Company Car, Expenses, Uniform/Clothes Allowance, etc.

6.3 Which of these is an effective bargain?
D is the only effective conditional bargain.

6.3 Rewrite the following as an assertive, conditional bargain:
  a) If you give me £500 off list price, then we will order the full kitchen today.
  b) If you give me a 5 per cent discount, then I will buy 100 more units.
  c) If you give me a three-month delivery date, then I will give you a 25 per cent deposit.
  d) If you give me a confirmed order for five machines, three months installation and a five-year warranty, then I will give you a 20 per cent Liquidated Damages cap.

Checkpoint 7

7.1
  1. Red, because it implies that the man with experience will teach the man with the money a lesson.
  2. Red, because it implies that a concern with your scruples (the 'heat') shows that you cannot take the pressure of success.
  3. Blue, because it implies you can trust his word even if it means he has lost.
  4. Red, because it implies that to get to the top you have to be tough, not soft-hearted.
  5. Red, because it implies that the toughest stance, the deepest pockets, wins.
  6. Blue, because it implies that there are other things besides a fast buck motivating them for a longer-term deal.
  7. Purple, because it combines a Red demand (Give me) with a Blue offer (I will give you).

Checkpoint 8

8.1 Why are John Nash's assumptions on bargaining so unrealistic?
Nash assumes that bargainers are equally skilled, which is unlikely as people have varying levels of experience and ability when it comes to negotiating.

Another assumption is that both negotiators have full knowledge of each other's tastes and preferences. This is extremely unlikely. We don't know for sure much about the other negotiator's wants, we can assume and we can ask them, but we can never really know for sure. It's also difficult to accurately predict the other negotiator's desires for various things. Again we can make assumptions and ask questions for an approximation, but can we accurately predict it? Probably not.

8.2 Fisher and Ury suggest that their principled negotiation is suitable for all types of negotiations. Do you consider this to be true?

For day-to-day business negotiations, the use of objective criteria is completely unrealistic and unsuitable. It would be time-consuming and expensive and the effort prohibitive. Who sets the objective criteria? You need to have an outside person oversee the objective criteria, otherwise there is a chance it won't be objective. But bringing in an outsider can give more delays and costs. For all but contentious legal matters it would seem to be overkill.

8.3 What does BATNA stand for, and what does it mean?

Best Alternative to a Negotiated Agreement. It means, what is the alternative if this negotiation fails? If that alternative is better than the current deal, it might give you the confidence to either walk away or press for more. If the alternative is worse than the current deal, it gives you the confidence to accept the deal.

Checkpoint 9

9.1 **Off limits**

Explain that you will be happy for them to pay you at 90 days as long as they realise that this will increase the price to cover your costs.

9.2 **Sell cheap/Get famous**

Explain that you will be happy to give a discount – on the last course in the series, not the first. You only discount when they have earned it.

9.3 **The Nibble**

The nibble works so well as it is often seen as such a small concession to get the deal, but that's exactly the problem: it's a concession. Instead, think of something you can trade it for. In this case, the salesman would do well to suggest that the customer pays a small amount towards the mats – is the customer really going to break the deal for the sake of car mats?

9.4 **Russian Front/Deadline**

What other alternatives do you have? Perhaps it's time to look at another supplier? Don't be pushed into making a decision on their terms.

Index

acceptance 13, 93, 114, 125, 172
'add-on' ploy 194
adjournment bargain 127
advice 4, 160, 171, 179, 183
agreements 6, 10, 139–41, 217, 219; and bargains 115–17, 119–20, 122–3, 125–9; and debate 61, 66, 69, 73–4, 80–2, 86; and distributive bargaining 15–18, 22–3, 25–6, 29; preparation 40, 43–6, 54–5; and ploys 182, 193–5, 197, 199; and proposals 97–8, 107–8, 110, 112; and rational bargaining 166–9, 171–3, 177–8, 180
ambiguity 114, 125, 207, 210
analysis 37–8, 76, 144, 148, 160, 183, 206–7, 212
anchoring 190, 217
anger 24, 64, 68, 75–6, 127, 141
antagonising 15, 88, 125
arbitration 5, 13, 217
arguments 4, 24, 29, 118, 153, 160, 165, 193; and debate 61–3, 67–9, 73, 86–7, 89; and proposals 94, 104, 107, 110
arrogance 88
assertion 64–5, 7–8, 92, 116, 139, 188, 204, 206
assumptions 38–9, 47, 64, 70, 72, 87, 108, 159, 162, 181, 204
assurance 153, 108, 150, 217; and debate 61, 69, 74–5, 77–8, 82, 86
attack 34, 58, 113, 150, 174, 219; and debate 62–3, 67–9, 79, 81
attitudes 11, 69, 75, 77, 87, 153, 167, 204–7, 210–12

bargaining power 54
bargaining problem 162, 167–8
bargains 113–29, 145, 218
beliefs 11, 79–81, 87, 174, 204–5, 209–11

Best Alternative to a Negotiated Agreement (BATNA) 35, 54, 178, 181, 197, 217
blame 56, 58, 62–3, 67, 76, 100, 118, 150, 174, 196
blocking 62, 66, 74, 151, 174, 179, 192, 195, 198, 203
Blue style 141–2, 144–6, 148–9, 151, 153, 156–8, 171, 174, 179, 202, 212, 217
bluff 11, 25, 88, 127, 143, 146, 156, 165, 196–7
brainstorming 174–5
buyers 9, 16, 20, 21, 28, 116, 125, 129, 187–9, 192–4

'Camel Question' 184–5
careless behaviour 71, 130
chance 4, 7, 136, 138
charm 75, 145
cheating 28, 133–4, 137–8, 152, 186
checkpoint answers 221
choices 7, 12, 31, 45, 51, 133, 136, 139, 142, 149, 167, 169, 192
circumstance 65, 79, 99, 115, 118, 122, 137, 170, 186, 188, 194, 205
claimers 168
clarification 86, 104, 106, 107, 110, 128
climbdown 79
closing ploys 186, 195–7
closing the deal 110, 125–6, 220
coercion 5–9, 217
communication 60–1, 64, 70, 139–41
compensation 2, 58, 64, 75–7, 83–8
competition 12–13, 39, 77, 83, 87–8, 142, 146, 171, 193, 204, 209
complaints 37, 76, 88, 118
compromise 5, 143–4, 174, 197, 223; and debate 67, 80–1, 87, 89

concessions 97, 102, 110, 126–7, 130, 159, 192, 195, 217, 227
conclusions 47, 205, 211
conditions 4–5, 9, 40, 52, 61, 142–3, 171, 175, 192–3; and bargains 114, 116, 130; and proposals 94, 98–9, 102, 111
constructive behaviour 62, 68–9, 87, 104, 108, 217–18, 220
co-operation 12, 55, 133, 140, 168
co-ordination 138–9
costs 5, 16, 21, 143, 155; and debate 58, 68, 83–4, 88; and preparation 36–7, 40–1, 45; and proposals 91, 96–8, 102, 105–6, 109
counselling 180
coverage 47, 99
creators 168
credibility 41, 66, 77, 79, 99, 143, 191, 196
criteria, objective 176–8, 227
cultural factors 201
cultural relativism 202, 204, 215, 218
Cultural Universalism 202, 208
culture and negotiation 201–16; definition 201–2

data 184–5, 207, 209–10; and preparation 37–9, 41, 47, 49, 52–6
deadlines 84, 151–3, 196
deadlock 36, 49, 94, 103, 106, 144, 154, 179–80, 190, 196, 218; and bargaining 117, 120–1, 126; and debate 63, 67, 69, 73, 78, 80, 88; and distributive bargaining 15, 23–7
debate 31, 47, 55, 57–90, 151, 158, 178, 193, 198–9, 202, 217–18; and bargaining 115–16, 118–19, 130; and proposing 94–5, 97–9, 104, 106–10
deception 194
decision making 1, 7–8, 10, 12–13, 38, 176, 179, 181
defection 133, 135, 137–41, 148
description 160
destructive behaviour 62, 218
details 86, 105–6, 121, 125, 128, 129, 154, 174, 176; and preparation 39, 41, 45–6, 48–9, 53
difficult negotiators 144, 146, 149–50, 171
dilemmas 15–16, 159, 166, 181, 211; and negotiating behaviours 134–5, 138–9, 141, 146, 148–9, 151, 157
disagreement, avoiding 6, 67, 72, 77–3, 89, 112, 223

disputes 5, 6, 143, 146, 150, 153, 172–3, 176–7
distributive bargains 10, 14–30, 51, 108, 218
dominance ploys 186–9

emotional behaviour 55, 63, 75, 77, 142, 171, 179, 189
entry points 16–17, 22–6, 52–3, 105, 190, 218
equity 28–9, 52, 122
error 77–9, 102, 110, 180
'escalating authority' ploy 195
estimating 133
ethics 159
exchange 8–10, 32–4, 48, 59, 93, 97, 99, 118, 190, 218; and negotiation behaviours 133–4, 136–7, 151, 158; and utility theory 160–5, 167, 180
exit points 17–19, 22, 24–5, 28–9, 44, 46, 50–3, 108, 173
expectation 14, 20–1, 39, 43, 61, 71, 75, 184–6, 190, 202
experience 7, 11, 15–16, 39, 47, 67, 70, 74, 86, 92, 103, 125, 129, 142, 157–8, 167, 196
explanation 61, 70, 101, 107, 216
exploitation 28, 152, 157, 202

'fait accompli' ploy 190
Fisher, Roger 169–74, 177, 181, 197, 217, 217, 227
'final offer' ploy 190
four phase/two style approach 31, 218
frustration 24, 68, 147

gains 53, 133–4, 140, 146, 163–9
gestures and tones 24
giving in 3, 6, 8, 13, 62, 81, 83, 85, 121, 171
goals 28, 63
grievances 150
guarantees 57, 60, 62, 138

haggling 6, 20, 159–60
'higher authority' ploy 195
honesty 4, 27, 65, 67, 142
humiliation 78–9

incentives 46, 53, 103
information 25, 27, 39, 47, 51, 66, 70, 72, 104, 106, 152–3, 165

inhibitions 70–1, 81–3, 86, 89, 110, 120, 126, 158, 180, 218
instruction 2–3, 6, 9
intangibles 5, 9, 167, 220
integrative bargaining 10, 31, 167
integrity 155
intentions 34, 106, 184, 186, 188, 190, 202, 211; and debate 61–2, 64, 71, 75, 88; and styles 135, 142, 152, 157
interests 12, 24, 28, 95, 153–5, 158, 198, 202, 216, 218; and debate 64, 67, 69, 71, 75, 81, 88–9; and preparation 35, 39–41, 43–4, 47, 52–3, 55–6; and principled negotiation 166, 169–75, 179–80
interruptions 62–6, 103, 195
intimidation 5, 55, 62, 103, 187
intransigence 93, 97
irrational behaviour 159, 190
irritation 25, 62–5
issues 10, 30, 119–26, 153–5, 188–9, 198, 218; and debate 59–60, 75, 80–1, 83; and preparation 31, 35–6, 39–56; and principled negotiation 169–74, 178–80; and proposals 97, 99, 107–9

joint ventures 1, 29, 82, 155–7, 213
judgement 54, 106, 125, 133, 142–3, 175, 190

Karrass, Chester 187, 190
Kennedy, Gavin 185

language 17, 25, 84, 92–7, 102, 114–16, 121, 130, 205
Lax and Sebenius 168
liability 83, 100
'limited authority' ploy 194–5
listening 66, 68–73, 85, 88, 109, 148, 153, 218
losses 39, 83–4

manipulations 24, 27, 143, 157, 182–6, 195
manners 147, 149–51, 202, 206, 214
marketing 13, 116, 143, 155–6
mediation 13, 23–4, 169, 179–80
mediator 179–80, 219
misunderstanding 125, 152
monopolies 162
moral issues 114, 142, 159, 211
motivation 32, 64, 80, 134, 138, 143
'Mother Hubbard' 191

movement 31, 44, 50, 53, 144, 172, 174, 180; and bargaining 115, 121–2, 124, 126–7; and debate 63, 83, 86–7; and distributive bargaining 8, 16–18, 26; and proposals 94, 96, 97, 101, 108–9

Nash, John 160, 162–7, 169
Negotek® Preparation Planner 34–5, 39, 43, 161, 163–4, 173
negotiating behaviours 44, 71, 110, 135, 145, 157, 160, 206, 211–12, 216
negotiation; in China 194, 203, 205, 208–9, 218–19; and culture 201–16; definition of 5, 8–11; in Japan 202, 207, 212
nerve, loss of 135
neutrality 69
'nibble' ploy 192–3, 198, 219
'non-negotiable' 188–9
non-zero sum 167
'now or never' ploy 196

offers 2–3, 5, 8, 13, 32–3, 54, 63, 86, 93, 145–6, 154, 190, 219; and bargaining 112–17, 119, 123, 125, 127, 130; and distributive bargaining 14–15, 18–21, 24, 29; and proposals 97–112
opinions 10, 65, 69, 75
or-else bargains 127–8, 219
overlapping 19–20, 22

penalties 42, 45–8, 52–3, 60, 62, 64
perceptions 11, 23, 25, 28, 41, 43, 99, 135, 137, 142, 161, 168, 184–7, 190, 216; and debate 59, 61, 71, 80
persuasion 4, 6–8, 13, 219
ploys 143, 168, 182–200
point scoring 66–7, 219
political negotiation 10, 12–13, 154, 172, 181, 204, 207–8
positional bargaining 169–70, 172–3, 178–9, 219
positional posturing 169–70, 172, 176, 178, 219
positions 17, 20, 66, 83, 89, 125, 186, 190, 198, 202, 215; and preparations 39–41, 44, 46–9, 51, 53, 55–6; and principled negotiation 153–5, 158, 165, 170–5, 177–8
postponement 6, 7, 46, 194
power 12, 23–4, 143, 168, 179, 184–7, 189–90, 194, 207–8, 212, 219
preconditions 188

Index

prediction 160
prejudice 41, 157
preparation 31–56, 77, 108, 124, 178, 219
prescription 171, 176–7
principled negotiation 169–71, 173, 176–81, 184, 219
priorities 35, 42, 45–8, 50, 55, 70, 104, 163–5, 180, 219
problem solving 4, 7
proposals 3, 27, 38, 41, 47, 52, 54, 91–112, 145, 153, 156, 172, 174, 201, 202, 219; and bargaining 114–18, 127, 130; and debate 60, 66, 68, 70, 83, 86, 88
props 187–8
protection, self 41, 78, 96, 137, 141, 177, 192
psychological behaviour 53, 130
punishment 77, 53
purple style 141, 150–1, 154–8, 202, 204, 219

qualification 65, 69, 80, 219
quality 39, 129, 174, 192, 206
questions 16, 21, 32, 70–3, 79, 81, 104–5, 108, 125, 152–3
'quivering quill' ploy 195–6, 198, 219

range, negotiation and settlement 17–20, 22–3, 25, 31, 35
rationality 159–60, 178
Red-style 142–4, 146, 148–50, 153, 157, 171, 192, 197–8, 219
rejection 97, 107, 125, 202
relationships 40, 69, 74, 78, 138, 142–5, 159, 170–1, 208
religion 80
reputation 74, 134, 145–6, 194
resentment 63, 77
responses 104, 144, 149, 175
revenue 47, 64, 155
rhetoric 80, 155, 178
'rigging the agenda' ploy 189
risks 5, 28, 44, 49, 97–8, 103, 108, 115, 175, 186–7; and debate 64, 79–81, 83, 85, 87; and negotiating behaviour 132, 137, 140–2, 153, 157
'Russian front' 192, 219

'salami' ploy 193–4
self-defeat and destruction 67, 95, 142, 193
self-protection 137, 141, 192

'sell cheap, get famous' ploy 194, 220
sensitivity 66, 175
settlements 31, 105–6, 108, 154, 158, 178–9, 186, 190, 195; and distributive bargaining 18–19, 22–5, 28; and debate 58, 60–2, 64, 67, 75, 80, 83, 87
shaping ploys 190–1
signalling 83–6, 89, 94, 109, 186
silence 103–4, 201–2
solutions 16, 33, 39, 43, 55, 75, 80, 94, 98, 108, 162, 167–8, 174–5, 180
'split the difference' ploy 5, 197
standard terms and conditions 94, 188
statements 37, 41, 66, 69–71, 74–5, 84, 94–5, 107, 128, 153
Statements, Listening, Assurance, Questions, Summaries and Signals (SLAQSS) 153
status quo 98, 166, 172, 208
streetwise approach 168, 183–4, 193
styles, negotiation 132–8, 183, 193
subcommittees 6
summarizing 73–4, 108–10, 128–9, 153, 220
summary bargains 127, 220
surplus 22–8

tactics 11, 16, 121, 155, 182–200
'take it or leave it' 13, 20, 29, 116–17, 127, 154, 196, 220
tension 4, 23–4, 75, 103, 135, 149
tentative 114, 117–18, 130, 153, 174, 219; and proposing 92–4, 96–8, 100, 103, 108–10
territory 122, 154, 205
threats 5, 8, 59, 62–3, 67–9, 147–8, 196
time: face to face interactions 34, 53, 61, 89, 130; pressures on 34, 196; trust in 135; wasted 33, 53
tones and gestures 24
'tough guy/soft guy' 191, 194, 198, 220
tradables 35, 53–4, 122–4, 220
traded concession bargain 126–7
trade-offs 83, 102, 155
training 4, 11, 59, 88, 104–6, 126, 159–60, 202
trust 4, 37, 71, 203, 211, 220; and negotiating behaviours 136–8, 140–1, 157–8

ultimatum 116, 170, 196–7
Ury, Bill 169–74, 179, 181, 197, 217, 219
utilities 163–5

vagueness 97–100, 102–5, 109
valuations 48–51, 53, 55, 108, 119, 163–4
verbal agreement 129
vulnerability 137–8, 141

welfare 209, 215

'win-win' 159, 166, 181, 220
working parties 6

'yes, but' ploy 196

zero sum 10, 167–8, 220